RACE AND ETHNICITY IN THE STUDY OF MOTIVATION IN EDUCATION

"Examining race and ethnicity is becoming an increasingly important area in motivation research. Finally, there is a book that comprehensively addresses motivation issues of students of color in the area of education. The strengths of this book are that it looks at how traditional motivational constructs can include sociocultural racial perspectives and how racial constructs can be placed in the center of motivational analysis. Both approaches are necessary in order to fully understand the motivational psychology of students of color. This is an indispensable resource for motivation researchers, faculty, and students who want to better understand how race and ethnicity impact motivation in education."

—**Kevin Cokley**, Director, The Institute for Urban Policy Research & Analysis, The University of Texas at Austin, USA

Race and Ethnicity in the Study of Motivation in Education collects work from prominent education researchers who study the interaction of race, ethnicity, and motivation in educational contexts. Focusing on both historical and contemporary iterations of race-based educational constructs, this book provides a comprehensive overview of this critical topic. Contributors to the volume offer analyses of issues faced by students, including students' educational pursuits and aspirations, as well as the roles of students' family and social networks in achieving educational success. A timely and illuminating volume, *Race and Ethnicity in the Study of Motivation in Education* is the definitive resource for understanding motivation issues posed by nondominant groups—including African American, Latino, Asian-Pacific Islanders, and Arab American students—in educational contexts.

Jessica T. DeCuir-Gunby is Associate Professor of Educational Psychology and University Faculty Scholar in the Department of Teacher Education and Learning Sciences at NC State University, USA.

Paul A. Schutz is Professor in the Department of Educational Psychology at the University of Texas at San Antonio, USA.

RACE AND ETHNICITY IN THE STUDY OF MOTIVATION IN EDUCATION

Edited by
Jessica T. DeCuir-Gunby
and Paul A. Schutz

NEW YORK AND LONDON

First published 2017
by Routledge
711 Third Avenue, New York, NY 10017

and by Routledge
2 Park Square, Milton Park, Abingdon, Oxon, OX14 4RN

Routledge is an imprint of the Taylor & Francis Group, an informa business

© 2017 Taylor & Francis

The right of Jessica T. DeCuir-Gunby and Paul A. Schutz to be identified
as the author of the editorial material, and of the authors for their
individual chapters, has been asserted in accordance with sections 77 and
78 of the Copyright, Designs and Patents Act 1988.

All rights reserved. No part of this book may be reprinted or reproduced
or utilised in any form or by any electronic, mechanical, or other means,
now known or hereafter invented, including photocopying and recording,
or in any information storage or retrieval system, without permission in
writing from the publishers.

Trademark notice: Product or corporate names may be trademarks or
registered trademarks, and are used only for identification and explanation
without intent to infringe.

Library of Congress Cataloging-in-Publication Data
Names: DeCuir-Gunby, Jessica T., author. | Schutz, Paul A., author.
Title: Race and ethnicity in the study of motivation in education /
   Jessica T. DeCuir-Gunby and Paul A. Schutz.
Description: New York : Routledge, 2016.
Identifiers: LCCN 2016004032 | ISBN 9781138859838 (hardback) |
   ISBN 9781138859845 (paperback) | ISBN 9781315716909 (e-book)
Subjects: LCSH: Motivation in education—Social aspects. |
   Minorities—Education.
Classification: LCC LB1065 .D28 2016 | DDC 370.15/4—dc23
LC record available at http://lccn.loc.gov/2016004032

ISBN: 978-1-138-85983-8 (hbk)
ISBN: 978-1-138-85984-5 (pbk)
ISBN: 978-1-315-71690-9 (ebk)

Typeset in Bembo
by Apex CoVantage, LLC

Printed and bound in the United States of America by Publishers Graphics,
LLC on sustainably sourced paper.

CONTENTS

Foreword: Motivation and Racial-Ethnic Dynamics   *viii*
Lyn Corno

PART I
An Introduction to Race and Ethnicity in the Study of Motivation in Education   **1**

1 Researching Race and Ethnicity in the Study of
Motivation in Educational Contexts: An Introduction   3
Paul A. Schutz and Jessica T. DeCuir-Gunby

PART II
Using Race-Reimaged Approaches to Examine Motivation in Educational Contexts   **11**

2 An Attributional Perspective on Motivation in Ethnic
Minority Youth   13
Sandra Graham

3 Retention Versus Persistence: A Self-Determination
Analysis of Students Underrepresented in STEM   36
Kelly A. Rodgers

vi Contents

4 Examining Associations Between Fitting In at School and Heart Rate Variability Among African American Adolescents 50
DeLeon L. Gray, LaBarron K. Hill, Lauren H. Bryant, Jason R. Wornoff, Oriana Johnson, and Lisa Jackson

5 STEM Motivation and Persistence Among Underrepresented Minority Students: A Social Cognitive Perspective 67
Shirley L. Yu, Danya M. Corkin, and Julie P. Martin

6 Out of the Book and Into the Classroom: Applying Motivational and Self-Regulated Learning Theories to Daily Instruction With English Language Learners 82
Rhonda S. Bondie and Akane Zusho

7 School Engagement and Future Academic Expectations Among U.S. High School Students: Variations by Ethnicity 99
Cynthia Hudley and Su-je Cho

PART III
Using Race-Focused Approaches to Examine Motivation in Educational Contexts 115

8 Identity, Motivation, and Resilience: The Example of Black College Students in Science, Technology, Engineering, and Mathematics 117
Tabbye M. Chavous, Samantha Drotar, Gloryvee Fonseca-Bolorin, Seanna Leath, Donald Lyons, and Faheemah Mustafaa

9 Asset-Based Pedagogies and Latino Students' Achievement and Identity 133
Francesca López

10 Role of Culture and Proximal Minority/Majority Status in Adolescent Identity Negotiations 152
Revathy Kumar, Stuart A. Karabenick, and Jeffery H. Warnke

11 Motivation and Achievement of Hispanic College Students in the United States 168
Tim Urdan and Veronica Herr

Contents vii

12 Desegregating Gifted Education for Culturally Different
Students: Recommendations for Equitable Recruitment
and Retention 183
Donna Y. Ford

PART IV
**Future Directions in Examining Race and Ethnicity in
the Study of Motivation** **199**

13 A Future Agenda for Researching Race and Ethnicity in
the Study of Motivation in Educational Contexts 201
Jessica T. DeCuir-Gunby, Paul A. Schutz, and Sonya D. Harris

About the Contributors *212*
Index *219*

FOREWORD: MOTIVATION AND RACIAL-ETHNIC DYNAMICS

Lyn Corno

Historically, human motivation theory has ignored important categories of potential difference, including factors traditionally framed as biographical such as gender and racial-cultural background. Principles from prominent information processing models such as theories of expectancy × value, attribution, efficacy, and self-regulation all assumed generality across population subgroups that were inflexible. Thus, research into the validity of such principles tends to reflect findings from general samples without disaggregating hypothetically important subgroups or to use samples that are relatively homogeneous. In addition, only recently have theorists begun to define constructs such as race and gender as dynamic social constructions rather than aspects of biology.

Thus, until now, scholars have done little to advance understanding of differences by racial-cultural identity. They have not clarified what it means for motivation and its consequences to be a person of color or a member of some other recognizable nondominant group. With this book, editors DeCuir-Gunby and Schutz focus on the motivation issues presented in education settings by students of varying racial-ethnic profiles, including African American and Latino students, as well as Arab Americans and Asian-Pacific Islanders.

Some of the questions to be raised in this discussion are: How do these students view themselves as learners and participants in school contexts? What are their aspirations for education in the short and long terms? What steps do they take to prepare for their future? What is the role of families, friends, and teachers—including the diversity reflected in these groups—in helping students gain equal access to opportunities for advanced education and jobs? And what specific skills or social networks are gaining prominence in these pursuits? How do these factors influence students' emotional responses in school and social situations? In short, the chapters presented address the strengths and struggles being faced by students with different racial-ethnic identities as they negotiate education and assume their journeys in life.

It is clear that research is shedding light as well on the complexities that underlie the goal of proportionately representing minorities in different education arenas (from special education programs to STEM courses to graduate schools), where sometimes there is overrepresentation and other times underrepresentation. It is likewise clear that there are patterns of motivated engagement and its consequences that are globally identifiable rather than limited to examples from just the United States. New and innovative programs are needed to address these and other concerns.

In my view, this edited book could not be more timely. Recent responses to police killings by organizations such as Black Lives Matter and the anti-Muslim sentiment blanketing the nations in the wake of Islam-connected acts of terror illustrate the costs when people feel the effects of violence. There are hidden ways that race and cultural heritage shape outcomes. Moreover, there is more at stake in modern society than motivation for education and how to address it in such contexts, although this volume clearly demonstrates the importance of education as a place to begin the dialogue.

The research presented here is complementary to efforts such as the work of Stanford social psychologist Jennifer Eberhardt (Eberhardt, Davies, Purdie-Vaughns & Johnson, 2006). Along with her students, Eberhardt has been documenting the "implicit bias, arising from America's tortured racial history [in which] still pervasive inequities . . . [are] underrecognized, especially in the context of criminal justice" (Scott, 2015, p. 48). Her experiments demonstrate that subconscious racial bias is a common human condition with stinging effects on motivation and outcomes well beyond education. To impact the criminal justice system is a current goal, so Eberhardt is developing and implementing active policies and programs with law enforcement agencies in several states. Her programs are intended not simply to raise awareness about dangerous consequences of implicit bias but to actually do something about them. No doubt contributors to the present volume on motivation would rise to this occasion and stand alongside her. Scholarship like this is ripe for comprehensive treatment, beginning with the chapters presented here.

References

Eberhardt, J. L., Davies, P. G., Purdie-Vaughns, V. J., & Johnson, S L. (2006). Looking death-worthy: Perceived stereotypicality of black defendants predicts capital-sentencing outcomes. *Psychological Science, 15*(5), 383–386.

Scott, S. (2015, September–October). A hard look at how we see race. *Stanford: A publication of the Stanford Alumni Association*, 46–51.

PART I

An Introduction to Race and Ethnicity in the Study of Motivation in Education

1

RESEARCHING RACE AND ETHNICITY IN THE STUDY OF MOTIVATION IN EDUCATIONAL CONTEXTS

An Introduction

Paul A. Schutz and Jessica T. DeCuir-Gunby

Issues related to race and ethnicity have always played a role in the history of the United States (e.g., see *Plessy v. Ferguson*, 1896; *Scott v. Sanford*, 1856), including the development of our schools (see *Brown v. Board of Education of Topeka*, 1954; *Mendez v. Westminster School District*, 1946). With the current prediction that people of color will represent nearly 50% of the population by 2050 (U.S. Census Bureau, 2012) and that schools are now almost 50% students of color (Kena et al., 2015), it seems clear that issues related to race and ethnicity will play an increasingly important role in all aspects of society, particularly the school system. As such, research related to the roles that race and ethnicity play in teaching, learning, and motivational processes is needed.

Although there is a clear need for research on motivation from a racial/ethnicity lens, it is also the case that inquiry from this perspective is challenging. That challenge begins with the attempt to define constructs like race and ethnicity. For example, because of the socially constructed nature of race, the definition of race and who is classified as a particular race has continued to change over time, as have definitions and notions of ethnicity (DeCuir-Gunby & Schutz, 2014; Haney Lopez, 1997; U.S. Census, 2012). To compound this challenge, scientists have found little genetic difference between racial groups (Jorde & Wooding, 2004; Omi & Winant, 1994; Smedley & Smedley, 2005). For example, Lehrman (2003) indicated that at the genetic level, *Homo sapiens* share around 99.9% of their DNA. This suggests that at the genetic level there should be few differences among racial and ethnic groups. Yet in our schools, students of color tend to be overrepresented in special education programs and underrepresented in gifted and advanced programs (DeCuir-Gunby & Schutz, 2014; Ford, Chapter 12, this volume), suggesting differential treatment based on social indicators. Thus, as indicated by DeCuir-Gunby and Schutz (2014), "although race may not have a genetic basis, it is important sociohistorically, and it is therefore vital for social scientists to investigate race as a sociohistoric phenomenon" (p. 4).

Given the aforementioned challenges and importance of research in this area, our aim in this edited book is to present in a single publication the work of researchers who use race-reimaged or race-focused constructs while investigating motivation within educational contexts (see DeCuir-Gunby & Schutz, 2014). A race-reimaged focus is where traditional motivational constructs (e.g., self-efficacy, self-regulation, achievement motivation, etc.) are reconceptualized to include racially influenced, sociocultural perspectives (e.g., history, context, multiple identities, etc.). A race-focused approach involves placing racial constructs at the center of analysis (e.g., influence of Hispanic/Latino students' racial/ethnic identity development on academic identity, motivation, and achievement). With such an approach, the racial constructs themselves are important for understanding the educational experience.

In doing so, this volume includes innovative approaches that will push the theoretical and methodological boundaries for researching race and ethnicity in educational contexts. For this reason, we expect this edited volume will become a standard source of reference for those researchers interested in studying the roles that race and ethnicity play in teaching, learning, and motivational processes. Additionally, this volume will make a contribution to ongoing debates regarding the study of motivation in educational contexts. In general, the objectives of this edited volume are to (1) interrogate the use of the social historical constructs of race and ethnicity and (2) discuss how those constructs can be best used in the study of teaching, learning, and motivation in educational contexts.

This volume features a number of important and influential scholars who represent a variety of disciplines (e.g., educational psychology, teacher education, gifted education, etc.), scientific paradigms (e.g., experimental research, nonexperimental field studies, critical perspectives, and postpositivist perspectives), and research methods (e.g., quantitative, qualitative, and mixed methods). Thus the authors take an eclectic and holistic look at research in this area, presenting current approaches from diverse perspectives, thereby making this volume a significant contribution to the field.

Book Structure

The book is organized into *five sections*. In the first section, Chapter 1, the present chapter, we begin the discussion of the goals of the book related to researching race and ethnicity in the study of teaching, learning, and motivation in educational contexts and set the stage for the remainder of the book.

The second section is titled "Using Race-Reimaged Approaches to Examine Motivation in Educational Contexts." The authors in this section, informed by many of the key traditional motivational theoretical frameworks (e.g., attribution theory, self-determination theory, social cognitive theory, achievement motivation theory), focus on developing understandings regarding race and ethnicity in educational contexts from those theoretical perspectives. This section features such scholars as Sandra Graham; Kelly A. Rodgers; DeLeon L. Gray, LaBarron K. Hill, Lauren H. Bryant, Jason R. Wornoff, Oriana Johnson, and Lisa Jackson; Shirley L. Yu, Danya M. Corkin, and Julie P. Martin; Rhonda Bondie and Akane Zusho; and Cynthia Hudley and Su-Je Cho.

In Chapter 2, Sandra Graham draws on her research that has used attribution theory as a framework for addressing the achievement motivation and social outcomes of ethnic minority youth. She focuses on four areas: the feedback provided by teachers and how it indirectly communicates a low ability attribution; the consequences of causal controllability (responsibility) on African American boys labeled as aggressive and our efforts to change their maladaptive attributions about responsibility in others; the controllability attributions that adults in the juvenile justice system make about adolescent offenders and how these attributions might help us understand racial disparities in the treatment of juvenile offenders; and the attributions of victimized youth and how the school racial context can be an antecedent to particular attributions. The goal of her chapter is to illustrate ways in which her research uses an attributional lens to shed light on the school experiences of ethnic minority youth and how educators can help make those experiences better.

In Chapter 3, Kelly A. Rodgers takes a look at the motivational issues underlying retention and persistence of college students of color in science, technology, engineering, and mathematics (STEM) programs. Specifically, in this chapter she examines the ideas of retention versus persistence, situating them within a self-determination framework to understand the motivation of students of color in STEM fields. She begins the chapter with a discussion of persistence, a student-centered variable, versus retention, an institution-centered variable. Then factors shown to be integral to both retention and persistence in STEM are discussed, with a focus on those factors that may apply to all students and with specific focus on those factors relevant to students of color. After an overview of the theory, she discusses the motivation of college students of color within the context of Deci and Ryan's (2000) self-determination theory. She concludes the chapter with directions for research, as well as suggestions for students and institutions.

In Chapter 4, DeLeon L. Gray, LaBarron K. Hill, Lauren H. Bryant, Jason R. Wornoff, Oriana Johnson, and Lisa Jackson, using unique research methods, examine the connections among students' social experiences and their emotions, motivation, and achievement by using heart rate variability as a biomarker of emotion regulation, physical health, and cognitive functioning. They point out that little research is available that examines whether—and under what conditions—students' social experiences are linked with their patterns of cardiovascular reactivity. They use a sample of African American high school students and provide results that reveal that patterns of cardiovascular activity are a function of students'

6 Paul A. Schutz and Jessica T. DeCuir-Gunby

perceptions of how much they fit in with their peers. Importantly, these patterns differ depending on whether the student is an African American male or an African American female. This work represents their effort to think beyond the current borders of educational psychology research in hopes of substantially advancing discourse on African American students' experiences in achievement contexts.

In Chapter 5, Shirley L. Yu, Danya M. Corkin, and Julie P. Martin examine the issue of the underrepresentation of students of color in engineering majors and careers. They point out that significant national efforts have been made during the last three decades to increase the number of underrepresented minority (URM) students in STEM disciplines, yet only modest increases have been realized. In addition, research that examines contextual and cultural factors among URM students that may promote or hinder their persistence in STEM remains important. Their chapter focuses on research informed by social cognitive career theory (SCCT; Lent, Brown, & Hackett, 1994), which has identified psychological and contextual factors that play a major role in students' persistence and success in different subjects and careers. They review studies that have examined the influence of racial and/or ethnic identity, acculturation, parent/teacher/peer support, and barriers such as racism on the motivation of URMs to persist in STEM domains. Their conclusions have implications for researchers and educators who wish to promote URMs' motivation to persist in STEM disciplines.

In Chapter 6, Rhonda S. Bondie and Akane Zusho describe their implementation of a motivationally based teacher professional development (PD) program called ALL-ED (*All Learners Learning Every Day*) across 15 New York City public high schools serving immigrant students with low literacy in their native languages. Their ALL-ED program is rooted in theories of motivation and self-regulated learning and focuses on improving teachers' abilities to integrate motivationally and cognitively supportive instructional routines into their daily practice so that teachers provide *all* students with equal and optimal opportunities to learn. More specifically, ALL-ED helps teachers instantiate a mastery-oriented approach to instruction by improving teachers' ability to develop and use clear, rigorous, and relevant *tasks* that are tied to instructional standards; formative *assessments* that promote monitoring and self-regulated learning (SRL); *group* routines that promote efficient and effective collaboration; and instructional practices that promote *choice* and *autonomy* (see http://all-ed.org for more information). They also present data collected during the 2013–2014 academic year on the 39 teachers who participated in the ALL-ED PD, focusing more specifically on the six teachers (two math, three science, and one social studies) for whom they have observational, survey, and teacher and student interview data.

In Chapter 7, Cynthia Hudley and Su-je Cho examine school engagement and future expectations in a culturally diverse sample of high school students. Most importantly, their analyses include an examination of ethnic diversity among the population subsumed under the racial label Asian-Pacific Islander (API).

Their analyses examine how students' future expectations are related to behavioral and affective engagement as well as to perceptions of classroom climate. Their results reveal that perceived climate and measures of student engagement are indeed related to future expectations, and this relationship is moderated by ethnicity. Overall, their findings speak to the powerful impact of relationships for sustaining student engagement, and they draw implications for schools about the broad variability that can be subsumed under monolithic racial labels such as API. In doing so, they demonstrate the importance of disaggregating data in order to reflect the heterogeneity in the API population.

The third section of the book, "Using Race-Focused Approaches to Examine Motivation in Educational Contexts," focuses on how educational contexts transact with culture to influence student identity, engagement, and achievement. This section features chapters by Tabbye M. Chavous, Samantha Drotar, Gloryvee Fonseca-Bolorin, Seanna Leath, Donald Lyons, and Faheemah Mustafaa; Francesca López; Revathy Kumar, Stuart A. Karabenick, and Jeffery H. Warnke; Tim Urdan and Veronica Herr; and Donna Y. Ford who investigate challenges and opportunities related to student identity, engagement, belonging, and achievement.

In Chapter 8, Tabbye M. Chavous, Samantha Drotar, Gloryvee Fonseca-Bolorin, Seanna Leath, Donald Lyons, and Faheemah Mustafaa highlight psychological, motivational, and contextual factors related to Black student achievement in predominantly White universities, with emphasis on STEM fields where Blacks are particularly underrepresented. In contrast to common deficit explanations of Black achievement, they take a risk and resilience approach. Specifically, they conceptualize Black students' normative experiences of racial stigma on campus (e.g., discrimination, microaggressions, token status) as a motivational risk factor. At the same time, they consider individual-level assets related to students' racial and cultural backgrounds—including their racial and gender identities—that may promote positive academic identity and motivation and help mitigate the negative impacts of stigmatizing experiences on motivation and persistence. Along with student-level assets, they note the importance of context-level characteristics—including institutional supports, resources, and opportunities—as critical to promoting motivation and academic resilience in settings where Black students normatively experience minority status and stigma due to race and gender.

In Chapter 9, Francesca López describes a framework that incorporates *critical awareness* and *asset-based pedagogy* (ABP) with *teacher expectancy* and *effectiveness* studies to address the paucity of evidence on classroom dynamics research focused on traditionally marginalized youth. She illustrates the application of the framework by describing a study in which she examines the extent to which dimensions of teacher-reported ABP beliefs and behaviors are associated with upper-elementary Latino students' identity and achievement outcomes in reading. Consistent with the assertions in extant literature that ABP is related to students' outcomes, López finds that teachers' beliefs and behaviors reflecting consideration of students' cultural backgrounds (e.g., incorporating students' culture into the curriculum) are positively related to students' reading and identity outcomes. Her research also uncovers issues with the current conceptualization of teacher expectancy, which has implications for educational psychology research. She discusses the need for future research to consider mixed-methods approaches to further refine the theories about the ways students' identities are shaped in the context of classrooms.

In Chapter 10, Revathy Kumar, Stuart A. Karabenick, and Jeffery H. Warnke discuss their interdisciplinary approach that utilized multiple research methods to frame the opportunities and constraints on adolescents' identity negotiations as well as their social and academic adjustment. They focus on their research project that examines Arab American and Chaldean adolescents' identity negotiations and adjustment in culturally diverse American schools. The theoretical perspectives framing the project include social identity theory, intergroup contact hypothesis, and the social cognitive theory of motivation—achievement goal theory. They utilize multiple data collection methodologies including focus-group interviews and survey data from students, web-based survey data from teachers and principals, and implicit association test data regarding attitudes toward minority students from teachers. In their chapter they discuss some of the findings based on qualitative and quantitative analysis of data from adolescents and teachers to highlight the importance of triangulation of findings from multiple sources using multiple methodologies. Their chapter also illustrates the importance for researchers to be mindful that *culture* is not merely a categorical variable in the study of learning and motivation, rather it is the foundation and framework that guides adolescents' motivations, identity negotiations, and behaviors.

In Chapter 11, Tim Urdan and Veronica Herr focus on how Hispanic students in the United States are a diverse and growing segment of the student body. They describe how these students differ in their familial country of origin, generational status, and socioeconomic background. In addition, Hispanic students engage in the complex developmental task of developing social, ethnic, and academic identities within two distinct cultural contexts: the native culture of the family and the broader culture of U.S. society. In this chapter, they explore how several of the factors associated with the bicultural identity of Hispanic students in the United States influence their motivation and achievement in school. In particular, they consider how both conscious processes (e.g., ethnic identity, possible selves, educational aspirations, goals, language proficiency) and nonconscious processes (e.g., acculturation, stereotype threat) interact and influence how Hispanic students in the United States view themselves and school. Their chapter includes a discussion of their recent research examining the motivation of academically successful Latino college students and concludes with recommendations for improving the motivational climate of schools serving Hispanic students.

In Chapter 12, Donna Y. Ford discusses how nationally and in the majority of states, Black and Hispanic students are underrepresented in gifted education. Underrepresentation is most extensive for Black males. In her chapter, Ford shares data on racially segregated gifted programs using information from the Office for Civil Rights Data Collection for several years. Recruitment and retention barriers are presented, along with recommendations for desegregating gifted education for such students. She also shares an equity formula, based on a 2013 court case, to guide decision makers in setting representation goals that help decrease discrimination and that increase access to gifted education. Finally, Ford focuses on the importance of preparing educators to be culturally responsive.

The final section, titled *Future Directions in Examining Race and Ethnicity in the Study of Motivation*, includes a chapter by Jessica DeCuir-Gunby, Paul A. Schutz, and Sonya D. Harris. In this chapter they synthesize the themes that emerged from the other chapters in the volume. They also discuss future directions for inquiry on race and ethnicity in the study of motivation in educational contexts and for educational research in general, as well as provide a discussion on methodological issues. Finally, they also discuss practical implications for teaching, learning, and educational policy as it pertains to motivation.

Conclusion

As indicated, the racial demographics of the United States are rapidly changing. The increase in racial/ethnic diversity undoubtedly means that race and ethnicity will play an increasingly important role in teaching-learning contexts. As such, research related to the roles that race and ethnicity play in teaching, learning, and motivational processes is needed. It is our hope that this edited book will begin to address more systematically several of those concerns.

References

Brown v. Board of Education of Topeka, 347 U.S. 483 (1954).
Deci, E. L., & Ryan, R. M. (2000). The "what" and "why" of goal pursuits: Human needs and the self-determination of behavior. *Psychological Inquiry, 11*, 227–268.
DeCuir-Gunby, J. T., & Schutz, P. A. (2014). Researching race within educational psychology contexts. *Educational Psychologist, 49*(4), 244–260.
Haney Lopez, I. F. (1997). Race, ethnicity, erasure: The salience of race to LatCrit theory. *California Law Review, 85*, 1143–1211.
Jorde, B. L., & Wooding, S. P. (2004). Genetic variation, classification and "race." *Nature Genetics, 36*, 528–533.
Kena, G., Musu-Gillette, L., Robinson, J., Wang, X., Rathbun, A., Zhang, J., Wilkinson-Flicker, S., Barmer, A., & Dunlop Velez, E. (2015). The condition of education 2015 (NCES 2015–144). U.S. Department of Education, National Center for Education Statistics. Washington, DC. Retrieved September 1, 2015 from http://nces.ed.gov/pubsearch
Lehrman, S. (2003). The reality of race. *Scientific American, 288*, 32.
Lent, R. W., Brown, S. D., & Hackett, G. (1994). Toward a unifying social cognitive theory of career and academic interest, choice, and performance. *Journal of Vocational Behavior, 45*(1), 79–122.
Mendez v. Westminster School District, 64 F. Supp. 544, 549 (S.D. Cal. 1946).

Omi, M., & Winant, H. (1994). *Racial formation in the United States: From the 1960s to the 1990s* (2nd ed.). New York, NY: Routledge.

Plessy v. Ferguson, 163 U.S. 537 (1896).

Scott v. Sanford 60, U.S. 393 (1856).

Smedley, A., & Smedley, B. D. (2005). Race as biology is fiction, racism as a social problem is real. *American Psychologist, 60*, 16–26.

U.S. Census Bureau. (2012). *The statistical abstract.* Retrieved June 19, 2013, from http://www.census.gov/compendia/statab/2012edition.html

PART II

Using Race-Reimaged Approaches to Examine Motivation in Educational Contexts

2

AN ATTRIBUTIONAL PERSPECTIVE ON MOTIVATION IN ETHNIC MINORITY YOUTH

Sandra Graham

Almost 30 years ago (Graham, 1988), I published an article with the title "Can Attribution Theory Tell Us Something About Motivation in Blacks?" That article appeared early in my academic career and still relatively early in the development of an attributional theory of motivation. But as an intellectually still maturing scholar conducting motivation research with an emergent theory, it was evident to me even in 1988 that many of our concerns about motivational patterns of African American youth—such as the relationships between self-esteem and academic achievement, expectations and aspirations, perceptions of powerful others, and coping with academic failure—were amenable to attributional analyses. We were just scratching the surface at the time.

In this chapter, I draw on my history as an attribution researcher for more than 30 years to describe some of my research that has used attribution theory as a framework for addressing the achievement motivation and social outcomes of ethnic minority youth, with a particular focus in some cases on African American youth. Researchers who study academic and social outcomes of ethnic minority youth are often studying challenges of enormous complexity—for example, the racial achievement gap and, increasingly, the racial discipline gap. I want to make the case that a good theory can help us manage some of that complexity. A good theory can help us choose the research problems that we study, frame those problems as questions that can be empirically studied, and guide our thinking about change. My goal is to illustrate some of the ways in which my research uses an attributional lens to shed light on the school experiences of ethnic minority youth and how we can help make those experiences better.

14 Sandra Graham

A Brief Summary of Attribution Theory

To lay the conceptual groundwork for the research presented in this chapter, I begin with an overview of the main principles of an attributional theory of motivation. Attribution theory originated with the publication of Fritz Heider's book, *The Psychology of Interpersonal Relations* (Heider, 1958). Many theorists associated with attributional analyses followed Heider, but in this chapter I focus on attribution theory as formulated and elaborated by Bernard Weiner (see reviews in Weiner, 1986, 1995, 2006). The main principles of the theory are depicted in Figure 2.1. Think of the linkages as a temporal sequence that begins with an outcome interpreted as a success or failure. Following an initial reaction of happiness or sadness (outcome-dependent emotions), individuals then undertake a causal search to determine why that outcome occurred. Attributions are answers to those "why" questions, such as "Why did I fail the exam?" when the motivational domain is achievement, or "Why don't I have any friends?" when the motivational domain is affiliation. Individuals make attributions about other people as well as themselves. For example, the American public continues to be riveted by a string of lethal police shootings of unarmed Black youth like 18-year-old Michael Brown in Ferguson, Missouri, 12-year-old Tamir Rice in Cleveland, and most recently 17-year-old LaQuan McDonald in Chicago. Most of the commentary associated with these shootings implicitly or explicitly asks "why?" Did the victims engage in threatening behavior? Did the perpetrators have malicious intent? Individuals especially make attributions about themselves and about other people following negative or unexpected outcomes (Gendolla & Koller, 2001; Stupnisky, Stewart, Daniels, & Perry, 2011). Causal search can therefore help us impose order on an unpredictable environment.

In the achievement domain, which has served as a model for the study of causality in other contexts, Figure 2.1 shows that success and failure often are attributed to an *ability* factor that includes both aptitude and acquired skills, an *effort* factor that can be either temporary or sustained, the difficulty of the task, luck, mood, and help or hindrance from others. Among these causal ascriptions, in this culture at least, ability and effort are the most dominant perceived causes of success and failure. When explaining achievement outcomes, individuals attach the most importance to how smart they are and how hard they try.

Because specific attributional content will vary among motivational domains as well as between individuals within a domain, attribution theorists have focused on the underlying dimensions or properties of causes in addition to specific causes per se. Here we ask, for example, how are ability and effort similar and how are they different? Are there other attributions that share the overlapping and non-overlapping properties of ability and effort? As I will illustrate, understanding the conceptual distinctions between ability and effort, or *can* and *want*, as attributions about oneself or other people provides insight into a number of important achievement-related experiences of ethnic minority youth.

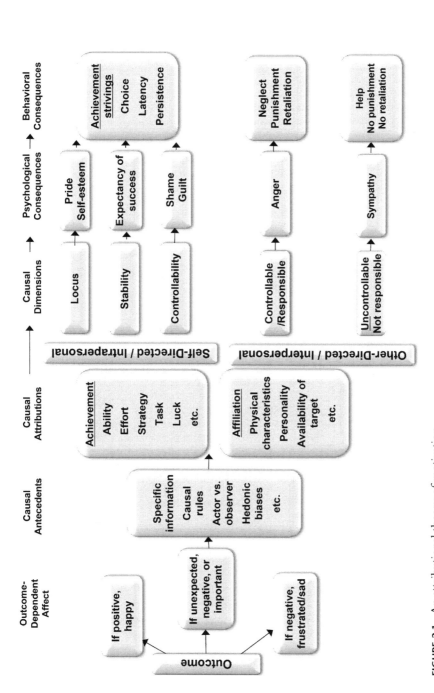

FIGURE 2.1 An attributional theory of motivation

16 Sandra Graham

Three causal dimensions have been identified with some certainty. These are *locus*, or whether a cause is internal or external to the individual; *stability*, which designates a cause as constant or varying over time; and *controllability*, or whether a cause is subject to volitional influence. All causes theoretically are classified according to each of these dimensions. For example, ability is typically perceived as internal, stable, and uncontrollable. When we attribute our failure to low ability, we tend to see this as a characteristic of ourselves, enduring over time, and beyond personal control. Effort, on the other hand, is also internal but unstable and controllable. Failure attributed to insufficient effort indicates a personal characteristic that is modifiable by one's own volitional behavior.

Each dimension is uniquely related to a set of cognitive, emotional, and behavioral consequences. As shown in Figure 2.1, the locus dimension of causality is related to self-esteem and esteem-related emotions like pride and shame. We feel more pride and shame when we succeed or fail because of internal rather than external causes. The stability dimension affects subjective expectancy about future success and failure. When achievement failure is attributed to a stable cause, such as low aptitude, one is more likely to expect the same outcome to occur again than when the cause is an unstable factor, such as lack of effort. These relations between the causal dimension of locus and stability and affect and expectancy are especially pertinent to the intrapersonal component of attribution theory (how I feel about myself; top right quadrant of Figure 2.1).

As the third dimension of causality, causal controllability relates largely to perceived responsibility in *others* and therefore is linked to a set of interpersonal cognitive, emotional, and behavioral consequences that are directed toward other people. These relations are depicted in the bottom right quadrant of Figure 2.1. When other people's failures are perceived as caused by controllable factors—the person is responsible—such as lack of effort, this elicits anger, retaliation, punishment, or withholding of help. For example, the able-bodied welfare recipient who refuses to work tends to elicit anger from taxpayers because that person is perceived as responsible for their plight. Others' failures perceived as caused by uncontrollable factors—the person is not responsible—evokes sympathy or pity and the desire to help. We tend to pity the physically disabled person and want to help because they are perceived as not responsible for their plight. These linkages suggest a particular set of relations between attributions, emotions, and behavior. Our causal thoughts tell us how to feel and our feelings in turn guide behavior.

With this overview of the theory as a guide, I now describe four programs of attribution research that capture parts of the intrapersonal and interpersonal sequences depicted in Figure 2.1. First, I turn to causal antecedents and describe how teacher feedback can indirectly communicate a low ability attribution. Next, I turn to the consequences of causal controllability (responsibility) as I describe research on African American boys labeled as aggressive and our efforts to change their maladaptive attributions about responsibility in others. Because children labeled as aggressive are at risk for involvement in the juvenile justice system, I then examine the controllability attributions that adults in that system make about adolescent offenders and how these attributions might help us understand racial disparities in the treatment of juvenile offenders. And finally I return to intrapersonal processes to study the attributions of victimized youth and how the school racial context can be an antecedent to particular attributions.

Teacher Feedback as an Attributional Antecedent

How do perceivers arrive at the attributions that they make about themselves or other people? One source of attributional information, particularly about effort and ability and especially relevant to motivation in school, is feedback from teachers. Teachers no doubt often directly and intentionally tell their students that they did not put forth enough effort, for trying hard has moral implications and is certainly compatible with the work ethic espoused in school. Although teachers typically do not intentionally tell their students that they are low in ability, this attributional information may be subtly, indirectly, and even unknowingly conveyed.

In a series of laboratory-experimental studies, we drew on basic attribution principles to document that three seemingly positive teacher behaviors can indirectly function as low ability cues (see Graham, 1990). The particular behaviors examined in these studies were communicated sympathy following failure; unsolicited offers of help; and the giving of praise following success, particularly at easy tasks.

We know from attribution theory that failure attributed to uncontrollable factors such as lack of ability elicits sympathy from others, and sympathy, in turn, promotes offers of help. This is in contrast to failure attributed to controllable causes such as lack of effort, which tends to evoke anger and the withholding of help. Now suppose that a teacher does respond with sympathy versus anger toward a failing student or with an unsolicited offer of help rather than neglect. It might be the case that students will then use these affective and behavioral displays to infer the teacher's attribution and his or her own self-ascription for failure.

We tested the attribution cue function of expressed sympathy and anger in a laboratory task involving manipulated failure (Graham, 1984). About 180 sixth-grade African American and White students were given four trials of repeated failure on a novel puzzle-solving task. The puzzles were tangrams requiring the student to construct geometric forms from sets of seven pieces (five different-size triangles, a square, a rhomboid). Each form to be constructed was depicted on a 7 × 11 in card with no indication of how the piece fit together. Participants had to put all the pieces in place to match a design within a limited amount of time—in this case 1 minute. All the puzzles were solvable but not within 1 minute based on pilot testing. Following "failure," a female experimenter posing as a teacher conveyed either mild sympathy, anger, or no affect. Children were randomly assigned to one of the three affect conditions. After the failure trials, four attributions were rated on nine-point scales including low ability and lack of effort.

Figure 2.2 shows the attributions to low ability and lack of effort as a function of the affect condition. The findings were the same across African American and White participants, so the data are combined. It is evident that affective displays of "teachers" communicated attributional information. Participants in the sympathy condition were more likely to attribute their failure to low ability. In the anger condition, compared to the other conditions, attributions to lack of effort were elevated. Thus, as predicted, a teacher display of sympathy can indirectly communicate low ability information.

Too much praise, like sympathy, can also function as a low ability cue. Two attribution principles are relevant here. First, praise is related to perceived effort expenditure in that the successful student who tries hard is maximally rewarded. Second, effort and ability are often perceived as compensatory causes of achievement: in both success and failure, the higher one's perceived effort, the lower one's perceived ability, and vice versa. Thus if two students achieve the same outcome, often the one who tries harder (and is praised) is perceived as lower in ability. George Barker and I had 5- to 12-year-old students watch videotapes of two students solving math problems, and both got the exact same number right (Barker & Graham, 1987). The teacher publically praised one student and gave only neutral feedback to the other student. Participants were then asked to rate the ability and effort of each student. It was documented that older students who were praised for success at a relatively easy task were inferred to be lower in ability

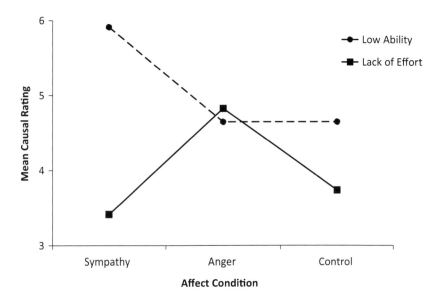

FIGURE 2.2 Teacher sympathy and anger as attributional cues (from Graham, 1984)

than their counterparts who received neutral feedback. In other words, the offering of praise following success, like communicated sympathy following failure, functioned as a low ability cue. Barker and I conducted a similar study in which we manipulated whether a teacher offered unsolicited help to one student and ignored the other (Graham & Barker, 1990). The student who was helped by the teacher, like praise and sympathy, was a low ability cue.

I believe these findings are just as relevant today to understanding some of the motivational challenges of ethnic minority youth as they were when I carried out the studies more than 20 years ago. Although not grounded in attributional analyses, there is quite a bit of contemporary research from social psychologists documenting how teacher behaviors similar to those I highlight can undermine motivation and performance of ethnic minority students. For example, in research on social stigma, African American students reported lower academic self-esteem when they received what the authors called *assumptive help* (help that is given without clear evidence of need) on an intelligence test from a White confederate than did their African American counterparts who received no such help (Schneider, Major, Luhtanen, & Crocker, 1996). Consistent with our attributional analysis, these authors proposed that help that is not requested can confirm a "suspicion of inferiority" among African Americans who regularly confront the negative stereotypes about their group's intellectual abilities.

Too much praise and, by implication, too little criticism for poor performance seems to be particularly directed toward ethnic minority students. For example, Harber and colleagues have documented a "positive feedback bias," defined as a tendency for teachers to provide fewer critical comments to African American and Latino students compared to White students with the same low achievement (Harber et al., 2012). The teachers in Harber's research appear to have been motivated by egalitarian concerns about not appearing prejudiced and the desire to protect the self-esteem of vulnerable minority students. The downside was that the minority students were not the beneficiaries of ability-confirming constructive feedback that communicated high expectations and more clarity about where to exert effort.

In summary, principles from attribution theory help explain how some well-intentioned teacher behaviors might sometimes function as low ability cues. Teachers might be more likely to engage in such feedback patterns when they desire to protect the self-esteem of failure-prone students. I am not suggesting that teachers should never help their students or that they should always be angry rather than sympathetic or critical as opposed to complimentary. The appropriateness of any communication, or what has been labeled "wise" feedback (criticism but with communicating high expectations; Yeager et al., 2014), will depend on many factors, including the characteristics of both students and teachers. Rather, the general message is that attribution principles can facilitate our understanding of how some well-intentioned teacher behaviors can have unexpected negative effects on the motivation of ethnic minority students.

20 Sandra Graham

Attributions of African American Boys Labeled as Aggressive

In this section I integrate social motivation and academic motivation to describe a program of research on African American boys labeled as aggressive. Here I draw on a set of attribution principles about relations between perceived responsibility, anger, and retaliation. As someone who began her career studying academic motivation, what led me to research on childhood aggression? The answer is simple. I was at the time and continue to be concerned about the serious consequences of antisocial behavior for young African American males. Black males are much more likely than their White counterparts to be labeled as aggressive by teachers and to be suspended or expelled from school for so-called aggressive behavior (e.g., Howard, 2014). Furthermore, a large empirical literature has documented the stability of aggression from childhood to young adulthood as well as its relation to a host of negative outcomes including low academic achievement, school dropout in adolescence, juvenile delinquency, and even adult criminality and psychopathology (Dodge, Coie, & Lynam, 2006). And most of these known correlates of childhood aggression are disproportionately prevalent among ethnic minorities, particularly African American males. The 20-year-old Black male dropout, inmate, or gang member is often the 10-year-old boy labeled as aggressive by teachers and peers.

When I first became interested in aggression in the early 1990s, I was drawn to the findings of developmental psychologists John Coie and Kenneth Dodge. A very robust finding in the peer aggression literature is that aggressive youth (primarily boys) display what is called a *hostile attributional bias* (Dodge et al., 2006). Aggressive boys overattribute negative intent to others, particularly in situations of ambiguously caused provocation. To illustrate, imagine a situation in which a youngster experiences a social transgression, such as being pushed by a peer while waiting in line, and it is unclear whether the peer's behavior was intended or not. Aggressive boys are more likely than their nonaggressive classmates to report that the push occurred intentionally ("he did it on purpose," he is *responsible*). Attributions to hostile intent then lead to anger and the desire to retaliate. Even among socially competent children, the individual who believes that another acted with hostile intent can feel justified in endorsing aggressive behavior. This goes back to basic attribution principles depicted in Figure 2.1 about responsibility inferences, feelings of anger, and their relations to punitive behavior. The problem with aggressive children is that they often inappropriately or prematurely assume hostile peer intent in ambiguous situations.

We started with the hostile bias finding and embraced an attributional lens to reason as follows: If attributions to others' negative intent instigate a set of reactions that leads to aggression, then it might be possible to train aggression-prone children to see ambiguous peer provocation as less intended. This should mitigate anger as well as the tendency to react with hostility. By the early 1990s, there

Attributional Perspective on Motivation **21**

were many successful attribution change programs in the achievement domain—training students to infer that failure was due to lack of effort rather than low ability or to unstable factors more generally (Wilson, Damiani, & Shelton, 2002). We reasoned that the same principles of attribution change could apply to the social domain and changing the perceived causes of others' aggression.

In dissertation research, my student Cynthia Hudley developed a school-based attributional intervention to alter the responsibility attributions of African American boys labeled as aggressive (Hudley & Graham, 1993). The fundamental goal of the intervention was to train aggressive boys to accurately detect responsibility and intentionality from social cues and to assume nonmalicious intent in ambiguous situations. The specific curriculum, *Brainpower*, consisted of 12 lessons clustered into three components. The first component strengthened aggressive participants' ability to detect others' intentions accurately. To achieve these skills, students learned to search for, interpret, and properly categorize the verbal, physical, and behavioral cues exhibited by others in social situations. After the participants gained skills in discerning social cues, the second component trained them to attribute ambiguous negative outcomes (i.e., when social cues are inconsistent or not interpretable) to uncontrollable or accidental causes. For example, students role-played ambiguous peer interactions (e.g., a peer spills your milk in the lunchroom). Students then brainstormed possible causes for the actions, categorized those causes as deliberate or unintentional, and then decided which attributions would be good decisions given uncertainty about the peer's intent. The third component linked negative social outcomes to appropriate nonaggressive behavioral responses. For example, lessons taught children to develop decision rules for potentially dangerous situations (e.g., "If someone threatens me, find an adult right away") to minimize the possibility of aggressive confrontations.

Brainpower was successful in changing the attributions and anger-related emotions of African American boys labeled as aggressive (see Hudley, 2008). We identified a particular population of African American males labeled as aggressive. We were able to conceptualize their status in terms of a motivational sequence relating feelings of anger to biased responsibility attributions and subsequent behavior. And by changing their causal thinking, we were able to show changes in the feelings and behavior that theoretically follow such thoughts. I think *Brainpower* may still be one of few programs to document the success of an attributional intervention with children in the social domain.

The success of *Brainpower* encouraged us to think more broadly. Social behavior problems and academic motivation problems often go hand in hand. Children who aggress against others often have histories of low achievement motivation, characterized by failing grades and school disengagement in general. So we began to think about whether we could combine a focus on both social and academic motivation: an intervention that could both *decrease* the motivation to aggress, as in *Brainpower*, but also *increase* the motivation to achieve as pathways to improving social and academic outcomes.

The organizing theme for this broader intervention approach was still the causal construct of perceived responsibility—in both other people and the self. We considered whether peers are perceived as responsible for negative events, which has implications for reducing the motivation to aggress against those peers; and we examined the degree to which individuals perceive themselves as responsible for their academic outcomes, which has implications for increasing their own motivation to achieve.

The intervention that we developed, titled *Best Foot Forward*, was designed for elementary school children who have been labeled as aggressive by their teachers and peers. It consisted of a 32-lesson curriculum with two separate but interrelated components. The social skills component focuses on reducing the tendency to infer hostile intent in others. We elaborated on *Brainpower* by also considering whether aggressive children are aware of the causal inferences that peers make *about them* and whether they have the social skills to manage the impressions of others through strategic account giving. Accounts are explanations or reasons for social transgressions, and they include apology (confession), excuses, justifications, and denials (Scott & Lyman, 1968). We included a set of lessons on account giving following a social transgression. We wanted participants to learn the adaptiveness of accepting responsibility for their own misdeeds (i.e., confession or apology) and of honoring the accounts of others by displaying greater forgiveness toward others who apologize for their transgressions.

The academic component of the intervention shifts the focus from holding others responsible for social dilemmas to holding oneself responsible for academic outcomes. That is, we use the same conceptual framework to guide both the social and the academic components of the intervention. Our basic assumption is that within an achievement context, like many social contexts, an individual is faced with the option (decision) to ascribe responsibility for outcomes to the self (e.g., to lack of effort following failure) or to factors for which the individual cannot be held responsible (e.g., low aptitude, poor teaching). That decision influences expectancy for success, affective reactions to task performance, and subsequent achievement strivings. It is further assumed that self-responsibility is the more adaptive motivational state because it is more likely to result in high expectancy, positive affect, and sustained effort. Strategies were taught in *Best Foot Forward* that encouraged participants to choose tasks of intermediate difficulty, be realistic goal setters, be task focused, and attribute academic failure to lack of effort rather than to factors that are not within their control. All of these strategies derive from principles of motivation, including attribution theory, that are known to increase academic motivation.

Participants were African American boys in third through fifth grades who were identified by their peers and teachers as most aggressive and by their teachers as having serious motivational problems. We recruited 66 third-, fourth-, and fifth-grade boys who met the eligibility criteria and whose custodial parent(s) or guardian provided informed consent. Thirty-one boys were randomly assigned to the intervention, and 35 were assigned to a no-treatment control group (a few parents only agreed to allow their son to participate if he was a control subject).

Although our sample was small and the effects therefore were modest, the results were encouraging. First, boys in the intervention learned the social skills of strategic account giving. Second, they learned the academic motivation skills of intermediate risk taking, realistic goal setting, task focus, and attributions for failure to factors within their control. Figure 2.3 shows the attribution data. Participants were asked at pretest and posttest to recall a time when they did poorly on a test and to rate the importance of four attributions for failure, including external factors (teacher bias or difficult test) and the internal factors of low ability and lack of effort. For boys in the control group (right panel), there were no changes in attributions for failure from pretest to posttest. However, boys in the intervention were significantly less likely to endorse external factors and low ability as causes for failure from pretest to posttest. Thus by the end of *Best Foot Forward*, intervention boys endorsed the most adaptive attribution pattern in terms of self-responsibility for achievement: few attributions to uncontrollable factors and more attributions to factors within one's control such as lack of effort.

Regarding actual behavior, boys in the intervention were rated by their teachers as showing more cooperation and persistence than control-group boys. They were also judged as having improved more in the social and academic domain based on end-of-semester written comments by teachers (see Graham et al., 2015, for a full description of findings).

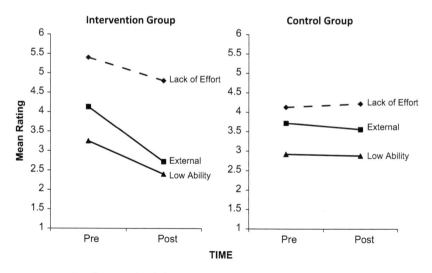

FIGURE 2.3 Attributions for failure pre- and postintervention as a function of treatment condition (from Graham, Taylor, & Hudley, 2015)

24 Sandra Graham

As currently implemented, *Best Foot Forward* was a pilot intervention, and we recognize that there are many things that we need to do better. But to my knowledge, this is the first successful intervention with aggressive youth that blended social skills training with motivation skills training under one unifying theoretical framework. If one's goal is to improve social behavior and academic achievement, altering maladaptive attributions about the self and others might be a reasonable starting point.

Stereotypes and Attributions About African American Adolescent Offenders

Because childhood aggression is a risk factor for juvenile delinquency, over the years I developed an interest in the plight of youth who have entered the juvenile justice system. This is the system in which the racial gap involving Black youth looms large. For example, African American youth ages 10 to 17 comprise about 16% of their age group in the population, yet they represent about 30% of all juvenile arrests, 35% of referrals to juvenile court, 40% of those incarcerated in juvenile facilities, and close to 60% of waivers to adult criminal court (National Research Council, 2013). Stated in comparative racial terms, Black youth are three to five times more likely than White youth to be confined in the criminal justice system. Moreover, African American youth often experience harsher treatment than White youth even after controlling for legal variables like crime severity and prior offense history. Some criminologists have argued that legally relevant variables account for only about 25% of the variance in the disposition of juvenile cases, which raises the possibility that race and other unknown factors can influence decision making in unpredictable ways (see Bridges & Steen, 1998).

What might be some of those race-related unknown factors? I was particularly interested in the consequences of negative racial stereotypes about African American adolescents. Even though privately held beliefs about African Americans have become more positive over the last 50 years, studies of cultural stereotypes continue to show that respondents associate being Black (and male) with hostility, aggressiveness, violence, and danger (Jones, Dovidio, & Vietze, 2014). Moreover, racial stereotypes often are activated and used outside of conscious awareness (Banaji & Greenwald, 2013). By automatically categorizing people according to cultural stereotypes, perceivers can manage information overload and make social decisions more efficiently.

Using my attributional lens, I then argued that unconscious stereotypes, once activated, influence conscious processes—in this case the attributions that decision makers endorse about the causes of adolescent offending. Stereotypes are attributional signatures in that they convey information about the locus, stability, and controllability of causes (Reyna, 2008). Stereotypes often evoke trait inferences, which are known to be internal, stable, and controllable (e.g., he's a violent person). Attributions to causes that are internal, stable, and controllable lead to greater expectations that that crime will occur again, more anger and blame, and harsher punishment. Thus racial disparity in the juvenile justice system might be the end result of a complex attributional process that begins with automatic activation of a negative racial stereotype and ends with a more punitive stance toward African American offenders.

Using a priming methodology with actual police officers and probation officers in the juvenile justice system, we examined the unconscious activation of racial stereotypes about adolescent males and their attributional consequences (Graham & Lowery, 2004). Participants in one condition were unconsciously primed to think about the construct *Black* using well-validated procedures from the cognitive priming literature (Bargh & Chartrand, 2000). These methods allow a researcher to activate a stereotype without any awareness on the part of the subject and then demonstrate that the activated stereotype influenced that subject's judgment or behavior in a completely unrelated task. Following the priming, officers were presented with hypothetical vignettes, written like actual crime reports, that described a juvenile allegedly committing a misdemeanor or felony with the cause of the crime portrayed as ambiguous. No information about the race of the alleged offender was provided. Participants then made inferences about the offender's traits, his culpability or blameworthiness, the likelihood that he would recidivate (commit the crime again), and severity of deserved punishment. Results showed that police officers and probation officers in whom racial stereotypes were unconsciously primed judged the hypothetical adolescent offender as more dangerous and violent, more responsible and blameworthy for his alleged offense, and more deserving of harsh punishment than did participants in an unprimed control condition. Using structural equation modeling, we tested a temporal sequence based on attribution principles in which unconsciously priming race influenced attribution-relevant judgments which in turn predicted perceived culpability of the offender, expected recidivism, and punishment. As shown in Figure 2.4, the data supported our attributional model with acceptable fit indices (see Graham & Lowery, 2004). I suggest that some of the racial disparity in the treatment of African American adolescent offenders can be explained by unconscious racial stereotypes and their associated attributional processes.

Our priming effects were documented irrespective of the respondents' gender, race/ethnicity, political orientation, or consciously held attitudes about African Americans. Hence, automatic stereotype activation does not require perceivers to endorse the stereotype, to dislike African Americans, or to hold any explicit prejudice toward that group. Even decision makers with good intentions can be vulnerable to racial stereotypes and their responsibility-related consequences (see Goff, Jackson, DiLeone, Culotta, & DiTomasso, 2014, for another recent example with police officers).

I believe that such findings also have implications for decision makers in our schools who make judgments about the social (mis)behavior of African American youth. Mirroring racial disparities in the juvenile justice system, reviews of school

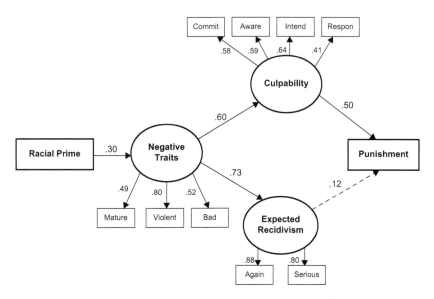

FIGURE 2.4 Structural model of relations among racial prime, attribution, expectancy, and punishment (from Graham & Lowery, 2004)

discipline policies reveal that African American youth are much more likely to be suspended or expelled from school than White youth who engage in similar or even more serious transgressions (e.g., Skiba et al., 2011). Particularly among perceivers at the front end of a system, like teachers dealing with classroom disorder, decisions often must be made quickly, under conditions of cognitive and emotional overload, and where much ambiguity exists. These are the very conditions that are known to activate unconscious beliefs (Fiske, 1998). Attributional analyses provide an ideal context for examining the unconscious racial stereotypes of well-intentioned teachers and administrators.

Attributions for Peer Victimization and School Racial Context

For my final topic, let me turn to the victims rather than the alleged perpetrators of peer-directed antisocial behavior. By peer victimization—also labeled peer harassment or bullying—I mean physical, verbal, or psychological abuse of a victim by a perpetrator who intends to cause harm. The critical features that differentiate peer victimization from simple conflict between peers are an imbalance of power between perpetrator and victim and the intent to cause harm (Olweus, 1994). Hitting, name calling, racial slurs, spreading of rumors, and social exclusion by powerful others are all examples of behaviors that constitute peer victimization. These types of harassment affect the lives of many youth and have been labeled a public health concern by the American Medical Association. Not only is peer victimization quite prevalent, it also is associated with a host of adjustment difficulties. Students who are chronic victims of school bullying often are rejected by their peers, and they feel depressed, anxious, and lonely (see Juvonen & Graham, 2014).

Why is it that victims of bullying feel so bad? In our work we have been bringing attributional analyses to the study of victimization–maladjustment relations. Repeated encounters with peer victimization, or even an isolated yet particularly painful experience, might lead that victim to ask, "Why *me*?" In the absence of disconfirming evidence, such an individual might come to blame him- or herself for their predicament, concluding, for example, that "I'm the kind of kid who deserves to be picked on." Self-blame and accompanying negative affect can then lead to many negative outcomes, including low self-esteem and depression. In the adult literature on causal explanations for rape (another form of victimization), attributions that imply personal deservingness, labeled characterological self-blame, are especially detrimental (Janoff-Bulman, 1979). From an attributional perspective, characterological self-blame is internal and therefore reflects on the self; it is stable and therefore leads to an expectation that victimization will be chronic; and it is uncontrollable, suggesting that there is no response in the victim's repertoire to prevent future harassment. Attributions for failure to internal, stable, and uncontrollable causes lead individuals to feel both hopeless and helpless (Weiner, 1986). Several researchers in the adult and child literatures document that individuals who make characterological self-blaming attributions for negative outcomes cope more poorly, feel worse about themselves, and are more depressed than individuals who make attributions to their behavior (Anderson, Miller, Riger, Dill, & Sedikides, 1994; Cole, Peeke, & Ingold, 1996; Tilghman-Osborne, Cole, Felton, & Cisela, 2008).

In the first study to directly examine attributions for peer victimization (Graham & Juvonen, 1998), we presented sixth-grade participants with a hypothetical vignette describing a typical harassment incident. We asked the students to imagine that the incident actually happened to them and to respond to a number of statements about what they would think, feel, or do if the incident indeed happened. Embedded in these statements were characterological self-blame attributions (e.g., "If I were a cooler kid, I wouldn't get picked on." "This kind of thing is more likely to happen to *me* than to other kids."). We also had information about which students in the sample were actual victims of bullying based on a combination of peer and self-report measures. We found that victims more so than nonvictims were especially likely to endorse characterological self-blame attributions and that self-blame partly explained the relationship between victimization and psychological maladjustment as measured by depression symptoms and social anxiety. It is as if the victim is saying to himself or herself, "It is something about me, things will always be this way, and there is nothing I can do about it." Those causal thoughts are then predicted to result in greater psychological distress.

Where does ethnicity fit into this research? A good deal of peer victimization research, including our earlier studies of attributions, is conducted in urban schools where multiple ethnic groups are represented, but very little of that research has systematically examined ethnicity-related context variables. This is disappointing because the factors that exacerbate or protect against peer victimization are likely to be influenced by such context factors as the ethnic composition of schools and neighborhoods, as well as the social and ethnic identities that are most significant to youth. In our research we bring the ethnic context to the study of peer victimization. We do this by making a case for the importance of attributions as a theoretical framework and school ethnic diversity as a central context variable, both of which can aid our understanding of the dynamics of peer victimization (see Graham, 2006, 2010).

There are three parts to our analysis. First, we know that students feel less victimized in schools that are more ethnically diverse (Juvonen, Nishina, & Graham, 2006). We proposed that in more ethnically diverse schools, there is a greater numerical balance of power among different racial/ethnic groups. Recall that the definition of peer victimization requires that there be an imbalance of power between perpetrator and victim. Second, in nondiverse schools, students who are both victims and members of the majority racial/ethnic group experience the most adjustment difficulties (Bellmore, Witkow, Graham, & Juvonen, 2004). Here we reasoned that majority group victims feel especially vulnerable because they deviate from the norm of their ethnic group to be numerically powerful. And third, based on the prior findings, we hypothesized that victims whose behavior deviated from local norms (i.e., victim status when one's group holds the numerical balance of power) would be particularly vulnerable to self-blaming attributions. As the number of same-ethnicity peers increases in one's social milieu, it becomes less plausible to make external attributions such as to the prejudice of others, which can protect self-esteem and buffer mental health.

We tested this hypothesis in a sample of about 1,500 sixth-grade Latino and African American students recruited from 11 middle schools that varied in ethnic diversity (Graham, Bellmore, Nishina, & Juvonen, 2009). In some schools African American and Latino students were the numerical majority group in their school, in some schools each was a numerical minority, and in the remaining schools they were one of several relatively equal-sized groups (i.e., the schools were ethnically diverse). Students reported on their experiences with victimization, their attributions for victimization including characterological self-blame (cf. Graham & Juvonen, 1998), and their feeling of depression and social anxiety. We then examined the temporal relations among victimization, self-blame, and maladjustment as a function of three ethnic diversity contexts.

Figure 2.5 displays the results of these analyses. As hypothesized, the temporal relations among victimization, self-blame, and maladjustment were strongest among students who were the ethnic majority group in their school ("It must be *me*"). For ethnic minority group members, the relations among victim status,

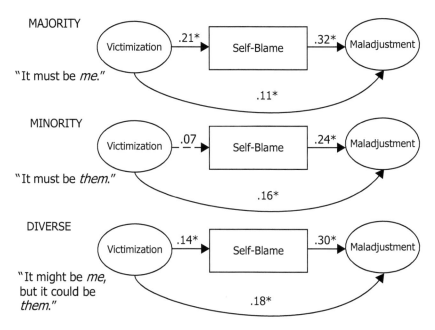

FIGURE 2.5 Attribution, self-blame, and adjustment relationships in three ethnic contexts (from Graham et al., 2009)

self-blaming tendencies, and maladjustment were the weakest. Being a victim and a member of the minority group can provide a context for external attributions to the prejudice of others that can protect self-esteem ("It must be *them*"). This goes back to a basic attribution principle of the relation between the locus of causes and esteem-related affect. Finally, in ethnically diverse contexts, with a greater balance of power, we found moderate relations between victimization and self-blame, which we interpreted as greater attributional ambiguity ("It might be me, but it could be them"). I suggest as a working hypothesis that ethnic diversity creates enough attributional ambiguity to ward off self-blaming tendencies, thereby allowing for attributions that have fewer psychological costs. In social contexts in which multiple social cues are present, attributional ambiguity can be particularly adaptive if it allows the perceiver to draw from a larger repertoire of causal schemes. Our analysis is one of few studies in the developmental literature to test whether ethnicity in context moderates a psychological process.

Summary and Conclusions

A focus on race and ethnicity in the study of motivation needs to be guided by strong theory. The research presented in this chapter is guided by attribution theory, one of the most enduring and robust contemporary theories of motivation.

As all of the chapters in this volume illustrate, issues of race, motivation, and achievement are enormously complex in that they cannot be disentangled from the historical circumstances and cultural forces that continue to shape the experiences of numerical ethnic minorities in this country. I gravitated toward attribution theory because it allowed me to manage some of that complexity. Moreover, the main constructs in the intrapersonal part of the theory—how I think and feel about myself—and in the interpersonal part—how others think and feel about me—shed light on the complex interplay between the individual and the larger sociocultural context in which experiences unfold.

What Have We Learned?

Conceptualizing motivation as a temporal sequence, I began with research on the antecedents of particular attributions. Here I reviewed our earlier work on how teachers might unintentionally be communicating low ability messages to youth. The legacy of that work can be seen in a rich contemporary literature emerging from stereotype threat research on the importance of "wise feedback" to ethnic minority students, who may worry about confirming negative stereotypes about race and intelligence (Yeager et al., 2014). A task for the future will be to bring this feedback research into closer contact with the ways in which teachers deliver real (high-stakes) feedback to students in actual instructional settings.

Acknowledging the close interplay between academic and social motivation, in the next section I described our research on changing the maladaptive attributions and related beliefs of African American boys labeled as aggressive. Ours is one of few intervention approaches to blend social skills training with academic motivation training under the unifying attribution principle of perceived responsibility in self and others. In neither *Brainpower* nor *Best Foot Forward* were we able to document changes in the academic achievement of boys labeled as aggressive. That was disappointing but not surprising. The low performance of aggressive youth is the result of cumulative challenges and not likely to be amenable to motivational interventions in the short run. Our hope is that we are arming youth with a set of social and academic motivation skills that will be empowering and will benefit them over the long run. A next step for us will be longitudinal research on our intervention approach.

In the third section I turned from childhood aggression to tackle one of the most pressing social problems in our nation today—racial disparities in the treatment of African American youth in the juvenile justice system. (The problem is even worse in the adult criminal system but that is beyond the scope of this chapter.) Although the public discourse on racial disparities has widely embraced the notion of unconscious biases or stereotypes, very little of that discourse has theorized about how unconscious stereotypes exert their influence. Drawing on attribution principles, we tested a model suggesting that racial disparities in the treatment of African American youth are the end result of a complex attributional process that begins with the automatic activation of unconscious stereotypes associating being Black and male with violence, threat, and danger. Black male teens are not perceived as the highly impressionable, immature, and less culpable adolescents that contemporary neuroscience research portrays them to be (see Steinberg, 2014). I worry that the emerging view of adolescent vulnerability and immaturity is trumped for Black male youth by racial stereotypes portraying them as violent, dangerous, and capable of adult-like negative intent. I focused on the juvenile justice system, but I think we also need studies of *teachers'* unconscious stereotypes and how they might affect the disproportionate discipline meted out to African American youth.

Finally, I brought an attributional perspective and an ethnic context perspective to some of the documented mental health consequences of chronic victimization by one's peers. Ethnicity matters in the study of peer victimization, but it is not so much ethnic group *per se* as ethnicity within context, or whether one's group is a numerical majority, minority, or residing in a diverse school with no numerical majorities. In other research, I have been making a case for the psychosocial benefits of ethnically diverse schools (Graham, 2010). The population in this country is becoming more ethnically diverse, but our schools are more segregated now than they have been in the last 40 years, with African American and Latino youth suffering the most academically from attending highly segregated schools (Ayscue & Orfield, 2015). I believe that many motivation-relevant experiences of ethnic minority youth will vary depending on overall school diversity as well as the numerical representation of their own ethnic group. In some cases numerical majority status might have challenges, as in our work on self-blame for victimization, whereas in other contexts there may be safety in numbers as, for example, when it comes to feelings of belonging (see Benner & Graham, 2009). Ethnic group representation is a context variable that is ripe for study in motivation research.

Motivational Methods

The chapters in this volume illustrate not only different theoretical approaches to motivation in ethnic minorities but also the multiple methods that researchers use to address this topic. I would like to make the case that role-playing paradigms should have a place in the motivation researcher's methodological toolkit. Most of the studies I described used role playing or simulation methods to some extent. For example, we asked about the *likelihood* of aggression among grade school boys given attributions rather than studying aggression per se (Graham et al., 2015). Similarly, we asked police officers and probation officers how punitive toward a hypothetical offender they would be given beliefs about offender culpability and recidivism rather than measuring actual legal decision making (Graham & Lowery, 2004). And we asked about imagined experiences with peer victimization rather than assessing those experiences during their state of activation (Graham et al., 2009).

These choices grow out of a belief among attribution theorists that simulation studies are both appropriate and useful when testing hypotheses and developing theory. We believe that what individuals *say* they would think, feel, or do in a particular situation maps closely onto how they *actually* think, feel, and behave in real-world contexts. A task for future research is more creative measurement that better captures attributional processes as they occur in real time and in real social settings.

Motivational Interventions

I stated at the beginning of this chapter that I was drawn to attribution theory because it can help guide our thinking about change. Our intervention research with aggressive youth illustrates our focus on attributional change. I believe that a logical next step is to target the victims of peer harassment with the goal of changing their maladaptive attributions about themselves. Interventions on school bullying have been so focused on a whole-school approach that the particular plight of the victim has not received adequate attention. Regarding my research on racial stereotypes in the juvenile justice system, a growing literature indicates that unconscious racial stereotypes are also amenable to intervention (see Lai et al., 2014). Just because biases get activated outside of conscious awareness does not mean that they cannot be changed. Experts on attribution theory and experts on reducing implicit racial bias should work together to determine what types of interventions show the most promise.

While the study of motivation in ethnic minority youth is ripe for intervention research, I believe that the best interventions will need to be multifaceted. A number of recent interventions emerging from social psychology research, some rooted in attributional analyses, have increased excitement about the potential of brief, even single-session treatments to increase achievement of stigmatized youth and college students (see Yeager & Walton, 2011). These interventions utilize constructs such as stereotype threat, mindsets, and self-affirmation to deliver short but powerful treatments that not only boost immediate achievement but also reduce the racial achievement gap.

I believe in theory-guided interventions, and I applaud the social psychologists engaged in new intervention approaches that can better uncover the mechanisms underlying motivational change. However, I am less convinced that changing one set of beliefs—be it worries about confirming racial stereotypes, mindsets, the importance of affirming personal values, or even causal attributions for failure—will have lasting effects on motivation and achievement no matter how powerfully they are delivered. Moreover, when the outcomes are pervasive problems like the racial achievement gap, effective interventions will need to address structural as well as psychological barriers to achievement.

The personality and motivation psychologist George Kelly reminded us that every good theory has a focus and range of convenience (Kelly, 1955). Focus refers to what the theory was designed to predict, and range refers to the breadth of phenomena to which the theory can be applied. As a model of motivation, attribution theory has great focus and range. But we must not lose sight of the fact that when we address issues associated with race/ethnicity, motivation, and contemporary educational challenges of ethnic minority youth, we are dealing with problems associated with poverty and social inequality that are far beyond the focus and range of convenience of attribution theory. As motivation researchers, the theory provides us with a good framework to ask some of the right questions in our effort to foster an educational (and juvenile justice) system that is fair to everyone. Finding solutions that last will require systemic change as well.

References

Anderson, C., Miller, R., Riger, A., Dill, J., & Sedikides, C. (1994). Behavioral and characterological attributional styles as predictors of depression and loneliness: Review, refinement, and test. *Journal of Personality and Social Psychology, 66*, 549–558.

Ayscue, J., & Orfield, G. (2015). School district lines stratify educational opportunity by race and poverty. *Race and Social Problems, 7*, 5–20.

Banaji, M., & Greenwald, A. (2013). *Blind spots: Hidden biases of good people.* New York: Delacorte Press.

Bargh, J. A., & Chartrand, T. L. (2000). The mind in the middle: A practical guide to priming and automaticity research. In H. T. Reis & C. M. Judd (Eds.), *Handbook of research methods in social and personality psychology* (pp. 253–285). New York: Cambridge University.

Barker, G., & Graham, S. (1987). A developmental study of praise and blame as attributional cues. *Journal of Educational Psychology, 79*, 62–66.

Bellmore, A., Witkow, M., Graham, S., & Juvonen, J. (2004). Beyond the individual: The impact of ethnic diversity and behavioral norms on victims' adjustment. *Developmental Psychology, 40*, 1159–1172.

Benner, A., & Graham, S. (2009). The transition to high school as a developmental process among multi-ethnic youth. *Child Development, 80*, 356–376.

Bridges, G. S., & Steen, S. (1998). Racial disparities in official assessments of juvenile offenders: Attributional stereotypes as mediating mechanisms of juvenile offenders. *American Sociological Review, 63*, 554–571.

Cole, D. A., Peeke, L. G., & Ingold, C. (1996). Characterological and behavioral self-blame in children: Assessment and development considerations. *Development and Psychopathology, 8*(02), 381–397.

Dodge, K., Coie, J., & Lynam, D. (2006). Aggression and antisocial behavior in youth. In N. Eisenberg (Ed.), *Handbook of child psychology*, Vol. 3: *Social emotional, and personality development* (6th ed., pp. 719–788). Hoboken, NJ: John Wiley & Sons.

Fiske, S. T. (1998). Stereotyping, prejudice, and discrimination. In D. T. Gilbert, S. T. Fiske, & G. Lindzey (Eds.), *Handbook of social psychology* (4th ed., pp. 357–411). New York: McGraw-Hill.

Gendolla, G., & Koller, M. (2001). Surprise and causal search: How are they affected by outcome valence and importance? *Motivation and Emotion, 25*, 237–250.

Goff, P., Jackson, M., DiLeone, B., Culotta, C., & DiTomasso, N. (2014). The essence of innocence: Consequences of dehumanizing Black children. *Journal of Personality and Social Psychology, 106*, 526–545.

34 Sandra Graham

Graham, S. (1984). Communicating sympathy and anger to black and white children: The cognitive (attributional) antecedents of affective cues. *Journal of Personality and Social Psychology, 47*, 40–54.

Graham, S. (1988). Can attribution theory tell us something about motivation in blacks? *Educational Psychologist, 23*, 3–21.

Graham, S. (1990). On communicating low ability in the classroom. In S. Graham & V. Folkes (Eds.), *Attribution theory: Applications to achievement, mental health, and interpersonal conflict* (pp. 17–36). Hillsdale, NJ: Lawrence Erlbaum.

Graham, S. (2006). Peer victimization in school: Exploring the ethnic context. *Current Directions in Psychological Science, 15*, 317–320.

Graham, S. (2010). School racial/ethnic diversity and disparities in mental health and academic outcomes. *Nebraska Symposium on Motivation, 57*, 73–96.

Graham, S., & Barker, G. (1990). The downside of help: An attributional-developmental analysis of help-giving as a low ability cue. *Journal of Educational Psychology, 82*, 7–14.

Graham, S., Bellmore, A., Nishina, A., & Juvonen, J. (2009). "It must be *me*": Ethnic diversity and attributions for victimization in middle school. *Journal of Youth and Adolescence, 38*, 487–499.

Graham, S., & Juvonen, J. (1998). Self-blame and peer victimization in middle school: An attributional analysis. *Developmental Psychology, 34*, 587–599.

Graham, S., & Lowery, B. (2004). Priming unconscious racial stereotypes about adolescent offenders. *Law and Human Behavior, 28*, 483–504.

Graham, S., Taylor, A. Z., & Hudley, C. (2015). A motivational intervention for African American boys labeled as aggressive. *Urban Education, 50*, 194–224.

Harber, K., Gorman, J., Gengaro, F., Butisingh, S., Tsang, W., & Ouellette, R. (2012). Students' race and teachers' social support affect the positive feedback bias in public schools. *Journal of Educational Psychology, 104*(4), 1149–1161.

Heider, F. (1958). *The psychology of interpersonal relations*. New York: John Wiley.

Howard, T. C. (2014). *Why race and culture matter in schools*. New York: Teachers College Press.

Hudley, C. (2008). You did that on purpose: Understanding and changing children's aggression. New Haven, CT: Yale University Press.

Hudley, C., & Graham, S. (1993). An attributional intervention with African American boys labeled as aggressive. *Child Development, 64*, 124–138.

Janoff-Bulman, R. (1979). Characterological and behavioral self-blame: Inquiries into depression and rape. *Journal of Personality and Social Psychology, 37*, 1798–1809.

Jones, J., Dovidio, J., & Vietze, D. (2014). *The psychology of diversity*. West Sussex, UK: John Wiley & Sons.

Juvonen, J., & Graham, S. (2014). Bullying in schools: The power of bullies and the plight of victims. *Annual Review of Psychology, 65*, 159–185.

Juvonen, J., Nishina, A., & Graham, S. (2006). Ethnic diversity and perceptions of safety in urban middle schools. *Psychological Science, 17*, 393–400.

Kelly, G. (1955). *The psychology of personal constructs: Volume 1 and 2*. New York: NW Simon.

Lai, C. K., Marini, M., Lehr, S. A., Cerruti, C., Shin, J.E.L., Joy-Gaba, J. A., & Nosek, B. A. (2014). Reducing implicit racial preferences: I. A comparative investigation of 17 interventions. *Journal of Experimental Psychology: General, 143*(4), 1765.

National Research Council. (2013). *Reforming juvenile justice: A developmental approach*. Committee on Assessing Juvenile Justice reform. Washington, DC: National Academies Press.

Olweus, D. (1994). Bullying at school: Basic facts and effects of a school-based intervention program. *Journal of Child Psychology and Psychiatry and Allied Disciplines, 35*, 1171–1190.

Reyna, C. (2008). Ian is intelligent but Leshaun is lazy: Antecedents and consequences of attributional stereotypes in the classroom. *European Journal of Psychology in the Classroom, 23*, 439–458.

Schneider, M., Major, B., Luhtanen, R., & Crocker, J. (1996). Social stigma and the potential cost of assumptive help. *Personality and Social Psychology Bulletin, 22*, 201–209.

Scott, M., & Lyman, S. (1968). Accounts. *American Sociological Review, 23*, 46–62.

Skiba, R., Horner, R., Chung, C., Rausch, M., May, S., & Tobin, T. (2011). Race is not neutral: A national investigation of African American and Latino disproportionality in school discipline. *School Psychology Review, 40*, 85–107.

Steinberg, L. (2014). *Age of opportunity: Lessons from the new science of adolescence.* New York: Houghton Mifflin Harcourt.

Stupnisky, R., Stewart, T. Daniels, L., & Perry, R. (2011). When do students ask why? Examining the precursors and outcomes of causal search among first-year college students. *Contemporary Educational Psychology, 36*, 201–211.

Tilghman-Osborne, C., Cole, D. A., Felton, J. W., & Cisela, J. A. (2008). Relation of guilt, shame, behavioral and characterological self-blame to depressive symptoms in adolescents over time. *Journal of Social and Clinical Psychology, 27*, 809–842.

Weiner, B. (1986). *An attributional theory of motivation and emotion.* New York: Springer.

Weiner, B. (1995). *Judgments of responsibility: A foundation for a theory of social conduct.* New York: Guilford Press.

Weiner, B. (2006). *Social motivation, justice, and the moral emotions: An Attributional approach.* Mahwah, NJ: Erlbaum.

Wilson, T., Damiani, M., & Shelton, N. (2002). Improving the academic performance of college students with brief attributional interventions. In J. Aronson (Ed.), *Improving academic achievement: Impact of psychological factors on education* (pp. 91–110). New York: Academic Press.

Yeager, D., Purdie-Vaughns, V., Garcia, J., Apfel, N., Brzustoski, P., Master, A., Hessert, W., Williams, M., & Cohen, G. (2014). Breaking the cycle of mistrust: Wise interventions to provide critical feedback across the racial divide. *Journal of Experimental Psychology: General, 143*, 804–824.

Yeager, D., & Walton, G. (2011). Social-psychological interventions in education: They're not magic. *Review of Educational Research, 81*, 267–301.

3

RETENTION VERSUS PERSISTENCE

A Self-Determination Analysis of Students Underrepresented in STEM

Kelly A. Rodgers

Concerns over the underrepresentation of students of color and women in STEM fields are far from new. From issues of recruitment to retention and degree completion, the (in some cases) extreme underrepresentation of African Americans, Hispanics and Native Americans has drawn the attention of researchers, administrators and practitioners from across K–12 and throughout higher education (Cromley et al., 2013; Gasman & Perna, 2011; Hurtado, Cabrera, Lin, & Arellano, 2009). Further, the research on retention and persistence in STEM has been mostly very consistent in its findings and suggestions to institutions moving forward. Institutions, broadly speaking, and specifically STEM programs within the university and college structure are consistently told that they must create an environment that is conducive to meaningful faculty–student interactions (Hurtado et al., 2011; Johnson, 2007) and that student–student interactions must likewise be available and authentic (Joseph, 2012; Perna et al., 2009). Academic resources should be plentiful, and institutions and programs have been informed that students of color, particularly those from African American, Hispanic, and Native American backgrounds, many of whom are still first-generation college students, may need to have their interest in STEM piqued and their attention drawn to the career options that a STEM degree may afford (Linley & George-Jackson, 2013).

Despite this somewhat intense and hardly new focus, the disparities persist. In 2011, 8.8% of bachelor's degrees in STEM fields were awarded to Black students, 10.3% to Hispanic students, 9.3% to Asian/Pacific Islanders, and a microscopic .06% to Native Americans. These percentages also represent only moderate gains for most minority groups. Though Hispanic students saw an increase from 7% to 10%, Asians saw only an increase from 9% to 10%, and other groups saw no increase from 2000 to 2011 (NSB, 2014). Asians, a group traditionally overrepresented in STEM, are also an exception in that both Asian males and females each earned about 9% of the bachelor's degrees in STEM, while for other minority groups, women generally outpaced men. At the graduate level, the numbers are even more troublesome, with Black, Hispanic, and Native American students earning only 6.6, 4.7, and 0.5%, respectively, of the master's degrees in STEM fields and only 2.5, 2.9, and 0.2% of doctoral degrees granted in these fields, with the men in each group become increasingly absent (NSF, 2010). This trend may be reflective of a wider issue in which Black, Hispanic, and Native American women attend college at higher rates than do their male counterparts (U.S. Department of Education, 2012).

These data illustrate the need to examine this old problem with new eyes. Accordingly, in the following sections, I take a look at the motivational issues underlying retention and persistence of college students of color in science, technology, engineering, and mathematics programs. Specifically, I examine the ideas of persistence, a student-centered variable, versus retention, an institution-centered variable, situating them within a self-determination framework to understand the motivation of students of color in STEM fields and how this motivation influences their decisions to persist and institutions' and STEM programs' ability to retain them. I discuss factors shown to be integral to both retention and persistence in STEM, with a focus on those factors relevant to students of color who have historically been underrepresented in STEM, namely African American, Hispanic/Latino, and Native American students. I conclude the chapter with a discussion of key ideas and directions for future research.

Motivation Theory, Retention, and Persistence

Academic motivation theory has been used to understand the behaviors that lead to outcomes such as student engagement and achievement. Such theory, however, like much of what we think we know about what drives students, both inside and outside the classroom, is based on the assumption that these motivational processes apply cross-culturally. This assumption may be faulty at best. Rodgers and Summers (2007), considering retention broadly, suggested that institutions, administrators, and practitioners should begin to question the applicability of what we think we know about retention to students who are typically not largely represented in the studies from which our current theories have derived. It is therefore important to reconsider our knowledge of retention and, as Rodgers and Summers (2007) suggest, question whether such models really tell the whole story of what is important for retention and persistence for these students.

When motivation theory has been applied to students of color, attribution theory (Graham, 1992; van Laar, 2000) has been used most often, with Deci and Ryan's (1985) expectancy-value theory garnering more recent attention (Anderson & Ward, 2014). However, self-determination theory, due to its dependence on the idea of the self and issues of control, both factors that have been zeroed in on as critical cultural components in understanding students of color (Cokley, 2003; Flowers,

Milner, & Moore, 2003), offers a unique look into the motivational patterns that can inform these students' intentions to persist in their STEM programs and institutions' and programs' ability to retain them.

Persistence Versus Retention

The research literature on college student continuity is replete with two terms: retention and persistence. These terms are sometimes used interchangeably, but to do so ignores a critical characteristic of their emphasis. In the context of the current discussion, *retention* refers to institutions' or programs' ability to keep or retain students. Persistence, on the other hand, refers to students' tendency or decision to continue or not continue along their current course. That is, retention can be thought of as an institution-controlled variable and persistence as a student-controlled variable. This distinction matters if we are to understand all of the barriers to completion in STEM and who controls those barriers. Indeed, they are connected and, in the most ideal circumstances, they work in concert. By fostering a supportive environment, an institution or program can create an atmosphere that is conducive to student persistence, leading the student being more likely to be retained. At the same time, they are two distinct processes in that a program may have proper supports in place and yet students may still choose not to persist for any number of reasons. So in choosing the correct terminology, it is important to consider from where the control originates: from within the student, within the institution, or both.

Vincent Tinto (1975, 1988) proposed that persistence (and, by extension, retention) is influenced by the extent to which students are able to *separate* from previous academic and social associations, *transition*, and ultimately become fully *incorporated* into the academic and social communities of the institution. Tinto refers to this incorporation as *academic integration* and *social integration*. That is, if students are socially and academically integrated into the institution or program, they will be more likely to persist and thus be retained.

However, Rodgers and Summers (2007), in questioning the applicability of traditional models of retention to Black students attending predominantly White institutions (PWIs), proposed that, unlike suggested by Tinto (1975), academic and social integration should be conceptualized as outcomes in the retention equation rather than as precursors that influence behaviors such as academic help seeking and formation of social friendships. Stressing the idea of "fit" between student and institution (the institution offers what the student needs), the authors contend that students' perceptions of the accessibility of faculty and other students, the comfort of the culture of their STEM program, and the overall sense of feeling welcomed by the program and fellow students all combine to influence students' motivation, which in turn influences their academic and social integration and ultimately leads to retention and persistence. For students of color, particularly those operating on predominantly White campuses and STEM programs, academic and social integration may take on a different appearance than was originally suggested by Tinto (1975), and the effects that these have on students' persistence or institutions' ability to retain them may also be different. In the following sections, I provide an overview of self-determination theory (SDT). I then situate retention and persistence issues within the context of SDT, with a specific focus on the role of intrinsic motivation in the retention and persistence process.

Self-Determination Theory

Self-determination theory is based on the belief that individuals have needs to feel competent, autonomous, and related (Deci & Ryan, 1985). Therefore, individuals are motivated by the desire to have these needs met, and this motivation comes generally in one of three forms: amotivation, extrinsic, and intrinsic. Deci and Ryan (1985) emphasize that, rather than think of motivation as either being controlled by the individual or not, it is more prudent to view intrinsic versus extrinsic motivation as less about from where the control comes and more about whether or not one is being controlled. *Amotivation* refers to a nondirectional lack of motivation, neither to have a need met nor to not have a need met. Comparatively, individuals who are driven more by extrinsic motivation tend to be controlled or compelled to act due to outside forces (e.g., approval of family members, admiration of classmates), while those who are more intrinsically motivated tend to be more free from outside control and can focus on needs that exist within the self (enjoyment, personal fulfillment). The focus on the self and systems of control make SDT a very relevant framework through which to examine retention and persistence in underrepresented students in STEM. In this way, we can consider to what extent the student is controlled by outside forces, which, for the purposes of the current discussion, are elements of the STEM program and the institution.

Ryan and Deci (2000) further describe SDT as a study not just of individuals' tendency or lack thereof to seek agency or control and to meet psychological needs, but SDT also considers the aspects of situations that foster these motivations. To this end, Deci and Ryan (1985) proposed cognitive evaluation theory (CET) as a subtheory to SDT, wherein CET specifically addresses the environmental and contextual factors that influence intrinsic motivation. Thus CET offers an additional subframework through which to further examine a self-controlled (internal) variable, *persistence*, and an institution-controlled (external) variable, *retention*, and how the two can interact to support students to degree completion.

Persistence

Persistence has been typically treated as a student-level or student-controlled variable (e.g., Marra, Rodgers, Shen, & Bogue, 2012; Morrow & Ackermann, 2012). Institutions can retain students, but students must also make the decision to persist.

Certainly, programmatic efforts to retain students can influence the likelihood that students will persist. As previously described, these student-level variables tend to fall into two categories: academic and social. Thus, there is some overlap between that which is considered to be necessary for institutions and programs to retain students and that which increases student persistence.

On the academic side, students who actively seek involvement in their courses, interact with faculty, display help-seeking behavior (contacting faculty, using academic support resources such as tutoring, etc.) in the face of trouble and are otherwise engaged in the academic life of their programs would be considered academically integrated. Academic preparation in high school and continued development during the program are also of great importance, as one would likely assume, and has been consistently found to be a predictor of student persistence in STEM (Russell & Atwater, 2005; Tyson, Lee, Borman, & Hanson, 2007). This academic preparation and the success, or lack thereof, that they might experience also informs students' feelings of competence, which has been shown to play into intention to persist in STEM (Marra, Shen, Rodgers, & Bogue, 2009). In Proctor and Truscott's (2012) study of African American students in school psychology, students identified poor relationships with faculty and classmates and lack of fit between personal career goals and the program as factoring into persistence decisions. Further, given that many students of color may be first-generation college students, economic support has also emerged as a critical piece in the persistence puzzle (Proctor & Truscott, 2012; St. John, Paulsen, & Carter, 2005; Tuttle & Musoba, 2013).

On the social side, sense of belonging has been a consistent predictor of intention to persist in college in general and in STEM in particular (Morrow & Ackermann, 2012; Marra, Rodgers, Shen, & Bogue, 2009). This social element is so strong that Hu (2011) found that, without similarly high levels of social engagement, high academic engagement negatively affected persistence. The importance of social interactions was underscored in Marra et al.'s (2012) study of persistence in engineering. The authors identified three factors that informed students' decisions to leave their engineering majors. Two factors were aspects of academic integration, curriculum difficulty, and faculty interactions, while the third factor, sense of belonging, was more attributable to social integration. Further, non-White students indicated that curriculum difficulty and belongingness factored more into their decision to leave engineering than they did for White students.

Underrepresented students' identity maintenance and development have also emerged as important to social interactions and ultimately to academic achievement, both broadly and specifically in STEM. In line with Rodgers and Summers's (2007) assertion that students of color operating in spaces where they are the minority must develop a bicultural identity, one that remains connected to one's culture and another that connects to their student lives, those in STEM must likewise develop a "science identity." Perez, Cromley, and Kaplan (2014) examined the relationship between students' STEM identity, defined as their sense of the fit between how they view themselves and how they perceive these things as being in accordance with what STEM offers and persistence. The authors found that students with more reflective STEM identities felt more competent and perceived fewer costs associated with pursuing STEM careers. Further, the development of this "scientist identity" has been linked to the achievement goals that are most closely associated with achievement and persistence (Hernandez, Schultz, Estrada, Woodcock, & Chance, 2013).

Retention

Given that retention and persistence, though separate constructs, are tied, suggestions for retention of students of color in general and in STEM necessarily follow the supportive needs of these students. As with persistence, Tinto (1975) suggested that these supports should attend to two goals: academic integration and social integration.

Seymour and Hewitt (1997) identified two categories of students who ultimately left their science/engineering programs: those who became bored or disengaged with the curriculum and those who suffered a blow to their self-confidence, likely as the result of some academic struggles or interactions with other students and faculty. Accordingly, in order to facilitate academic integration, institutions are typically advised to provide academic supports such as tutoring and effective advising and to foster positive interactions between faculty and students (Williamson, 2010).

Within STEM programs, especially at PWIs, fostering social integration might be more difficult. As with the campus as a whole, interactions between students from similar cultural backgrounds are likely to be few and far between, with Black, Hispanic, and Native American students often finding themselves in classes with just a few others, if any, of the same cultural or racial background. To facilitate social gatherings between students, many campuses also offer cultural centers, such as Black or Hispanic cultural centers, where students from similar cultural backgrounds can meet and participate in activities that they may find more relevant.

The potential for a sense of alienation may be exacerbated in programs that require students to work in labs or assist in research, such as is expected in many STEM disciplines. In these situations, not only are students of color operating in a space where they will still be the minority, but research labs are where academic and social integration collide. Those spaces, probably more than the traditional classroom format, promote an atmosphere of collaboration and, potentially, competition. Thus a student who has not built relationships with both faculty and other students may find themselves limited in a critical area of academic and social development. Further, failure to socially connect may undermine students' intrinsic motivation, which can, in turn, negatively impact their persistence.

Russell and Atwater (2005) found that intrinsic motivation was positively related to African American student science persistence. Consequently, next I take a closer look at the tenets of intrinsic motivation with a critical eye toward understanding how these aspects inform what we know about retention and persistence patterns for students of color pursuing degrees in STEM fields.

Intrinsic Motivation

Deci and Ryan (2000) describe intrinsic motivation as "the inherent tendency to seek out novelty and challenges, to extend and exercise one's capacities, to explore and to learn" (p. 70). In terms of control, a student who is intrinsically motivated in STEM is one who is not, at least solely, controlled by external factors and is therefore driven in part or whole by their own desires. The authors go on to describe intrinsic motivation as a natural curiosity that environmental contexts can either promote or undermine. This is where we can readily observe the synergy that can exist between retention and persistence. According to CET, there are ways that institutions and programs can free students from the control of outside forces by offering them opportunities to meet the need for competency, relatedness, and autonomy. That is, students are more likely to maintain the intrinsic motivation with which they began their STEM programs as long as the program and the institution as a whole offers them a chance to feel competent, connected, and self-sufficient.

Competence

Classroom settings offer students several clues by which to judge their competence, the most obvious of which are coursework, past success, and academic preparedness (Cromley et al., 2013). However, beyond these, students also receive messages regarding their academic competence from other students, from faculty, and from society at large. Societal impressions can trigger issues related to stereotype threat (Cromley et al., 2013; Steele, 1997).

Interactions with faculty and fellow students in particular have the potential to shape the ways in which students of color see themselves as students in STEM. The students of color in Hurtado et al.'s (2009) study of underrepresented students in the sciences cited not only their confidence in their own abilities in science but also the encouragement from teachers and professors as important contributors to their interest and pursuit of STEM careers. Hurtado et al. (2011) echoed these findings in their examinations of underrepresented students' interactions with faculty. Utilizing a sample of mostly students of color in STEM attending five institutions (two predominantly White, two Hispanic serving, and one HBCU), the authors found that school selectivity and size were important factors, with students at larger and more selective schools being more likely to interact with faculty. Overall, Black students interacted with faculty less often than did White students, although students at the HBCU interacted more frequently than did their counterparts at other institutions. In the final section of this chapter, I discuss the unique position and success that HBCUs and other minority-serving institutions have in promoting retention and persistence in their STEM students of color.

These findings are important in the current discussion for a couple of reasons. First, they highlight the role that teachers and university faculty play in encouraging students of color to pursue careers in STEM. Second, because faculty are an important link, likely the main link, to the academic culture of an institution, students who do not find faculty to be accessible, whether it is because of time constraints, culturally related discomfort, or a lack of racially or culturally congruent faculty, may find themselves locked out of opportunities to succeed. These students may not be chosen to do research with faculty or simply be able to seek additional academic help at times of struggle, which can affect their overall sense of competence.

Connectedness

The importance of connectedness to students from particular ethnic backgrounds has been somewhat extensively covered in the literature (Green & Glasson, 2009; Hurtado et al., 2007). Some of this work relates the need for connectedness to collectivist cultural orientation, which is one in which members of the cultural group view themselves as interconnected (Triandis, 1989). Though much of the literature on this cultural orientation has utilized Asian American samples, Hispanic Americans as well as African Americans have been noted as having collectivistic communities. Research points to the importance of family and friendship networks in supporting African American and Latino students through college (Oyserman, Coon, & Kemmelmeier, 2002; Russell & Atwater, 2005). Sayed, Azmitia, and Cooper (2011) describe the role of these friendship and familial connections as that of "identity agents," because they allow students to maintain a cultural identity and a connection to home, which facilitates adjustment into the university culture.

Within STEM fields, many of which are dominated by White males, the support of identity agents becomes especially critical. As generally male-dominated spaces, the culture of many STEM programs has been described as aggressive, competitive, and consequently very supportive of an individualistic mindset (Seymour & Hewitt, 1997). Further, faculty in these fields are likely to be mostly male, which means that not only is the culture of the classroom male oriented, but interactions outside of the classroom can also take on this complexion. In her study of women of color in science, Johnson's (2007) participants described a science culture in which success depended in part on the extent to which one was visible and vocal, behavioral expectations that run counter to the ways in which many women are raised. An African American student in Hurtado et al.'s (2009) study who had transferred from a predominantly White university to an HBCU described the importance of connectedness to his overall motivation:

> I felt so disconnected from everybody, not necessarily because it was a racial difference, but just the motivational factor. I didn't feel motivated, I felt as if I was just a social security number, so I decided to come to [HBCU] and that's when I felt at home, you know, because I got individual attention, I got motivation, I was able to see professors that were African American, bio-chemistry PhD professors, people that look like me, which motivated me to say, "OK, I can do this. It's possible for me not only to get an undergraduate degree, but also to pursue a higher level degree," so it's the motivational factor that I would say an HBCU provides.
>
> *(p. 207)*

In addition to highlighting the importance of connectedness to motivation, the student also hints at another aspect of the minority STEM experience addressed by self-determination theory, autonomy.

Autonomy

According to Deci and Ryan (2000), feelings of competence only positively influence intrinsic motivation if these feelings are accompanied by an internal locus of causality. However, Chirkov, Ryan, Kim, and Kaplan (2003) questioned autonomy as an actual need in the quest for self-determination. From a collectivist standpoint, the self is tied to others in the group. Thus to be self-determined requires not that one has individual control over one's destiny, but as a group you have control over your collective destiny. Iyengar and Lepper (1999) found that, among collectivistic groups, adopting the choices of respected others can have the same positive effect on intrinsic motivation as others may gain in making autonomous decisions, suggesting a cultural variation in this perceived "need." These findings run counter to Deci and Ryan's (1985) initial supposition that environments that stifled autonomy by overly controlling or removing individuals' choice undermined their intrinsic motivation.

This underscores the importance of faculty again in the process of retaining students of color in STEM. Iyengar and Lepper's (1999) findings suggest that respected others, such as the African American faculty described by the student at the HBCU, may be seen by some students as extensions of themselves, thereby helping maintain students' sense of autonomy, positively influencing their intrinsic motivation and increasing the likelihood that the student will be retained to degree completion. Hence, the underrepresentation of Black, Hispanic, and Native American faculty in STEM (Towns, 2010) offers definite cause for concern. In the earlier quote from Hurtado et al.'s (2009) study, the African American male student expresses how important it is to have faculty who looked like him,

Retention Versus Persistence **45**

who had similarly achieved what he hoped to achieve, and who would provide him with more personal interaction. Hence, in this way, he was able to draw a sense of power and control over his outcomes from respected others (in this case, faculty), just as the Asian American students in Iyengar and Lepper's (1999) study did, thereby increasing his intrinsic motivation.

Closing Discussion

I began this chapter making the point that the concerns relating to the continued underrepresentation of students from certain racial or ethnic backgrounds in STEM disciplines was hardly new, especially given the rather consistent findings about the supposed "keys" to retention and persistence of students of color in these disciplines. Throughout this chapter, I have covered the main issues and suggestions, from both persistence and retention perspectives, as well as from institutional and programmatic perspectives. I will not further rehash them here. Instead, I want to conclude this discussion by addressing a couple of key takeaways that are critical in this process.

Cokley (2003) noted that the task that sits before us is about understanding the psychology of African American students, how these students view themselves, their motivation, and how this all connects to achievement and, relative to the current discussion, their degree completion. Many years after Cokley published his study, I believe we can say the same of the need for truly understanding the psychology and motivation of students of color as they make their way through their STEM programs.

Beyond what we already know about retention and persistence of underrepresented students in STEM, the first takeaway I gather from a review of the literature is that students' conceptualizations of the self matter. I chose self-determination theory to illustrate the motivational responses of students of color in STEM because I believe that it centers on a very important piece of the persistence and retention puzzle, which is the self and how students situate themselves in their understanding of themselves and in their environments. In this retention/persistence interplay, you have the individual student "self" and you have institutions attempting to serve that "self." However, this might be an incomplete approach. Institutions and programs have typically been assumed to be serving the student by serving what they view as the individual student's self. Yet if the self extends beyond the student, then serving the student alone will be insufficient. For underrepresented students in STEM, the literature tells us that this self includes the family, the faculty, other students, and generally the students' identification with others of their same ethnic or racial background. Thus, STEM programs hoping to increase retention of underrepresented students must affect in some way all aspects of the student self, and not just tend to students' individual academic needs. In addition to offering academic resources and even encouraging social interactions on campus, programs might seek, for example, to engage the family by offering a sibling day in the lab or a parent day of research presentations.

Programs and institutions should also always be striving for diversity in their faculty and be purposeful in their hiring of other social and academic support staff, as well as in seeking the same diversity in its student body. Such diversity is imperative if there is to be change to the climate and culture of many STEM disciplines so that the student experience is not one note in that only one cultural approach is practiced and respected. If students of color are to believe that the institution is committed to them, then they must see evidence of that commitment not only in the people with whom they interact but also in the way the program functions.

This brings me to my second takeaway, which involves the success that minority-serving institutions (MSIs), such as HBCUs and Hispanic-serving institutions (HSIs), have had in attracting and graduating large numbers of under-represented students. In data that was collected in 2006, 20% of Black students attended HBCUs, but graduates of these institutions accounted for nearly 22% of bachelor's degrees awarded to Black students in STEM, including 20.1% of engineering degrees and a staggering 45% and 49% of degrees in biology and physics, respectively. A possible argument against this success is that since these institutions, by mission, serve mostly students of color, then it would make sense that they also graduate large numbers of students in STEM. However, though most Black students attend PWIs, you can see that, from the previously stated data, graduates of HBCUs account for a disproportionately high percentage of degrees awarded to Black students in STEM in general, and this is especially true in certain STEM fields, such as biology and physics, where, despite educating only 20% of Black college students, HBCUs account for about half of graduates in these disciplines. I do not believe that this is by accident.

By their very nature, MSIs offer a learning environment that tends to the self-needs of their students of color. They offer more diverse faculty and higher numbers of faculty who share racial or ethnic backgrounds with their students, a presence that cannot be undervalued. Hence, as suggested by Gasman and Perna (2011), PWIs and other institutions seeking to increase retention and encourage persistence should take a page from how many HBCUs run their STEM programs, oftentimes without the financial resources available at more selective PWIs. Indeed, as cuts in federal funding have impacted most public institutions, as described by Rivard (2014), HBCUs and other MSIs have been especially hard hit. These institutions tend to serve higher percentages of students dependent on need-based aid, and with the rising costs of higher education and fewer economic resources, STEM programs at MSIs may soon feel the sting even more (Arnett, 2014).

Both of these take-aways suggest a few new directions that we should take in the quest to understand and continue to effectively address the barriers facing students of color pursuing STEM careers. First, new research should seek to understand the differences in STEM disciplines, acknowledging that some disciplines have been more successful at attracting and retaining both women and students of color. Engineering and technology programs, which continue to be overwhelmingly White and male, may have much to gain from examining the culture and structure of biology programs, which have been among the most successful in attracting and retaining students of color (National Science Board, 2014). In the spirit of continuing to understand what drives Black, Hispanic, and Native American students, future research should also examine the role that identity plays in integrating students into their STEM programs while also allowing them to maintain those necessary familial and cultural connections. Additional work on many of these same issues is also sorely needed for Hispanic and especially for Native American students, who are all but absent from higher education in general and extremely so in STEM. On the other hand, if institutions and programs are to make the important adjustments to what their programs have traditionally valued and how they have operated, future research should also examine faculty agency in implementing these changes. In this way, we can, as I initially suggested, look at an old problem with new eyes.

References

Anderson, L., & Ward, T. J. (2014). Expectancy-value models for the STEM persistence plans of Ninth-grade high-ability students: A comparison between Black, Hispanic and White students. *Science Education, 98*, 216–242.

Arnett, A. A. (2014). State of HBCUs. *Diverse Issues in Higher Education, 31*, 18–20.

Chirkov, V., Ryan, R. M., Kim, Y., & Kaplan, U. (2003). Differentiating autonomy from individualism and independence: A self-determination theory perspective on internalization of cultural orientations and well-being. *Journal of Personality and Social Psychology, 84*, 97–110.

Cokley, K. O. (2003). What do we know about the motivation of African American students? Challenging the anti-intellectual myth. *Harvard Educational Review, 73*, 524–558.

Cromley, J. G., Perez, T., Wills, T. W., Tanaka, J. C., Horvat, E. M., & Agbenyega, E. T. (2013). Changes in race and sex stereotype threat among diverse STEM students: Relation to grades and retention in the majors. *Contemporary Educational Psychology, 38*, 247–258.

Deci, E. L., & Ryan, R. M. (1985). *Intrinsic motivation and self-determination in human behavior.* New York: Plenum.

Deci, E. L., & Ryan, R. M. (2000). The "what" and "why" of goal pursuits: Human needs and the self-determination of behavior. *Psychological Inquiry, 11*, 227–268.

Flowers, L. A., Milner, H. R., & Moore, J. L. (2003). Effects of locus of control on African American high school seniors' educational aspirations: Implications for preservice and inservice high school teachers and counselors. *High School Journal, 87*, 39–50.

Gasman, M., & Perna, L. W. (2011). Promoting attainment of African American women in the STEM fields: Lessons from historically Black colleges and universities. In J. Gaetane & B. Lloyd-Jones (Eds.), *Women of color in higher education: Changing directions and new perspectives* (pp. 73–88). Bingley, UK: Emerald Group Publishing Limited.

Graham, S. (1992). Most of the subjects were white and middle class: Trends in reported research on African-Americans in selected APA journals, 1970–1989. *American Psychologist, 47*, 629–639.

Green, A., & Glasson, G. (2009). African Americans majoring in science at predominantly white universities (a review of the literature). *College Student Journal, 43*, 366–374.

Hernandez, P. R., Schultz, P. W., Estrada, M., Woodcock, A., & Chance, R. C. (2013). Sustaining optimal motivation: A longitudinal analysis of interventions to broaden participation of underrepresented students in STEM. *Journal of Educational Psychology, 105*, 89–107.

Hu, S. (2011). Reconsidering the relationship between student engagement and persistence in college. *Innovative Higher Education, 36*, 97–106.

Hurtado, S., Cabrera, N. L., Lin, M. H., & Arellano, L. (2009). Diversifying science: Underrepresented student experiences in structured research programs. *Research in Higher Education, 50*, 189–214.

Hurtado, S., Eagan, M. K., Cabrera, N. L., Lin, M. H., Park, J., & Lopez, M. (2007). Training future scientists: Predicting first-year minority student participation in health science research. *Research in Higher Education, 49*, 126–152.

Hurtado, S., Eagan, M. K., Tran, M. C., Newman, C. B., Chang, M. J., & Velasco, P. (2011). "We do science here": Underrepresented students' interactions with faculty in different college contexts. *Journal of Social Issues, 67*, 553–579.

Iyengar, S. S., & Lepper, M. R. (1999). Rethinking the value of choice: A cultural perspective on intrinsic motivation. *Journal of Personality and Social Psychology, 76*, 349–366.

Johnson, A. C. (2007). Unintended consequences: How science professors discourage women of color. *Science Education, 91*, 805–882.

Joseph, J. (2012). From one culture to another: Years one and two of graduate school for African American women in STEM fields. *International Journal of Doctoral Studies, 7*, 125–142.

Linley, J. L., & George-Jackson, C. E. (2013). Addressing underrepresentation in STEM fields through undergraduate interventions. *New Directions for Student Services, 144*, 97–102. doi:10.1002/ss.20073

Marra, R. M., Rodgers, K. A., Shen, D., & Bogue, B. (2012). Leaving engineering: A multi-year single institution study. *Journal of Engineering Education, 101*, 6–27.

Marra, R. M., Shen, D., Rodgers, K. A., & Bogue, B. (2009). Women engineering students and self-efficacy: A multi-year, multi-institutional study of women engineering students. *Journal of Engineering Education, 98*, 27–38.

Morrow, J. A., & Ackermann, M. E. (2012). Intention to persist and retention of first-year students: The importance of motivation and sense of belonging. *College Student Journal, 46*, 483–491.

National Science Board. (2014). *Science and Engineering Indicators 2014*. Arlington VA: National Science Foundation (NSB 14–01). Retrieved from http://www.nsf.gov/statistics/seind14/index.cfm/chapter-2

National Science Foundation. (2010). *Science and Engineering Degrees, by Race/Ethnicity of Recipients: 1997–2006*. Detailed Statistical Tables NSF 10-300. Arlington, VA: National Science Foundation. Retrieved from http://www.nsf.gov/statistics/nsf10300/

Oyserman, D., Coon, H. M., & Kemmelmeier, M. (2002). Rethinking individualism and collectivism: Evaluation of theoretical assumptions and meta-analyses. *Psychological Bulletin, 128*, 3–72.

Perez, T., Cromley, J. G., & Kaplan. A. (2014). The role of identity development, values, and costs in college STEM retention. *Journal of Educational Psychology, 106*, 315–329.

Perna, L., Lundy-Wagner, V., Drezner, N. D., Gasman, M., Yoon, S., Bose, E., & Gary, S. (2009). The contribution of HBCUs to the preparation of African American women for STEM careers: A case study. *Research in Higher Education, 50*, 1–23.

Proctor, S. L., & Truscott, S. D. (2012). Reasons for African American student attrition from school psychology programs. *Journal of School Psychology, 50*, 655–679.

Rivard, R. (2014). Fighting for survival. *Inside Higher Ed*. Retrieved from https://www.insidehighered.com/news/2014/06/24/public-hbcus-facing-tests-many-fronts-fight-survival

Rodgers, K. A., & Summers, J. J. (2008). African American students at predominantly White institution: Towards a revised retention model. *Educational Psychology Review, 20*, 171–190.

Russell, M. L., & Atwater, M. M. (2005). Traveling the road to success: A discourse on persistence throughout the science pipeline with African American students at a predominantly White institution. *Journal of Research in Science Teaching, 42*, 691–715.

Ryan, R. M., & Deci, E. L. (2000). Self-determination theory and the facilitation of intrinsic motivation, social development, and well-being. *American Psychologist, 55*, 68–78.

Sayed, M., Azmitia, M., & Cooper, C. R. (2011). Identity and academic success among under-represented ethnic minorities: An interdisciplinary review and integration. *Journal of Social Issues, 67*, 442–468.

Seymour, E., & Hewitt, N. (1997). *Talking about leaving*. Boulder, CO: Westview Press.

St. John, E. P., Paulsen, M. B., & Carter, D. F. (2005). Diversity, college costs, and postsecondary opportunity: An examination of the financial nexus between college choice and persistence for African Americans and Whites. *The Journal of Higher Education, 76*, 545–569.

Steele, C. M. (1997). A threat in the air: How stereotypes shape intellectual identity and performance. *American Psychologist, 52*, 613–629.

Tinto, V. (1975). Dropout from higher education: A theoretical synthesis of recent research. *Review of Educational Research, 45*, 89–123.

Tinto, V. (1988). Stages of student departure: Reflection on the longitudinal character of student leaving. *Journal of Higher Education, 59*, 438–455.

Towns, M. H. (2010). Where are the women of color? Data on African American, Hispanic, and Native American faculty in STEM. *Journal of College Science Teaching, 39*, 6–7.

Triandis, H. C. (1989). The self and social behavior in differing cultural contexts. *Psychological Review, 96*, 506–520.

Tuttle, L. V., & Musoba, G. D. (2013). Transfer student persistence at a Hispanic-serving university. *Journal of Latinos & Education, 12*, 38–58.

Tyson, W., Lee, R., Borman, K. M., & Hanson, M. A. (2007). Science, technology, engineering and mathematics pathways: High school science and math coursework and postsecondary degree attainment. *Journal of Education for Students Placed at Risk, 12*, 243–270.

U.S. Department of Education, National Center for Education Statistics. (2012). *The condition of education 2012* (NCES 2012–045). Washington, DC: Author.

van Laar, C. (2000). The paradox of low academic achievement but high self-esteem in African American students: An attributional account. *Educational Psychology Review, 12*, 33–60.

Williamson, S. Y. (2010). Within-group ethnic differences of Black male STEM majors and factors affecting their persistence in college. *Journal of International & Global Studies, 1*, 45–73.

4

EXAMINING ASSOCIATIONS BETWEEN FITTING IN AT SCHOOL AND HEART RATE VARIABILITY AMONG AFRICAN AMERICAN ADOLESCENTS

DeLeon L. Gray, LaBarron K. Hill, Lauren H. Bryant, Jason R. Wornoff, Oriana Johnson, and Lisa Jackson

Theoretical arguments regarding the role of positive social experiences in students' motivation and achievement are easy to find (e.g., Martin & Dowson, 2009; Weiner, 1990), but studies that test these predictions among African American students exist in rare form. This chapter makes two contributions. First, we contribute to the limited number of empirical studies examining the African American experience of fitting in at school. Second, we move beyond traditional research methods employed in educational psychology by examining African American adolescents' physiological responses to fitting in at school.

In this chapter we provide an initial examination of the prediction that unmet belongingness needs result in psychological distress (also referred to as the psychological distress hypothesis) among African American adolescents. A number of models of academic functioning implicate psychological distress as an intervening factor linking students' social experiences with their engagement and performance. Indicators of psychological distress—including depression, anxiety, low self-worth, low well-being, moodiness, and anger (Kessler, Foster, Saunders, & Stang, 1995; Wentzel, 1998)—are thought to negatively impact engagement and performance. Students who report receiving less social support from peers also report greater psychological distress; and those who report greater psychological distress have lower interest in school (Wentzel, 1998). Students who are bullied report being less engaged in scholastic activities due to greater psychological distress; in turn, they have lower academic achievement (Totura, Karver, & Gesten, 2014). Students who report a lack of peer acceptance earn lower grades—an effect that is partially mediated by teachers' perceptions of students' somatic complaints, behavioral withdrawal, and anxious and depressed behaviors (Flook, Repetti, & Ullman, 2005). As Roeser, van der Wolf, and Strobel (2001) explain, such affective mediums can have an impact on school functioning "through disruption of self-regulatory processes essential to learning, through an activation of debilitating motivational beliefs (e.g., lack of efficacy), and through an activation of avoidance-behavioral scripts aimed at self-protective rather than educational ends in the classroom" (p. 133). These findings—when coupled with basic research highlighting the need to belong as essential for healthy human functioning (Baumeister & Leary, 1995)—provide suggestive support for the importance of students' social experiences in general and have implications for the role of fitting in at school more specifically.

Uniquely, we examine the relationship between fitting in and heart rate variability—an established biomarker of psychological distress (Appelhans & Leucken, 2006; Kemp & Quintana, 2013; Thayer & Lane, 2000). If this prediction is upheld, the findings reinforce our current understanding of fitting in at school. If the psychological distress hypothesis is not upheld, then our general theoretical understanding of fitting in at school becomes more nuanced, qualified, and perhaps even falsified.

Belonging at School Among Ethnic Minority Adolescents

A core developmental task during adolescence involves social contact and relationships among peers (Higgins & Parsons, 1983). Each weekday, adolescents traditionally spend at least 7 hours around their peers in school. While navigating the social terrain of hallways, buses, cafeterias, and classrooms, students absorb the norms, standards, and cultural mores of this *autonomous adolescent social system* (Higgins & Parsons, 1983, p. 27). Their experiences within these spaces give rise to their perceptions of belonging (or relatedness)—which is not only a hallmark of adolescence and emerging adulthood but is also a basic human need (Baumeister & Leary, 1995; Deci & Ryan, 1985). This assumption underlies several studies conducted on ethnic minority adolescents. These studies reveal fluctuations in belonging across time, school contexts, and gender and draw attention to the contingencies upon which belongingness is experienced and expressed. For instance, Wang and Eccles (2012) examined the developmental trajectories of school belonging in a predominantly African American sample of adolescents in the Washington, DC, metropolitan area. These authors found that adolescents' school belonging declines significantly from seventh grade to eleventh grade—as does adolescents' self-regulated learning and behavioral participation in school. Relative to White students, ethnic minority students demonstrate significantly steeper declines in school belonging over time. Moreover, declines in school belonging are associated with lower educational aspirations over time. Within the scope of stage–environment fit theory (Eccles et al., 1993), Wang and Eccles explain that these declines are likely a function of a lack of fit between the adolescents' developmental needs and the school environment's opportunity structures for satisfying these needs.

For ethnic minority adolescents, perceptions of "fit" may stem, in part, from opportunities to interact with other members of their same ethnic group. There is some empirical support for this notion. Benner and Graham (2007) assessed the effects of transitioning to high schools with a lower proportion of students from one's own ethnic group, relative to the proportion of same–ethnic group students at one's middle school. When adolescents move to a high school with a lower proportion of students from their own ethnic group, they also experience significant declines in school belonging—especially if they are African American or male. Taken together, these studies emphasize the developmental importance of the school's social context for all students—but especially for ethnic minority adolescents who exhibit more acute responses to a lack of fit and who also process their school fit in terms of racial/ethnic group interactions.

African American males and females also respond differently to their school's social environment, and these responses have implications for academic adjustment. In a study of African American urban high school students in the Southern United States, Adelabu (2007) found school belonging to be a significant predictor of achievement. However, when this association was disaggregated, school belonging was positively associated with academic achievement for African American females but not for African American males. This disconnect between African American males' perceptions of their school's social environment and their scholastic engagement and performance epitomizes a theoretical and practical issue in education that has intrigued researchers for decades.

Studies employing peer nomination procedures have further shown that African American male adolescents uniquely process information about their social experiences. For example, when asked to nominate peers whom they admired, respected, and wanted to be like, African American males disproportionately nominate more low-achieving compared to high-achieving, same-sex peers (Graham, Taylor, & Hudley, 1998). Hamm, Lambert, Agger, and Farmer (2013) extended this work in a study of African American males' peer networks. Findings demonstrated that sustained involvement in a peer network whose norms included academic effort and scholastic achievement had positive benefits for students, including an increased valuing of school. At the same time, sustained involvement in these peer networks did not result in a greater sense of belonging at school. In fact, individuals who sustained involvement in these academically supportive networks received significantly fewer peer nominations when their peers were asked to identify which classmates they most wanted to be like. Together, these studies suggest that African American males may not always (1) see achieving as a way to belong at school, (2) achieve when they belong at school, or (3) belong when they achieve in school. Just as these social cognition studies provide a more nuanced understanding of the ways in which belonging is manifested in school among African American males, studies of physiological activity may also yield theoretical insights into the social experiences of African American males in school.

The Role of Heart Rate Variability: A Proxy for Psychological Distress

Cardiovascular activity has long been viewed as a general index of physiological arousal in response to psychological stress caused by events in one's environment (Cannon, 1922; Selye, 1950). During stress the activity of the heart is largely governed by the autonomic nervous system (ANS), which is further divided into two complementary branches, the sympathetic (SNS) and parasympathetic (PNS). Whereas the sympathetic nervous system is largely responsible for the well-known "fight or flight" (i.e., see snake, run), reaction to stressors, the parasympathetic branch has been termed the "rest and digest" system because it promotes calming and buffering of SNS activity (Thayer, Hansen, & Johnsen, 2010). In broad terms, this indicates that the relative impact of distress can be assessed by examining changes in heart rate. Specifically, extensive theoretical and empirical research has demonstrated that the influence of the parasympathetic branch on the heart, measured as heart rate variability (HRV), is an important and sensitive index of the effects of both acute and chronic forms of psychological distress (cf. Porges, 1995, 2007; Thayer & Lane, 2000, 2009). Generally, when the body is at rest, HRV is typically high and resting heart rate is low—a pattern that generally reflects a low degree of physiological and psychological arousal to stimuli in one's environment. Conversely, increases in an individual's level of arousal will generally produce a corresponding decrease in HRV and subsequently an increase in heart rate (Appelhans & Leucken, 2006).

Scholars as far back as Darwin have theorized that the heart and brain are interconnected in such a manner that factors affecting one organ will influence the activity of the other (Thayer & Lane, 2009). Contemporary research has largely substantiated this notion. For instance, medical research has shown that temporary deactivation of the prefrontal cortex (PFC), the so-called executive center of the brain, is associated with an increase in heart rate via a reduction in HRV (Ahern, et al., 2001). Significantly, this effect was observed in individuals as young as 13 years old, for whom neural integration between the heart and prefrontal regions of the brain is likely not complete. Moreover, neuroimaging studies have further shown that increased activity in the PFC during the processing of emotional stimuli is positively associated with resting HRV (Lane et al., 2009), while brain activation during the experience of explicitly negative emotions that signal distress (e.g., anger) has been inversely related to HRV (Marci, Glick, Loh, & Dougherty, 2007). There is also growing evidence that lower HRV may be a common feature of psychological states characterized by poor or diminished emotion regulation such as anxiety and depression (Chalmers, Quintana, Maree, Abbott, & Kemp, 2014; Kemp & Quintana, 2013; Tully, Cosh, & Baune, 2013). In contrast, higher HRV has been associated with better performance on cognitively and emotionally challenging tasks (Mezzacappa, Kindlon, Saul, & Earles, 1998) and better self-reported emotion regulation and coping (Fabes & Eisenberg, 1997). As these findings suggest, examinations of HRV may not only be relevant for understanding basic social processes in education—HRV examinations also are potential sources of insight into practical outcomes related to student behavior and achievement.

Overview of Research

In the present study, we employ the term *fitting in* as we attempt to capture the "essence" of being part of the school environment in its broadest and most basic form—similarity, or mere belonging (Walton, Cohen, Cwir, & Spencer, 2012). From a psychological distress perspective, fitting in at school should predict better functioning (as indicated by higher resting HRV). We tested the psychological distress hypothesis among a sample of African American students from an inner-city school.

We adjusted for additional factors that might account for the association between fitting in and HRV. Health-related factors including BMI and physical activity have previously been shown to impact HRV (Koenig et al., 2014), so we controlled for these factors. We also considered other social factors that might account for any shared variance between fitting in and HRV. Research indicates that students have a desire to fit in—yet they also wish to stand out (Snyder & Fromkin, 1980). Although the desire for distinctiveness is not often examined in educational studies, social identity researchers have shown that these desires are often associated with one another (Sheldon & Bettencourt, 2002). In addition, considering that the need to belong differs in intensity from person to person (Brewer & Roccas, 2002), we also adjusted for this individual difference characteristic. Finally, in an effort to explore the boundary conditions of the psychological distress hypothesis, we tested whether the relations between fitting in and psychological distress were the same across gender groups.

Method

Participants were 65 sophomores across three social studies classrooms at a predominantly African American, inner-city high school in the southern region of the United States. The sample was 42% male, and all but one student was African American (Latino). We were unable to obtain individual data points on socioeconomic status. In terms of school statistics, 66% of students were free-reduced lunch eligible, and the school was 83% African American.

Procedure

We administered questionnaires and conducted cardiovascular recording during the school day in spring 2014.

Survey Administration

On the day the surveys were administered, students completed 15-minute questionnaires during their social studies class period. Students were instructed to access the questionnaire using their school-issued laptops. Researchers were present to ensure that students were able to access the questionnaire. All students were instructed to work quietly on their laptops after submitting their survey electronically.

Cardiovascular Recording

Heart rate data was collected using the Polar™ RS800CX Heart Rate (HR) Monitor. After viewing a 2-minute instructional video, participants applied the device and sat quietly in their chairs for 2 minutes prior to recording. Participants were then instructed to rest for an additional 5 minutes during cardiovascular recording. Raw interbeat interval (IBI) series was written to a single text file and analyzed using the Kubios HRV analysis software, Version 2.0 (Tarvainen, Niskanen, Lipponen, Ranta-aho, & Karjalainen, 2009), to derive estimates of HRV. Using spectral analysis, estimates of high-frequency HRV (HF-HRV; 0.15–0.40 ms^2/Hz) were obtained.

Measures

Standing Out and Fitting In

We adapted Gray's (2013) Standing Out and Fitting In (SOFI) measures to assess how satisfied students were in terms of their level of similarity and uniqueness among their peers at school (fitting in α = .75, three items, sample item: "The amount of similarity I feel to students in this school meets my standards," 1 = *Not at all true*, 5 = *Very true*; standing out α = .72, three items, sample item: "I am satisfied with how unique I am from other students in this school," 1 = *Not at all true*, 5 = *Very true*). Social identity research suggests that it is possible for individuals simultaneously to fulfill their desires to stand out and fit in (Brewer, 1991). Higher scores on the SOFI measures indicate that students' desires to stand out and fit in are being met.

Need to Belong

We used the Need to Belong Scale (Leary, Kelly, Cottrell, & Schreindorfer, 2013) to assess individual differences in the desire to belong to social groups. Internal consistency for this 10-item measure was acceptable (α = .73, sample item: "I have a strong need to belong." 1 = *Strongly disagree* to 5 = *Strongly agree*).

Recent Physical Activity

We administered the Patient-Centered Assessment and Counseling for Exercise Plus Nutrition (PACE+) Adolescent Physical Activity Measure—a screening measure of recent physical activity that has validity evidence and has demonstrated test-retest reliability in prior research (Prochaska, Sollis, & Long, 2001). This measure assesses participants' physical behavior over the past week (single item: "Physical activity is any activity that increases your heart rate and makes you get out of breath some of the time (i.e., sports, playing with friends, walking to school).

56 DeLeon L. Gray et al.

Over the past 7 days, on how many days were you physically active for a total of at least 60 minutes per day?").

Body Mass Index (BMI)

Participants self-reported their height and weight. BMI was calculated as weight in kilograms (kg) divided by height in meters squared (m^2).

Results

Means, standard deviations, and correlations are presented in Table 4.1.

TABLE 4.1 Means, standard deviations, and correlations

	Mean	SD	1	2	3	4	5	6
1 Fitting In	4.62	1.31						
2 Need to Belong	2.53	0.61	−0.16					
3 Body Mass Index	225.10	5.85	0.08	−0.28				
4 Male	0.42	0.49	0.26	−0.35	0.40★★			
5 Standing Out	6.10	0.99	0.37★★	−0.42★	0.15	0.18		
6 Physical Activity	5.53	2.1	0.04	−0.20	0.16	0.20	0.32	
7 Heart Rate Variability (pHF)	0.31	0.43	−0.26	0.12	−0.10	−0.15	0.01	0.25

Note. $p < .05$:★; $p < .01$:★★; $p < .001$★★★

To test whether the psychological distress hypothesis regarding students' social experiences was upheld in a sample of African American adolescents, bounded by gender, we regressed resting HRV onto recent physical activity, need to belong, standing out, BMI, fitting in, gender, and a fitting in-by-gender cross-product. Results revealed a significant interaction between fitting in and gender, $b = -.05$, 95% CI [−.08, −.01]. This interaction accounted for 16% of the variation in HRV, $sr^2 = .159$. As shown in Figure 4.1, gender does not predict resting HRV at low perceptions of fitting in, $b = .04$, 95% CI [−.01, .09]. However, gender does predict resting HRV at high perceptions of fitting in, $b = -.05$, 95% CI [−.09, −.01]. Among these male students, fitting in negatively predicts resting HRV, $b = -.04$, 95% CI [−.06, −.01]. No effect of fitting in is seen among these female students, $b = .01$, 95% CI [−.02, .03]. No covariates were significant except for recent physical activity, $b = .02$, 95% CI [.01, .03], $sr^2 = .114$. All coefficients are presented in Table 4.2, and all simple slope coefficients are visualized in Figure 4.2.

As Figure 4.2 shows, the effects of fitting in on HRV are conditional upon gender such that these females exhibit higher HRV at high levels of fitting in, and males exhibit higher levels of HRV at low levels of fitting in. The gender simple slope coefficient is largest for students with fitting-in scores that are 2.5 standard deviations below the mean. We interpret this coefficient as follows: Among

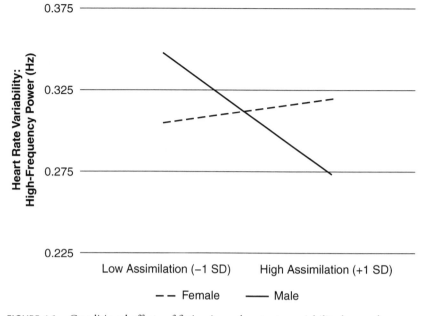

FIGURE 4.1 Conditional effects of fitting in on heart rate variability by gender

TABLE 4.2 Unstandardized Regression Coefficients in a High-Frequency Power Spectrum Analysis of Heart Rate Variability

Variable	b	SE	t	p	95% CI Lower	95% CI Upper
Intercept	**0.32**	**0.03**	**10.55**	**<0.001**	**0.25**	**0.38**
Fitting In	0.01	0.01	0.64	0.53	−0.02	0.03
Male	0.00	0.02	−0.14	0.89	−0.03	0.03
Male × Fitting In	**−0.04**	**0.02**	**−2.75**	**0.01**	**−0.08**	**−0.01**
Standing Out	0.01	0.01	0.62	0.54	−0.01	0.02
Recent Physical Activity	**0.02**	**0.01**	**2.33**	**0.03**	**0.00**	**0.03**
Need to Belong	0.00	0.01	0.07	0.94	−0.02	0.02
BMI	0.00	0.00	−0.11	0.92	0.00	0.00
R^2	0.35					

Note. [a]Standardized continuous variable. Bold coefficients are significant

two students of different gender groups who are very low in their perceptions of how much they fit in at school (−2.5 SD), the female student is estimated to exhibit resting HRV that is more than 1 Hz lower than the male student, $b = .11$, 95% CI [.03, .20]. The magnitude of the gender simple slope coefficient is half as small at a standardized fitting-in score of 1.1, $b = .05$, 95% CI [.01, .10].

58 DeLeon L. Gray et al.

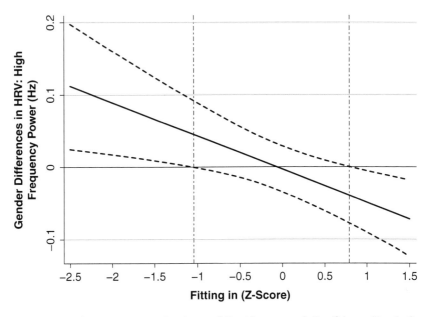

FIGURE 4.2 Johnson-Neyman Regions of Significance and Confidence Bands for the Conditional Relation between Gender and Mean-Adjusted Heart Rate Variability as a Function of Fitting In. This figure depicts the relation between gender and HRV at different levels of fitting in. Students' standardized fitting in scores are presented horizontally along the abscissa from 2.5 standard deviations below the mean to 1.5 standard deviations above the mean. Based on recommendations for probing conditional effects, Hayes and Matthes (2009), these values along the *x*-axis represent observations that fall within range of scores observed on the moderator variable. Estimated gender differences are presented along the ordinate. The descending solid line depicts the gender simple slope at each point along the continuous fitting-in moderator variable. The descending dashed lines are confidence bands (Bauer & Curran, 2005), which represent 95% confidence intervals that accompany simple slope estimates for gender at each level of the continuous moderator variable. When the upper and lower bounds of a 95% confidence interval contain zero, the effect of a regression coefficient is not statistically significant. Similarly, when the confidence bands contain a value of zero (as represented by the horizontal line within the figure), the simple slope for gender is not significant. These confidence bands appear narrowest around average fitting-in levels, indicating that our estimation of the gender simple slopes is most precise for individuals with average fitting-in scores.

Note in Figure 4.2 that the dashed vertical lines mark the values of fitting in at which the 95% confidence interval around the gender simple slope includes zero—thus indicating that the association of gender and HRV is nonsignificant for students whose standardized fitting-in scores range between −1.00 and 0.70. Starting again with students who have a standardized fitting-in score of .080, the gender differences in HRV are significant but reversed. Specifically, among two students of different gender groups who are high in their perceptions of how much they fit in at school (+.08 SD), the male student is estimated to exhibit resting HRV that is .04 Hz lower than the female student, $b = −.04$, 95% CI [−.08, −.01]. This gender effect remains significant and is exacerbated among students at even higher levels of fitting in.

Discussion

Over the past decade, motivation researchers have conducted seminal work that explains the role of self-reported affective responding in achievement contexts (e.g., Pekrun, Goetz, Frenzel, Barchfeld, & Perry, 2011; Schutz & Lanehart, 2002). Prior research has linked HRV to cognitive, emotional, social, and academic functioning among children and adolescents (i.e., Fabes & Eisenberg, 1997; Mezzacappa et al., 1998), but few educational psychologists have incorporated measures of HRV when examining students' social experiences in actual educational settings. With the long-term goal of extending the boundaries of educational psychology research to document how scholastic, social, and health perspectives inform our understanding of motivation in education contexts, we examined whether students who fit in with peers at school exhibit more adaptive patterns of cardiovascular activity.

Results demonstrate that fitting in is associated with HRV but not in ways that are consistent with a psychological distress hypothesis. Because higher HRV is indicative of greater parasympathetic nervous system activity, a psychological distress perspective would predict that—relative to students who do not fit in with their peers—those who do fit in will exhibit higher HRV when they are in a resting state. In our sample of inner-city African American adolescents, fitting in is positively—albeit nonsignificantly—associated with higher HRV in African American females. For African American males, the effect is reversed: fitting in predicts lower HRV. In prior research, stronger social ties at school predicted lower psychological distress (e.g., Roeser et al., 2001; Wentzel, 1998); and to our knowledge, significant moderating effects of gender have not been reported. A logical question becomes, why did African American students in this sample respond differently than what conventional predictions might suggest? Proceeding cautiously in our interpretation, we speculate first by considering theoretical arguments that have been offered in prior research.

Can These Results Be Explained by Considering Opportunity Structures to Fit In at School?

Our approach of testing a well-documented theoretical argument with urban African American adolescents positions us to consider the kind of process that might have led to this disconfirming pattern of results. A stage–environment fit perspective might help us characterize how African American students' desires to fit in might function in the context of an inner-city school.

Stage–environment fit theory focuses on the intersection of adolescents' developmental needs and the structural features of their school environments. The general argument advanced by Eccles and colleagues is that a match between the adolescents' developmental needs and the opportunity structures of their school environment will curb academic and psychological maladjustment to school (Eccles & Midgley, 1989; Eccles et al., 1993). This focus is conceptually similar to Juvonen's (2006) characterization of how adolescents' heightened concerns for identity are manifest in their school engagement, except that Juvonen explicitly suggests that a school environment may present opportunity structures that are need satisfying yet incompatible with healthy development. Juvonen argues that adolescents' identity concerns result in a perceptual exaggeration of in-group–out-group distinctions—with peers being the in-group and adult socializers being the out-group. And to the extent that adolescents want to fit in with their peers, they will adopt the behaviors that are deemed desirable by this in-group—whether these behaviors are consistent with or "antithetical to the mission of the school" (p. 667). By considering Juvonen's perspective in the context of stage–environment fit theory, it is possible to envision a student who fits in at school but who does so in ways that are counterproductive to their healthy development.

Taking Juvonen's (2006) perspective on need-satisfying opportunity structures seriously, it is possible that some African American males in this sample deem it viable to place energy, for instance, into behaviors that are incompatible with the school's mission, such as being successful at working jobs that will allow them to fund a name-brand wardrobe—thereby enhancing their style or physical appearance at the expense of sleep and academic success (Gray et al., in press). Whereas these need-satisfying behaviors may ultimately lead to rather unhealthy outcomes physically, behaviorally, emotionally, and academically, they may, in fact, meet the needs of some African American males within this school context. Theoretically, this argument applies to any student, regardless of race, and should play out depending on the student's subjective construal of which behaviors constitute fitting in at their school. However, this argument seems particularly relevant to African American males—a group of individuals who do not always evaluate their peers more favorably on the basis of scholastic achievement (Graham et al., 1998; Hamm et al., 2013). Taken together with prior research, this study underscores the potential relevance of sources of belongingness need satisfaction within school contexts. Moreover, our approach to testing a well-documented theoretical argument in the context of inner-city, African American adolescents highlights the need for a rigorous, complementary analysis of structural and organizational school features (Eccles & Roeser, 1999) moving forward. Next, we offer a number of methodological considerations that are essential for advancing this line of inquiry.

Methodological Considerations for Progress and Theory Development

The results presented in this chapter can serve as a building block for future investigations that test whether well-grounded predictions, such as the psychological distress hypothesis, are upheld in predominantly ethnic minority samples. However, a number of caveats must be addressed in future work. First, we are aware of and fully appreciate the diversity that exists among African American students with respect to social class. We also understand that, without adjusting for SES, it is difficult for motivational psychologist who studies the experiences of African Americans to disentangle race and class effect (Graham, 1994). These data points were not made available to us in the present study and would have allowed us to further examine patterns of variability in our outcome of interest.

Second, our sample was notably smaller than is common in education research. However, this sample size is typical of exploratory studies of psychophysiological phenomena. Further, significant results are more difficult to observe in studies with smaller samples due to larger standard errors. Whereas larger standard errors are not ideal for precision, statistical power was not a barrier to observing significant results in the present study. For the purposes of greater precision, larger sample sizes are ideal and should be secured where possible.

Third, we conceptualized HRV broadly as an indicator of psychological distress, but we did not assess self-reports of stress or well-being. It would have been ideal to examine the correspondence between self-reported distress and HRV. This should be an important aim of future research in this area. In addition, while there has been relatively little research on HRV and African Americans, our finding regarding African American males is especially intriguing in light of emerging data that suggests that African Americans may actually possess greater resting HRV compared to Whites (Hill et al., 2015). This pattern would suggest that HRV is potentially a protective mechanism among African Americans. Previous research provides some support for this notion. For example, in one laboratory-based investigation, African American college students exposed to audio recordings of blatantly racist commentary from either a Black or White assailant exhibited decreases in HRV during the imaginal exposure. However, the decrease in HRV was smaller for individuals who endorsed moderately positive views toward their own racial identity when exposed to the scenario featuring a Black assailant (Neblett & Roberts, 2013). In another study, researchers examined the moderating role of resting HRV on the association between race-related stress and psychological distress in a sample of African American college students. These researchers found that greater levels of institutional racism were associated with greater psychological distress in both men and women; however, the magnitude of this relationship was attenuated in African American males with higher HRV (Utsey & Hook, 2007). As these illustrative findings indicate, the ramifications of possessing higher or lower HRV may be especially complex among African

Americans—and particularly among males. It is resoundingly clear that additional research is needed to further elucidate the connections between environmental stimuli and HRV among African Americans.

Fourth, our measure of fitting in assesses students' general perceptions of how satisfied they were in terms of their level of similarity with their peers. However, this measure does not account for whom students wish to fit in with or the characteristics of these social targets. The present emphasis on social need-satisfaction, coupled with state-of-the art peer nomination procedures (e.g., Hamm, Farmer, Lambert, & Gravelle, 2014), could provide further assurance and clarification necessary for understanding the dynamic ways in which fitting in is linked with psychological distress.

Conclusion

Research on cardiac vagal function continues to illuminate important theoretical insights regarding students' socioemotional functioning, linking physiological states to peer rejection (Gunther Moor, Crone, & van der Molen, 2010), internalizing and externalizing problems (Grazianoa & Derefinko, 2013), and both asocial and prosocial behaviors (Beauchaine, 2015). In this chapter, we employed similar psychophysiology methods in an effort to push the boundaries of educational psychology research regarding (1) students' social experiences at school, (2) cardiovascular responding in school environments, and (3) the experiences of inner-city African American adolescents. There is much more to know about the study of race in teaching, learning, motivation, and emotion. We hope this chapter serves as a springboard for new methodological, practical, and theoretical considerations in future research on ethnic minority adolescents' social experiences in achievement contexts.

References

Adelabu, D. H. (2007). Time perspective and school membership as correlates to academic achievement among African American adolescents. *Adolescence, 42*, 525–538.

Ahern, G. L., Sollers, J. J., Lane, R. D., Labiner, D. M., Herring, A. M., Weinand, M. E., Hutzler, R., & Thayer, J. F. (2001). Heart rate and heart rate variability changes in the intracarotid sodium amobarbital (ISA) test. *Epilepsia, 42*, 912–921. doi:10.1046/j.1528–1157.2001.042007912.x

Appelhans, B. M., & Leucken, L. J. (2006). Heart rate variability as an index of regulated emotional responding. *Review of General Psychology, 10*(3), 229. doi:10.1037/1089–2680.10.3.229

Bauer, D. J., & Curran, P. J. (2005). Probing interactions in fixed and multilevel regression: Inferential and graphical techniques. *Multivariate Behavioral Research, 40*, 373–400. doi:10.3102/10769986031004437

Baumeister, R. F., & Leary, M. R. (1995). The need to belong—desire for interpersonal attachments as a fundamental human-motivation. *Psychological Bulletin, 117*(3), 497–529. doi:10.1037/0033–2909.117.3.497

Beauchaine, T. P. (2015). Future directions in emotion dysregulation and youth psychopathology. *Journal of Clinical Child & Adolescent Psychology*, *44*(5), 875–896. doi:10.1080/15374416.2015.1038827.

Benner, A. D., & Graham, S. (2007). Navigating the transition to multi-ethnic urban high schools: Changing ethnic congruence and adolescents' school-related affect. *Journal of Research on Adolescence*, *17*(1), 207–220. doi: 10.1111/j.1532-7795.2007.00519.x

Brewer, M. B. (1991). The social self: On being the same and different at the same time. *Personality and Social Psychology Bulletin*. *17*, 475–482.

Brewer, M. B., & Roccas, S. (2002). Individual values, social identity, and optimal distinctiveness. In C. Sedikides & M. B. Brewer (Eds.), *Individual self, relational self, collective self* (pp. 219–237). New York: Psychology Press.

Cannon, W. B. (1922). New evidence for sympathetic control of some internal secretions. *American Journal of Psychiatry*, *79*(1), 15–30.

Chalmers, J. A., Quintana, D. S., Maree, J., Abbott, A., & Kemp, A. H. (2014). Anxiety disorders are associated with reduced heart rate variability: A meta-analysis. *Frontiers in Psychiatry*, *5*. Retrieved from http://journal.frontiersin.org/article/10.3389/fpsyt.2014.00080/full

Deci, E. L., & Ryan, R. M. (1985). *Intrinsic motivation and self-determination in human behavior.* New York: Plenum Press.

Eccles, J., & Midgley, C. (1989). Stage/environment fit: Developmentally appropriate classrooms for young adolescents. In R. Ames & C. Ames (Eds.), *Research on motivation and education: Goals and cognitions* (vol. 3., pp. 139–186). New York: Academic Press

Eccles, J., Midgley, C., Wigfield, A., Buchanan, C., Reuman, D., Flanagan, C., & Mac Iver, D. (1993). Development during Adolescence: The impact of stage-environment fit on young adolescents' experiences in schools and families. *American Psychologist, 48*(2), 90–101. doi:10.1037/0003–066X.48.2.90

Eccles, J. S., & Roeser, R. (1999). School and community influences on human development. In M. Bornstein & M. Lamb (Eds.), *Developmental psychology: An advanced textbook* (4th ed., pp. 503–554). Mahwah, NJ: Lawrence Erlbaum.

Fabes, R. A., & Eisenberg, N. (1997). Regulatory control and adults' stress-related responses to daily life events. *Journal of Personality and Social Psychology*, *73*(5), 1107.

Flook, L., Repetti, R. L., & Ullman, J. B. (2005). Classroom social experiences as predictors of academic performance. *Developmental Psychology*, *41*(2), 319–327. doi:10.1037/0012–1649.41.2.319

Graham, S. (1994). Motivation in African Americans. *Review of Educational Research, 64*(1), 55–117. doi:10.3102/00346543064001055

Graham, S., Taylor, A. Z., & Hudley, C. (1998). Exploring achievement values among ethnic minority early adolescents. *Journal of Educational Psychology*, *90*(4), 606–620. doi:10.1037/0022-0663.90.4.606

Gray, D. L. (2013, April). *Assessing the synergism between adolescents' needs to "fit in" and "stand out": A window into classroom identities, values, and emotions.* Paper presented at the 2013 annual meeting of the American Educational Research Association, San Francisco, CA.

Gray, D. L., Leach, N., Zimmerman, S., Wornoff, J., Johnson, D., & Baker, Q. (in press). "This is me, all day!" A standing out and fitting in (SOFI) perspective on black males' sense of school belonging in high school. Manuscript to appear in T. L. Strayhorn (Ed.), *Interrogating black masculinity in higher education: A collection of critical race analyses.*

Graziano, P., & Derefinko, K. (2013). Cardiac vagal regulation and children's adaptive functioning outcomes: A meta-analysis. *Biological Psychology*, *94*, 22–37. doi: 10.1037/a0038189

Gunther Moor, B. G., Crone, E. A., & van der Molen, M. W. (2010). The heartbrake of social rejection—heart rate deceleration in response to unexpected peer rejection. *Psychological Science, 21*(9), 1326–1333. doi:10.1177/0956797610379236

Hamm, J. V., Farmer, T. W., Lambert, K., & Gravelle, M. (2014). Enhancing peer cultures of academic effort and achievement in early adolescence: Promotive effects of the SEALS intervention. *Developmental Psychology, 50*(1), 216–228. doi:10.1037/a0032979

Hamm, J. V., Lambert, K., Agger, C. A., & Farmer, T. W. (2013). Promotive peer contexts of academic and social adjustment among rural African American early adolescent boys. *American Journal of Orthopsychiatry, 83*(2–3), 278. doi: 10.1111/ajop.12030

Hayes, A. F., & Matthes, J. (2009). Computational procedures for probing interactions in OLS and logistic regression: SPSS and SAS implementations. *Behavior Research Methods, 41*(3), 924–936. doi:10.3758/BRM.41.3.924

Higgins, E. T., & Eccles[Parsons], J. S. (1983). Social cognition and the social life of the child: Stages as subcultures. In E. T. Higgins, D. W. Ruble, & W. W. Hartup (Eds.), *Social cognition and social behavior: Developmental issues* (pp. 15–62). Cambridge, England: Cambridge University Press.

Hill, L. K., Hu, D. D., Koenig, J., Sollers III, J. J., Kapuku, G., Wang, X., . . . & Thayer, J. F. (2015). Ethnic differences in resting heart rate variability: A systematic review and meta-analysis. *Psychosomatic Medicine, 77*(1), 16–25. doi:10.1097/PSY.0000000000000133

Juvonen, J. (2006). Sense of belonging, social relationships, and school functioning. In P. A. Alexander & P. H. Winne (Eds.), *Handbook of educational psychology* (2nd ed., pp. 655–674). Mahwah, NJ: Lawrence Erlbaum Associates.

Kemp, A. H., & Quintana, D. S. (2013). The relationship between mental and physical health: Insights from the study of heart rate variability. *International Journal of Psychophysiology, 89*(3), 288–296. doi:10.1016/j.ijpsycho.2013.06.018

Kessler, R. C., Foster, C. L., Saunders, W. B., & Stang, P. E. (1995). Social consequences of psychiatric disorders, I: Educational attainment. *American Journal of Psychiatry, 152*, 1026–1032. doi:0.1176/ajp.152.7.1026

Koenig, J., Jarczok, M. N., Warth, M., Ellis, R. J., Bach, C., Hillecke, T. K., & Thayer, J. F. (2014). Body mass index is related to autonomic nervous system activity as measured by heart rate variability—a replication using short-term measurements. *The Journal of Nutrition, Health & Aging, 18*(3), 300–302.

Lane, R. D., McRae, K., Reiman, E. M., Chen, K., Ahern, G. L., & Thayer, J. F. (2009). Neural correlates of heart rate variability during emotion. *NeuroImage, 44*, 213–222. doi:10.1016/j.neuroimage.2008.07.056

Leary, M. R., Kelly, K. M., Cottrell, C. A., & Schreindorfer, L. S. (2013). Individual differences in the need to belong: Mapping the nomological network. *Journal of Personality Assessment, 95*, 610–624. doi:10.1080/00223891.2013.819511

Marci, C. D., Glick, D. M., Loh, R., & Dougherty, D. D. (2007). Autonomic and prefrontal cortex responses to autobiographical recall of emotions. *Cognitive, Affective, & Behavioral Neuroscience, 7*(3), 243–250. doi:10.3758/CABN.7.3.243

Martin, A. J., & Dowson, M. (2009). Interpersonal relationships, motivation, engagement, and achievement: Yields for theory, current issues, and educational practice. *Review of Educational Research, 79*(1), 327–365. doi:10.3102/0034654308325583

Mezzacappa, E., Kindlon, D., Saul, J. P., & Earles, F. (1998). Executive and motivational control of performance task behavior, and autonomic heart-rate regulation in children: Physiologic validation of two-factor solution inhibitory control. *Journal of Child Psychology and Psychiatry, 39*(04), 525–531.

Neblett, E. W., & Roberts, S. O. (2013). Racial identity and autonomic responses to racial discrimination. *Psychophysiology, 50*(10), 943–953.

Pekrun, R., Goetz, T., Frenzel, A. C., Barchfeld, P., & Perry, R. P. (2011). Measuring emotions in students' learning and performance: The Achievement Emotions Questionnaire (AEQ). *Contemporary Educational Psychology, 36*, 36e48. doi:http:/dx.doi.org/10.1016/j.cedpsych.2010.10.002.

Porges, S. W. (1995). Cardiac vagal tone: A physiological index of stress. *Neuroscience and Biobehavioral Reviews, 19*, 225–233. doi:10.1016/0149-7634(94)00066-A

Porges, S. W. (2007). A phylogenetic journey through the vagus and ambiguous Xth cranial nerve: A commentary on contemporary heart rate variability research. *Biological Psychology, 74*, 301–307.

Prochaska, J. J., Sollis, J. F., & Long, B. (2001). A physical activity screening measure for use with adolescents in primary care. *Archives of Pediatric and Adolescent Medicine, 155*, 554–559. doi:10.1001/archpedi.155.5.554

Roeser, R. W., van der Wolf, K., & Strobel, K. R. (2001). On the relation between social-emotional and school functioning during early adolescence: Preliminary findings from Dutch and American samples. *Journal of School Psychology, 39*(2), 111–139. doi:10.1016/S0022-4405(01)00060-7

Schutz, P. A., & Lanehart, S. L. (2002). Emotions in education: Guest editors' introduction. *Educational Psychologist, 37*, 67–68. doi:10.1207/S15326985EP3702_1

Selye, H. (1950). Stress and the general adaptation syndrome. *British Medical Journal, 1*(4667), 1383.

Sheldon, K. M., & Bettencourt, B. A. (2002). Psychological need-satisfaction and subjective well-being within social groups. *British Journal of Social Psychology, 41*, 25–38. doi:10.1348/014466602165036

Snyder, C. R., & Fromkin, H. L. (1980). *Uniqueness: The human pursuit of difference.* New York: Plenum Press.

Tarvainen, M. P., Niskanen, J., Lipponen, J. A., Ranta-aho, P. O., & Karjalainen, P. A. (2009). Kubios HRV—a software for advanced heart rate variability analysis. *4th European Conference of the International Federation for Medical and Biological Engineering, 22*(1–3), 1022–1025.

Thayer, J. F., Hansen, A. L., & Johnsen, B. H. (2010). The non-invasive assessment of autonomic influences on the heart using impedance cardiography and heart rate variability. In A. Steptoe (Ed.), *Handbook of behavioral medicine* (pp. 723–740). New York: Springer. doi:10.1007/978-0-387-09488-5_47

Thayer, J. F., & Lane, R. D. (2000). A model of neurovisceral integration in emotion regulation and dysregulation. *Journal of Affective Disorders, 61*(3), 201–216. doi:10.1016/S0165-0327(00)00338-4

Thayer, J. F., & Lane, R. D. (2009). Claude Bernard and the heart–brain connection: Further elaboration of a model of neurovisceral integration. *Neuroscience & Biobehavioral Reviews, 33*(2), 81–88.

Totura, C. M. W., Karver, M. S., & Gesten, E. L. (2014). Psychological distress and student engagement as mediators of the relationship between peer victimization and achievement in middle school youth. *Journal of Youth and Adolescence, 43*(1), 40–52. doi:10.1007/s10964-013-9918-4

Tully, P. J., Cosh, S. M., & Baune, B. T. (2013). A review of the affects of worry and generalized anxiety disorder upon cardiovascular health and coronary heart disease. *Psychology, Health & Medicine, 18*(6), 627–644. doi:10.1080/13548506.2012.749355

Utsey, S. O., & Hook, J. N. (2007). Heart rate variability as a physiological moderator of the relationship between race-related stress and psychological distress in African Americans. *Cultural Diversity and Ethnic Minority Psychology, 13*(3), 250. doi:10.1037/1099–9809.13.3.250

Walton, G. M., Cohen, G. L., Cwir, D., & Spencer, S. J. (2012). Mere belonging: The power of social connections. *Journal of Personality and Social Psychology, 102*(3), 513–532. doi:10.1037/a0025731

Wang, M., & Eccles, J. S. (2012). Adolescent behavioral, emotional, and cognitive engagement trajectories in school and their differential relations to educational success. *Journal of Research on Adolescence, 22*(1), 31–39. doi: 10.1111/j.1532-7795.2011.00753.x

Weiner, B. (1990). The history of motivation research in education. *Journal of Educational Psychology, 82*(4), 616–622. doi:10.1037/0022–0663.82.4.616

Wentzel, K. R. (1998). Social relationships and motivation in middle school: The role of parents, teachers, and peers. *Journal of Educational Psychology, 90*(2), 202–209. doi:10.1037//0022–0663.90.2.202

5

STEM MOTIVATION AND PERSISTENCE AMONG UNDERREPRESENTED MINORITY STUDENTS

A Social Cognitive Perspective

Shirley L. Yu, Danya M. Corkin, and Julie P. Martin

Significant national efforts have been made during the last three decades to increase the number of underrepresented minority (URM) students in science, technology, engineering, and mathematics (STEM) disciplines, yet only modest increases have been realized. The sociopolitical and historical dimensions of minority students' underrepresentation in higher education and STEM in particular are complex. Minorities were largely and systemically excluded from educational opportunities during much of the 20th century, creating a stubborn gap in educational attainment between minority and White students in STEM higher education that continues to this day (National Academy of Sciences, National Academy of Engineering, and Institute of Medicine, 2011). While this gap has narrowed somewhat in recent decades, the challenges faced by URM students pursuing undergraduate STEM degrees have been described as unique and persistent (Chang, Sharkness, Hurtado, & Newman, 2014).

Many national calls to action to increase the diversity in the national STEM workforce have been asserted in recent years. National economic competitiveness and security are often cited as driving forces for diversifying URM students studying STEM disciplines and subsequently helping meet projected workforce demands. The effect of the historical marginalization of URMs in STEM is compounded by the anticipated high retirement rates in the current STEM workforce and declining STEM enrollments (Carnevale, Smith, & Milton, 2011; Drew, 2011; National Academy of Sciences et al., 2011; National Action Council for Minorities in Engineering [NACME], 2012).

A key report published in 2011 by the National Academy of Sciences emphasizes diversity as both a societal and economic resource. They call for broadened participation in STEM by examining the issue from an opportunity cost perspective, asserting that the United States can no longer afford to waste the participation and viewpoints of URMs (National Academy of Sciences et al., 2011). The potential human capital gained by greater participation of URMs in STEM will not only increase the number of citizens participating in the STEM workforce, but also widen the diversity of thought that will ultimately strengthen the solutions that the workforce will be able to develop in response to today's complex problems for a diverse society (National Academy of Sciences et al., 2011). A well-known example of a problem in overlooking diversity in a STEM setting is the predominantly male engineering team that designed the first generation of automobile airbags that were designed based only on men's body sizes; these airbags therefore deployed at forces that increased injuries and fatalities for women and children passengers (Margolis & Fisher, 2002).

The abovementioned national calls to action are concomitant with the changing domestic U.S. talent pool, in which African American and Hispanic/Latino groups are the fastest growing populations. The U.S. Census Bureau predicts that by 2030, these two groups will comprise 34% of the population. As of yet, African Americans and Latinos represent a small fraction of students pursuing undergraduate STEM degrees, for example, making up only 5% and 3.8% of undergraduate engineering students, respectively (not including Puerto Rico). However, their 2013 representation in the overall population is estimated to be 14.3% and 17.4% of the United States, respectively (Colby & Ortman, 2015; NACME, 2012; Yoder, 2012). The rising population predictions suggest that large increases in the numbers of African American and Hispanic students studying STEM subjects will be needed even if we are only to maintain current proportions in undergraduate education.

As such, a number of theoretical approaches and research studies have been conducted to understand influences on URMs' persistence and achievement in STEM. We focus this chapter specifically on social cognitive career theory (SCCT; Lent, Brown, & Hackett, 1994; Lent et al., 2015). SCCT identifies social and psychological factors that play a major role in whether students succeed and persist in subjects and careers. Several facets of personal motivation stemming from socializing agents predict academic and career outcomes related to achievement, choice, and persistence. A subset of this research has focused on URM students in STEM, which has led to the exploration of additional cultural and contextual influences on motivation that are salient in these students' lives (e.g., Lent et al., 2001). This subset of research will be the focus of this chapter. First, we will briefly discuss how this theory is informed by social cognitive theory (Bandura, 1986) and explain the major motivational constructs within SCCT. Second, we will highlight several of the personal, cultural, and contextual factors that have been studied as predictors of STEM motivation among URM students.

Social Cognitive Career Theory

Through a social cognitive theoretical perspective, people are neither solely motivated by internal influences nor regulated by environmental factors. Instead, environmental factors, person factors (e.g., cognitive states), and behavior jointly influence each other in a reciprocal manner (Bandura, 1986). Lent and his colleagues (1994) explicitly apply Bandura's (1986) social cognitive theory in their comprehensive SCCT model to explain career development processes. Within SCCT, models of interest, choice, satisfaction, and performance have typically been examined as separate segments, although more recent work has identified the advantages of combining components into an integrative model (Lent et al., 2015). The main variables in SCCT related to student motivation are self-efficacy, outcome expectations, and interest. These variables act as mediators linking personal and environmental factors to subsequent career decisions and outcomes.

Self-Efficacy

Self-efficacy is defined as "a judgment of one's capability to accomplish a certain level of performance" (Bandura, 1986, p. 391). SCCT researchers examining self-efficacy beliefs among URM students have measured self-efficacy pertaining to several academic domains and outcomes, such as mathematics, science (Anderson & Ward, 2014), college completion (Flores, Navarro, & DeWitz, 2008), and career decision making (Gushue & Whitson, 2006). Studies have indicated that URM students with higher self-efficacy for math and/or science are more likely to have goals to persist and have higher academic performance within these domains (Austin, 2010; Byars-Winston, Estrada, Howard, Davis, & Zalapa, 2010; Else-Quest, Mineo, & Higgins, 2013; Gainor & Lent, 1998). Thus, it is important to understand the antecedents of students' self-efficacy beliefs to understand URM students' likelihood of persisting in STEM.

Consistent with Bandura's (1986) social cognitive theory, SCCT highlights four major sources of self-efficacy that stem from a person's learning experiences: prior mastery experiences, verbal persuasion, vicarious learning (models), and affective and physiological reactions. Previous researchers have noted how these sources of self-efficacy may manifest themselves differently in the lives of URMs compared to their White counterparts given, for example, the differential performance feedback and educational inequities experienced by students of color (Hackett & Byars, 1996; Johnson-Ahorlu, 2012; Lent et al., 1994). These contextual influences on URM students' self-efficacy will be elaborated further in subsequent sections.

Outcome Expectations

Related to a person's self-efficacy beliefs are outcome expectations, which are judgments of the likely outcomes (e.g., rewards or punishments) that are obtained from engaging in specific behaviors (Bandura, 1986). For example, students may anticipate certain outcomes for performing well, such as praise from teachers and parents. These anticipated consequences are separate from students' beliefs in their capability to do so (Bandura, 1986); outcome expectations and self-efficacy work jointly to influence career-related interests and outcomes (Lent et al., 1994). However, Bandura (1986) suggests that outcome expectations play a weaker role in determining behavior. For example, people may anticipate positive outcomes from successfully performing a particular activity, but if they have doubts about their capability to do so, outcome expectations may serve as a poor determinant for engaging and persisting in that activity (Bandura, 1986).

Researchers have noted that the outcome expectations for engaging in certain academic or career-related activities among URM students may be markedly different from their White peers, based on the systemic structural inequalities and discrimination that still exist in American institutions. Because URM students may perceive their efforts as not having the same outcomes as students from other racial and/or ethnic groups, their likelihood to persist in certain academic and career-related activities may diminish. Thus, despite valuing education, if the anticipated consequences of succeeding in educational domains are not equally rewarded, these perceptions may affect motivation, performance, and persistence (Hackett & Byars, 1996).

Interest (Values)

In addition to self-efficacy, Lent et al. (1994) indicate that personal values play an inherent role in the extent to which outcome expectations are determinants of behavior. Specifically, in order for outcome expectations to have an influence on career behavior, one must value the anticipated consequence of enacting a particular career-related activity. SCCT focuses on a form of value-labeled interest, defined as "patterns of likes, dislikes, and indifferences regarding career-relevant activities and occupations" (Lent et al., 1994, p. 88). Interests are posited to be influenced by both self-efficacy and outcome expectations. Individuals develop stronger, long-lasting interests in activities for which they both believe they can succeed and expect positive outcomes. The assertion that self-efficacy and outcome expectations influence interests and, in turn, academic goals, has been found to generalize to the career development of URM students (Byars-Winston et al., 2010).

Researchers have noted that because of the varying influence of culture and socializing agents on identity, one might expect that students' value and interest for engaging in certain academic and career domains would differ across racial/ethnic groups (Anderson & Ward, 2014). For example, because racial and ethnic stereotypes are pervasive in our culture, it is not surprising that URM students' awareness of these stereotypes plays a role in shaping their identity, which can in turn influence the extent to which they value STEM disciplines and careers (Aronson & McGlone, 2009; Hudley & Graham, 2001; Sinclair, Hardin, & Lowery, 2006). In addition, URM students may be less likely to see themselves as a math/science person or as someone "fitting" in to the STEM profession, as they are not typically exposed to people of the same racial/ethnic background working in

STEM careers (Seymour & Hewitt, 1997). Recent findings provide support for this contention, as one particular study indicated that among high-ability ninth-grade students, White students valued science more than did their Black and Hispanic peers (Anderson & Ward, 2014).

Personal, Cultural, and Contextual Influences Within SCCT

In addition to the main psychological components of SCCT, researchers recognize the importance of personal and contextual influences on learning experiences and, in turn, motivational processes within the models (Lent et al., 1994). These components include person inputs, which include race/ethnicity, as well as background contextual affordances and more proximal contextual influences, such as supports and barriers (Lent, Brown, & Hackett, 2000; Lent, Sheu, Gloster, & Wilkins, 2010). The next several sections will review some of these influences and provide examples of research examining the extent to which these variables influence URM students' STEM motivation.

Person Inputs

Lent et al. (1994) highlighted the importance of including "developmental models of race/ethnicity/culture" (p. 118) to understand how the special issues and challenges that come with minority membership play a role in the career development of URM students. Accordingly, the focus of SCCT research has included attempts to understand how sociocultural factors can influence students' perceptions of themselves and, in turn, their academic and career attitudes. SCCT studies have examined both racial and ethnic identity and the developmental stages of these identities as influences on students' motivation for pursuing STEM (Gainor & Lent, 1998).

Racial and Ethnic Identity

Racial identity is defined as "the significance and qualitative meaning that individuals attribute to their membership within the . . . racial group within their self-concepts" (Sellers, Smith, Shelton, Rowley, & Chavous, 1998, p. 23), whereas ethnic identity centers more on the extent to which one identifies with "the culture of one's ancestors' national or tribal groups" (Helms, 1994, p. 293). Researchers have used these terms interchangeably (Yip, Douglass, & Sellers, 2014), and various theoretical conceptualizations of these two forms of identity have been examined in relation to STEM motivation among URM students. Therefore, it is difficult to synthesize previous research to develop a comprehensive understanding of the extent to which racial and ethnic identity influence students' motivation to pursue STEM fields. Nevertheless, we will summarize the various developmental stages and dimensions of racial and ethnic identity that have been examined within SCCT, discuss associations found between racial or ethnic identity and STEM motivation, and make some inferences about the aspects that may promote or hinder STEM persistence.

Austin (2010) incorporated SCCT to investigate the relations of racial identity with intentions to persist in math and science domains among African American high school students. Racial identity was assessed through a multidimensional instrument measuring three facets: connections toward one's race (sense of belonging), awareness of racism, and pride for the achievements of members within one's own race (Oyserman, Harrison, & Bybee, 2001). Students who expressed greater pride for achievements and who viewed race as being important to their identity expressed greater intentions to persist in math/science-related fields compared to students who reported lower identification with their race. In addition, a significant positive relation was found between African American students' racial identity and math/science self-efficacy (Austin, 2010).

Relatedly, Gainor and Lent (1998) surveyed first-year Black college students attending a predominantly White university. Their measure of racial identity represented various sequential developmental stages of Black identity, ranging from least developed (pre-encounter) to the most developed (internalization; Cross & Vandiver, 2001). None of the stages of racial identity was associated with Black students' mathematics self-efficacy beliefs. However, students at the pre-encounter stage, considered to be the least developed stage of racial identity where one's race is neither central nor salient to one's identity, tended to report greater interest in mathematics. Conversely, students who reported greater ascription to the encounter stage, exemplified by an emerging awareness for and identification with being Black while at the same time holding neutral to negative feelings towards Whites and White culture, expressed lower intentions to persist in math-related majors. Researchers concluded that the lower levels of intentions to persist in math-related disciplines might have emerged during this stage because it encapsulates feelings of identity confusion and conflict. Despite the statistically significant relations reported, the effects of racial identity on attitudes related to math persistence were very small (Gainor & Lent, 1998).

In terms of the effect of ethnic identity on STEM motivation, one study examined these beliefs among African American, Latino/a, South East Asian, and Native American college students majoring in engineering or the biological sciences at a predominantly White university (Byars-Winston et al., 2010). Three dimensions of ethnic identity (sense of belonging, exploration, and ethnic practices/behaviors) were aggregated into a composite score. Researchers also examined students' willingness and enjoyment in engaging with students from other ethnic groups (other-group orientation). Results indicated that ethnic identity did not relate to math or science motivation-related variables. However, students with other-group orientation tended to have higher math or science self-efficacy, which in turn was associated with greater value for obtaining a math or science degree and higher interests in math or science (Byars-Winston et al., 2010).

While the aforementioned studies have varied in their conceptualization and measurement of racial/ethnic identity, several inferences can be made regarding which facets of racial/ethnic identity may promote or hinder STEM persistence among students of color. First, even though racial and ethnic identity had a very small to nonsignificant effect on college students' STEM motivation, stronger statistically significant effects were found in the study with high school students (Austin, 2010). It is uncertain whether variations in racial or ethnic identity effects can be attributed to the education level of the population examined. However, one distinction between the aforementioned SCCT studies is Austin's (2010) inclusion of a dimension that assessed pride for the achievements of members within one's own race labeled as embedded achievement. Previous research has found the embedded achievement facet of racial identity to be the strongest predictor of academic efficacy among African American students (Oyserman et al., 2001). Based on this finding, Oyserman and colleagues (2001) stated, "it seems that making one's racial identity salient may be promotive or deflating of competence depending on whether the content of one's racial identity is positive with regard to academics or leaves one vulnerable to negative stereotypes about one's group" (p. 379).

Taken together, these findings suggest that when trying to understand the role of racial and/or ethnic identity on student motivation, future research should hone in on how salient the value of academic achievement is embedded within identification with a particular race/ethnicity. The findings also underscore the importance of having positive feelings toward and being able to work with members of other racial/ethnic groups, as findings indicated that getting along with members of other groups is related to STEM persistence (Byars-Winston et al., 2010; Gainor & Lent, 1998).

In conclusion, given the varying findings across studies examining the effects of racial and ethnic identity on STEM motivation, it seems important for future research to differentiate the effects of each racial/identity dimension rather than include composite measures. This may help further clarify which facets of racial/ethnic identity are most important in influencing URM students' motivation to pursue STEM fields. It is also important to distinguish between racial/ethnic identity dimensions given that some dimensions used in previous research were more aligned with the construct of acculturation (e.g., ethnic practices; Byars-Winston et al., 2010), which will be the focus of the next section.

Acculturation

Acculturation is related to ethnic identity but distinct in that it mostly represents the *behaviors* that may express an identity (Berry, Phinney, Sam, & Vedder, 2006; Phinney & Ong, 2007). More specifically, acculturation is described as "those phenomena which result when groups of individuals having different cultures

74 Shirley L. Yu et al.

come into continuous first-hand contact, with subsequent changes in the original cultural patterns or behaviors of either or both groups" (Cuellar, Arnold, & Maldonado, 1995, p. 278). Perhaps because on average, Hispanics have the lowest educational attainment in the United States compared to their White, Black, and Asian counterparts (U.S. Census Bureau, 2014), researchers have examined acculturation status as a contextual influence on the educational aspirations of Mexican Americans (e.g., McWhirter, Hackett, & Bandalos, 1998).

Two SCCT studies were identified that examined the relations between acculturation status using the Acculturation Rating Scale for Mexican Americans (ARSMA-II; Cuellar et al., 1995) and motivational beliefs related to STEM (Flores & O'Brien, 2002; Navarro, Flores, & Worthington, 2007). The ARSMA-II includes a scale with two distinct dimensions (Anglo orientation and Mexican orientation) that assess language use, ethnic identity, behaviors, and interactions for each cultural orientation (Berry, 1980; Cuellar et al., 1995). Flores and O'Brien (2002) examined the extent to which acculturation level, measured by subtracting mean scores on the Anglo orientation dimension from those on the Mexican orientation dimension, predicted Mexican American female high school students' self-efficacy for pursuing careers underrepresented by females (e.g., mechanical engineering). In this study, Mexican American females who were highly assimilated were more likely to choose traditionally female careers compared to their less assimilated peers (Flores & O'Brien, 2002). While the researchers focused on the traditionality of career choices as an outcome rather than specifically examining motivation to persist in STEM, this finding suggests that highly Anglicized Mexican American females may be less likely to choose STEM careers compared to their bicultural and Mexican-oriented counterparts. The researchers inferred that acculturated Mexican American females may be aware of the social challenges women encounter in predominantly male work environments and thus choose to avoid these types of careers. However, questions remain as to why the level of traditionality of career choices among more assimilated Mexican American females differed from their bicultural and Mexican-oriented counterparts.

Navarro and colleagues (2007) also tested an SCCT model in which both Anglo orientation and Mexican orientation, along with generation status and social class were hypothesized to predict math/science past performance and, in turn, math/science self-efficacy and outcome expectations among eighth-grade Mexican American students. Bivariate correlation results indicated that students who identified more highly with Anglo culture tended to report slightly higher math/science self-efficacy, interests and goal intentions compared to those reporting lower levels of identification with Anglo culture. Conversely, Mexican orientation was not associated with any of the math/science motivation variables.

Collectively, SCCT studies have varied on how they have utilized the ARMSA-II to measure acculturation level, which makes it challenging to make comparisons across studies. Specifically, some studies have calculated levels of acculturation by combining the Anglo and Mexican orientation dimension scores (Flores,

STEM Motivation and Persistence **75**

Navarro, Smith, & Ploszaj, 2006; Flores & O'Brien, 2002), whereas others have used the scores on each dimension as separate continuous variables to determine if a person is highly orientated in each respective dimension (Flores & O'Brien, 2002; Flores et al., 2008; Garriott & Flores, 2013; Navarro et al., 2007). Nevertheless, findings from Navarro et al. (2007) are somewhat consistent with other studies suggesting that higher levels of assimilation are associated with adaptive motivational processes (Garriott & Flores, 2013) and higher educational attainment aspirations and expectations (Flores et al., 2008). Some researchers have concluded that higher levels of assimilation may emerge as more adaptive because Mexican American students in the United States are typically immersed in educational environments where Anglo cultural values are predominant (Garriott & Flores, 2013).

Although Anglo orientation tends to emerge as more adaptive, the fact that the effects of acculturation on career-related motivational outcomes are small cannot be overlooked. These small effects may result from the way that acculturation status has been measured. Using Anglo and Mexican orientation as separate continuous variables may obfuscate the effect of biculturalism (high orientation to both dominant and heritage cultures) on motivation. Distinguishing biculturalism from other levels of acculturation in relation to STEM motivation seems particularly important for several reasons. First, results from a recent meta-analysis indicate that a consistent and strong association exists between biculturalism and psychological and sociocultural adjustment (Nguyen & Benet-Martinez, 2013). In addition, studies show that bicultural individuals are more proficient at adjusting to various people and environments both in the dominant culture and in their native culture, as well as other cultures (e.g., Leung, Maddux, Galinsky, & Chiu, 2008). This suggests that bicultural students of color who have adjusted to straddling two cultures may be better equipped to navigate educational and career systems in which they are the minority group, such as in STEM academic and career environments.

Background Contextual Affordances and Proximal Contextual Influences

According to SCCT, both objective and perceived environmental factors influence choice behaviors, with important consideration given to people's active sense making and response to positive and negative contextual influences (Lent et al., 2000). These environmental factors include both distal background contextual affordances (e.g., support or discouragement for participation in certain activities) as well as proximal contextual influences (e.g., career network contacts, external barriers). Supports and barriers exist at both temporal periods and are examined next.

Supports

The proximal contextual influences include the roles of socializers and others who may provide support, for example, through encouragement or endorsement of academic and career choices. A variety of people have socializing influences on students. These individuals include parents, teachers, and peers. Parents are a child's first socializing agents; thus, the role of parents has been examined as critical influences on students' STEM motivation. For example, in Navarro et al.'s (2007) examination of Mexican American middle school students' mathematics and science goal intentions from a modified social cognitive career theory perspective, perceptions of parental support (e.g., "My parent(s) show that they are proud of me") significantly predicted math/science self-efficacy, which in turn was related to intentions to pursue and persist in mathematics and science courses in high school and future careers.

In a study examining an ethnically diverse sample of female engineering majors, social supports were assessed utilizing mixed methods, specifically, quantitative survey and qualitative interview methods (Trenor, Yu, Waight, Zerda, & Sha, 2008). Analysis of survey data indicated that social supports, including perceptions that family members supported their choice of major, were positively correlated with intentions to persist in engineering. Further, in the interviews, women reported family support and encouragement as influential in their pursuit of their career goals, although for the Hispanic students, the familial support was directed toward college completion in general and not a specific field. The benefits of social supports have also been demonstrated by Lent and colleagues (2001, 2003, 2005) in mathematics, science, and engineering with other college student samples.

In addition to parents' support, school personnel, including teachers, faculty, and academic advisors also provide important influences on students' motivation for STEM. Through their instruction and interactions with students, STEM teachers and faculty play direct roles in shaping students' motivation in those areas. For example, when students have success in the classroom, these mastery experiences can serve as a source of self-efficacy. Through the manner in which they teach STEM material and convey their own motivation for the subject matter during instruction, teachers and faculty can influence students' interests and attitudes toward those domains as well. Furthermore, teachers, faculty, and academic advisors can also provide support for STEM during out-of-class interactions. In an examination of a nationally representative cohort of 6,300 URM college student participants in the Education Longitudinal Study of 2002, Wang (2013) found that postsecondary academic interaction, which included talking with faculty about academic matters outside of class and meeting with one's advisor about academic plans, was directly related to choosing a STEM major. While the roles of parents and school personnel have been examined specifically, other adult influences also impact students' motivation in STEM. In some studies, researchers have investigated the possible influence of adults in general without specifying who these adults may be and the nature of their relationship with students. For example, in a study of mostly African American tenth graders in underserved communities, perceived adult support was positively related to intent to pursue health science education in college, controlling for other cognitive, personal, and environmental factors (Zebrak, Le, Boekeloo, & Wang, 2013). In this study, extent of perceived adult support was assessed with self-report survey items such as, "I know adults who encourage me often in sciences" and "I have good adult science role models."

Barriers

Contextual influences include not only supports but also barriers. Barriers include environmental influences that can have a negative impact on students' motivation and achievement. For example, parents and teachers may discourage students from pursuing STEM. Trenor et al. (2008) found that for female undergraduates majoring in engineering, experiences with faculty were negatively related to perceived barriers to achieving college and career plans. In other words, the more that students indicated discussing with faculty things such as their academic program or course selection, the less pressure they felt to change their major to another field. These results were correlational, however, so causality cannot be determined.

In addition, racism creates barriers, both actual and psychological, that reduce students' opportunities to prepare for STEM careers (Alliman-Brissett & Turner, 2010). Using an extended SCCT framework, Alliman-Brissett and Turner (2010) investigated African American middle school students' perceptions of racism and several SCCT–related variables within the math domain. They found that several types of perceived racism were negatively related to math self-efficacy, math outcome expectations, math-related career interests, and academic achievement in math.

Johnson-Ahorlu (2012) conducted focus group interviews with African American undergraduates in order to explore how campus racial climate, particularly experiences of racism and stereotypes, influenced students' academic opportunities. Although from a critical race theory perspective and not SCCT, the findings are relevant to the previous study in that students recounted instances of faculty members demonstrating low expectations and lack of support for them because of their minority status. For example, one student indicated that faculty did not expect them to achieve and did not encourage them to go to graduate or professional programs because they did not feel they had the intellectual capabilities to succeed in those programs. Students reported being discouraged by faculty from majoring in certain undergraduate degree programs, which limited their academic opportunities and prevented them from pursuing their dreams and finding a suitable major (Johnson-Ahorlu, 2012).

To summarize, background contextual affordances and proximal contextual influences include both supports and barriers that are perceived at various times within the SCCT model. Both objective and perceived supports and barriers are included, which serve to encourage or constrain, respectively, the motivation and career-related processes among students.

Conclusions

In this chapter, we discussed SCCT with a specific focus on the personal, cultural, and contextual factors that influence motivation and academic and career outcomes in STEM for URM students. As a whole, research related to the role that racial/ethnic identity and acculturation has on URM students' STEM motivation has been mixed (e.g., Austin, 2010; Gainor & Lent, 1998). This may be due to inconsistencies in conceptualization and operationalization of these constructs. However, overall findings suggest that the extent to which the value of academic achievement is salient within one's racial/ethnic group identity may be an important predictor of STEM motivation among URM students beyond the centrality of race in one's identity. Also, positive feelings toward members of other racial/ethnic groups and being able to work with individuals outside one's racial and/or ethnic group has academic benefits when it comes to STEM persistence (Gainor & Lent, 1998).

Research related to contextual supports and barriers has been more consistent. For example, studies indicate that parental and teacher/faculty support positively influence motivation to persist in STEM among URM students (Lent et al., 2001, 2003, 2005; Trenor et al., 2008; Zebrak et al., 2013). Conversely, barriers such as discouragement and racism limit and constrain the motivation of URM students (Alliman-Brissett & Turner, 2010; Johnson-Ahorlu, 2012).

There are a number of recommendations for future research that can be made. First, more research needs to be conducted utilizing the established SCCT framework, but with a specific focus on URM in STEM. Although it was not possible to include every study that did fit these criteria in this review, it is notable that there were not many more studies available. Given the strength of this social cognitive perspective in understanding majority populations, it would be beneficial to see more work conducted examining URM students.

Relatedly, another suggestion is that researchers and educators should develop interventions aimed at addressing contextual factors that have been shown to positively influence motivation among URM students in STEM and then conduct evaluations of their effectiveness. For example, given findings that parental support is related to math/science self-efficacy and intentions to pursue and persist in these domains, programs that provide parent education on how to provide effective encouragement and support, as well as programs aimed at providing the support itself, could be very helpful for parents and students alike.

Through additional research investigations utilizing the established framework of SCCT, researchers and educators can continue to better understand the factors affecting URM students' motivation and pursuit of STEM courses and careers. More importantly, this work has the potential to allow educators, parents, and other important socializing agents to learn how to adequately support these students so that there are fewer differences in participation rates in the future. These changes are necessary if we are to address the projected workforce demands and provide a diverse talent pool capable of adequately tackling our society's technological and scientific problems.

References

Alliman-Brissett, A. E., & Turner, S. L. (2010). Racism, parent support, and math-based career interests, efficacy, and outcome expectations among African American adolescents. *Journal of Black Psychology, 36*, 197–225.

Anderson, L., & Ward, T. J. (2014). Expectancy-value models for the STEM persistence plans of ninth-grade, high-ability students: A comparison between Black, Hispanic, and White students. *Science Education, 98*(2), 216–242.

Aronson, J., & McGlone, M. S. (2009). Stereotype and social identity threat. In T. Nelson (Ed.), *The handbook of prejudice, stereotyping and discrimination* (pp. 153–177). New York, NY: Psychology Press.

Austin, C.Y. (2010). Perceived factors that influence career decision self-efficacy and engineering related goal intentions of African American high school students. *Career and Technical Research, 35*, 119–135.

Bandura, A. (1986). *Social foundations of thought and action.* Englewood Cliffs, NJ: Prentice Hall.

Berry, J.W. (1980). Acculturation as varieties of adaptation. In A. M. Padilla (Ed.), *Acculturation: Theory models and new findings* (pp. 9–25). Boulder, CO: Westview.

Berry, J.W., Phinney, J. S., Sam, D. L., & Vedder, P. (2006). Immigrant youth: Acculturation, identity, and adaptation. *Applied Psychology, 55*, 303–332.

Byars-Winston, A., Estrada, Y., Howard, C., Davis, D., & Zalapa, J. (2010). Influence of social cognitive and ethnic variables on academic goals of underrepresented students in science and engineering: A multiple-groups analysis. *Journal of Counseling Psychology, 57*, 205–218.

Carnevale, A. P., Smith, N., & Milton, M. (2011). *STEM: Science technology engineering mathematics.* Washington, DC: Georgetown University Center on Education and the Workforce. Retrieved from http://cew.georgetown.edu/stem

Chang, M. J., Sharkness, J., Hurtado, S., & Newman, C. B. (2014). What matters in college for retaining aspiring scientists and engineers from underrepresented racial groups. *Journal of Research in Science Teaching, 51*, 555–580.

Colby, S. L., & Ortman, J. M. (2015). *Projections of the size and composition of the U.S. population: 2014 to 2060. Current population reports.* Washington, DC: U.S. Census Bureau. Retrieved from https://www.census.gov/content/dam/Census/library/publications/2015/demo/p25-1143.pdf

Cross, W. E., & Vandiver, B. J. (2001). Nigrescence theory and measurement: Introducing the Cross Racial Identity Scale (CRIS). In J. G. Ponterott, J. M. Casas, L. A. Suzuki, & C. M. Alexander (Eds.), *Handbook of multicultural counseling* (2nd ed., pp. 371–393). Thousand Oaks, CA: Sage.

Cuellar, I., Arnold, B., & Maldonado, R. (1995). Acculturation rating scale for Mexican Americans-II: A revision of the original ARSMA scale. *Hispanic Journal of Behavioral Sciences, 17*, 275–304.

Drew, D. E. (2011). *STEM the tide: Reforming science, technology, engineering, and math education in America.* Baltimore, MD: The Johns Hopkins University Press.

Else-Quest, N. M., Mineo, C. C., & Higgins, A. (2013). Math and science attitudes and achievement at the intersection of gender and ethnicity. *Psychology of Women Quarterly, 37*(3), 239–309.

Flores, L.Y., Navarro, R. L., & DeWitz, S. J. (2008). Mexican American high school students' postsecondary educational goals: Applying social cognitive career theory. *Journal of Career Assessment, 16*(4), 489–501.

80 Shirley L. Yu et al.

Flores, L.Y., Navarro, R. L., Smith, J. L., & Ploszaj, A. M. (2006). Testing a model of nontraditional career choice goals with Mexican American adolescent men. *Journal of Career Assessment, 14*, 214–234.

Flores, L.Y., & O'Brien, K. M. (2002). The career development of Mexican American adolescent women: A test of social cognitive career theory. *Journal of Counseling Psychology, 49*, 14–27.

Gainor, K. A., & Lent, R. W. (1998). Social cognitive expectations and racial identity attitudes in predicting the math choice intentions of black college students. *Journal of Counseling Psychology, 45*(4), 403–413.

Garriott, P. O., & Flores, L.Y. (2013). The role of social cognitive factors in Mexican American students' educational goals and performance: A longitudinal analysis. *Journal of Latina/o Psychology, 1*(2), 85–94.

Gushue, G. C., & Whitson, M. L. (2006). The relationship of ethnic identity and gender role attitudes to the development of career choice goals among black and Latina girls. *Journal of Counseling Psychology, 53*(3), 379–385.

Hackett, G., & Byars, A. M. (1996). Social cognitive theory and the career development of African American women. *Career Development Quarterly, 44*(4), 322–340.

Helms, J. E. (1994). The conceptualization of racial identity and other "racial" constructs. In E. J. Trickett & R. J. Watts (Eds.), *Human diversity: Perspectives on people in context* (pp. 285–311). San Francisco, CA: Jossey-Bass.

Hudley, C., & Graham, S. (2001). Stereotypes of achievement striving among early adolescents. *Social Psychology of Education, 5*, 201–224.

Johnson-Ahorlu, R. N. (2012). The academic opportunity gap: How racism and stereotypes disrupt the education of African American undergraduates. *Race Ethnicity and Education, 15*, 633–652.

Lent, R. W., Brown, S. D., Brenner, B., Chopra, S. B., Davis, T., Talleyrand, R., & Suthakaran, V. (2001). The role of contextual supports and barriers in the choice of math/science educational options: A test of social cognitive hypotheses. *Journal of Counseling Psychology, 48*, 474–483.

Lent, R. W., Brown, S. D., & Hackett, G. (1994). Toward a unifying social cognitive theory of career and academic interest, choice, and performance. *Journal of Vocational Behavior, 45*, 79–122.

Lent, R. W., Brown, S. D., & Hackett, G. (2000). Contextual supports and barriers to career choice: A social cognitive analysis. *Journal of Counseling Psychology, 47*, 36–49.

Lent, R. W., Brown, S. D., Schmidt, J., Brenner, B., Lyons, H., & Treistman, D. (2003). Relation of contextual supports and barriers to choice behavior in engineering majors: Test of alternative social cognitive models. *Journal of Counseling Psychology, 50*(4), 458–465.

Lent, R. W., Brown, S. D., Sheu, H. B., Schmidt, J., Brenner, B. R., Gloster, C. S., . . . & Treistman, D. (2005). Social cognitive predictors of academic interests and goals in engineering: Utility for women and students at historically Black universities. *Journal of Counseling Psychology, 52*, 84–92.

Lent, R. W., Miller, M. J., Smith, P. E., Watford, B. A., Hui, K., & Lim, R. H. (2015). Social cognitive model of adjustment to engineering majors: Longitudinal test across gender and race/ethnicity. *Journal of Vocational Behavior, 86*, 77–85.

Lent, R. W., Sheu, H.-B., Gloster, C. S., & Wilkins, G. (2010). Longitudinal test of the social cognitive model of choice in engineering students at historically Black universities. *Journal of Vocational Behavior, 76*, 387–394.

Leung, A. K.Y., Maddux, W. W., Galinsky, A. D., & Chiu, C.Y. (2008). Multicultural experience enhances creativity: The when and how. *American Psychologist, 63*, 169–181.

Margolis, J., & Fisher, A. (2002). *Unlocking the clubhouse: Women in computing.* Cambridge, MA: The MIT Press.

McWhirter, E. W., Hackett, G., & Bandalos, D. L. (1998). A causal model of the educational expectations of Mexican American high school girls. *Journal of Counseling Psychology, 45,* 166–181.

National Academy of Sciences, National Academy of Engineering, and Institute of Medicine. (2011). *Expanding underrepresented minority participation: America's science and technology talent at the crossroads.* Washington, DC: The National Academies Press.

National Action Council for Minorities in Engineering. (2012, August). Latinos in engineering. *NACME Research and Policy, 2*(5), 1–2. Retrieved from http://www.nacme.org

Navarro, R. L., Flores, L. Y., & Worthington, R. L. (2007). Mexican American middle school students' goal intentions in mathematics and science: A test of social cognitive career theory. *Journal of Counseling Psychology, 54,* 320–335.

Nguyen, A. D., & Benet-Martinez, V. (2013). Biculturalism and adjustment: A meta-analysis. *Journal of Cross-Cultural Psychology, 44,* 122–159.

Oyserman, D., Harrison, K., & Bybee, D. (2001). Can racial identity be promotive of academic efficacy? *International Journal of Behavioral Development, 25*(4), 379–385.

Phinney, J., & Ong, A. D. (2007). Conceptualization and measurement of ethnic identity: Current status and future directions. *Journal of Counseling Psychology, 54,* 271–281.

Sellers, R. M., Smith, M. A., Shelton, J. N., Rowley, S. A. J., & Chavous, T. M. (1998). Multidimensional model of racial identity: A reconceptualization of African American racial identity. *Personality and Social Psychology Review, 2,* 18–39.

Seymour, E., & Hewitt, N. M. (1997). *Talking about leaving: Why undergraduates leave the sciences* (Vol. 12). Boulder, CO: Westview Press.

Sinclair, S., Hardin, C. D., & Lowery, B. S. (2006). Self-stereotyping in the context of multiple social identities. *Journal of Personality and Social Psychology, 90,* 529–542.

Trenor, J. M., Yu, S. L., Waight, C. L., Zerda, K. S., & Sha, T.-L. (2008). The relations of ethnicity to female engineering students' educational experiences and college and career plans in an ethnically diverse learning environment. *Journal of Engineering Education, 97,* 449–465.

U.S. Census Bureau. (2014). *Statistical abstract of the United States: 2014.* Washington, DC: Author.

Wang, X. (2013). Why students choose STEM majors: Motivation, high school learning, and postsecondary context of support. *American Educational Research Journal, 50*(5), 1081–1121.

Yip, T., Douglass, S., & Sellers, R. M. (2014). Ethnic and racial identity. In F. T. L. Leong, L. Comas-Diaz, & G. C. Nagayama Hall (Eds.), *APA handbook of multicultural psychology* (pp. 179–205). Washington, DC: American Psychological Association.

Yoder, B. L. (2012). Engineering by the numbers. In American Society for Engineering Education (ASEE) (Ed.), *Profiles of engineering and engineering technology colleges* (pp. 11–47). Retrieved from https://asee.org/papers-and-publications/publications/college-profiles/2011-profile-engineering-statistics.pdf

Zebrak, K. A., Le, D., Boekeloo, B. O., & Wang, M. Q. (2013). Predictors of intent to pursue a college health science education among high achieving minority tenth graders. *Current Issues in Education, 16,* 1–9.

6

OUT OF THE BOOK AND INTO THE CLASSROOM

Applying Motivational and Self-Regulated Learning Theories to Daily Instruction With English Language Learners

Rhonda S. Bondie and Akane Zusho

Teachers confront considerable diversity in today's classrooms. In terms of academic diversity, the average public school classroom, for example, contains students with abilities that can span multiple grade levels (Latz, Speirs Neumeister, Adams, & Pierce, 2009). Research also suggests that our schools are increasingly becoming racially, ethnically, and linguistically diverse. Correspondingly, statistics demonstrate that the number of English language learners (ELLs) is increasing. For example, between 2002–03 to 2011–12, the percentage of ELLs grew in all but 10 states (Kena et al., 2014). In New York City, the setting of the current study, 41% of the public school population speaks a language other than English at home (NYC Department of Education, 2014).

The solution to such diversity is often a one-size-fits-all approach in which teachers focus on the middle range of students' academic abilities and primarily employ whole-class instruction that may or may not be culturally relevant (Gay, 2010; Tomlinson, 2014). As a consequence, mounting evidence suggests that most teachers do not provide students with equal and optimal opportunities to learn; some are left consistently unchallenged, whereas others remain unable to grasp fundamental concepts. Research further suggests that students of color, including ELLs, are often among those who are left behind. Accordingly, there is an urgent need for teachers to learn how to differentiate instruction so that they can effectively and efficiently serve *all* youth.

To that end, the overarching purpose of this chapter is to describe a model of professional development aimed at increasing teachers' skills in differentiation, namely All Learners Learning Every Day (ALL-ED), and its impact on one NYC public high school serving immigrant students who have low literacy in their native languages. In what follows, we define the components and theoretical bases of ALL-ED and further describe how seven teachers used ALL-ED routines to serve ELLs.

What Is ALL-ED?

We approach these issues with the idea that there is no instructional silver bullet that will eliminate achievement disparities. Thus, rather than a single practice, ALL-ED encourages teachers to employ a network of behaviorally, motivationally, and cognitively supportive instructional routines into their daily practice so that teachers provide *all* students with equal and optimal opportunities to learn. Theoretically, ALL-ED is based in the literatures of student engagement, achievement motivation, and self-regulated learning (SRL). Corresponding to these theoretical bases, we briefly review below how ALL-ED promotes behavioral engagement, motivation, and SRL.

Increasing Active Participation

All too often, we see classrooms in which not every student actively participates in the lessons. Participation and academic learning time—key indicators of behavioral engagement—have been linked with important educational outcomes, including dropout rates (Reschley & Christenson, 2012). Finn's (1989) participation-identification model of student engagement, for example, identifies behavioral engagement as a key component of student engagement. Engagement theories, therefore, recognize behavioral engagement (e.g., paying attention to the teacher, responding to teachers' questions, completing assignments) as a fundamental and necessary component of academic success.

In many classroom settings, behavioral engagement cannot be taken for granted. Thus, one of the key goals of ALL-ED is to provide teachers with instructional routines to promote behavioral engagement. Group learning routines (GPLRs)—one of the hallmarks of the ALL-ED professional development (PD)—were specifically designed for this purpose.

Common to all ALL-ED GPLRs are two features intended to prevent many of the common pitfalls of group work: roles and rounds. Similar to the jigsaw group strategy, we assume that GPLRs is more efficient when each member of the group takes on specific roles to accomplish a common goal and when the successful completion of the group work depends on each group member carrying out their role (see Figure 6.1 below).

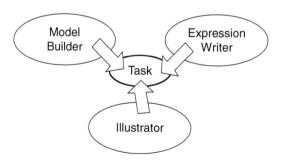

FIGURE 6.1 GPLRs roles for math problem solving

Rounds, in turn, are when everyone in the group takes turns completing the same task in a circular fashion. For example, a group may use rounds to share a favorite part of the story, evidence to support a statement, or an answer to a problem. Rounds ensure that everyone talks and listens in a specified amount of time, thus ensuring behavioral engagement of all group members. In short, through roles and rounds, the teacher can prevent social loafing and facilitate productive collaborations, thereby promoting the effectiveness of group work (Kuhn, 2015).

It is important to note that we refer to these as GPLRs because we expect students to repeat the same steps—be it roles or rounds—until the process becomes habitual. We assume that in doing so, the learning process becomes more efficient by allowing students to focus on mastering new content rather than taking up limited class time to (re-)negotiate rules for group work, thus increasing time spent on tasks.

Facilitating Adaptive Motivation

Simply getting students to *do* the work only gets them so far. In order to sustain engagement in learning, students must also *want* to do the work. Indeed, we, like others (see Eccles & Wang, 2012; Skinner & Pitzer, 2012), generally assume motivation to be an important precursor to behavioral engagement. Overall, the collective body of research on achievement motivation demonstrates that when students feel competent in their abilities, find value in what they are learning, and perceive their learning environment to be inclusive and supportive, they are more likely to actively participate in their learning and ultimately achieve academic success (Maehr & Zusho, 2009).

Promoting Competence

ALL-ED promotes students' perceptions of competence in several ways. First, research suggests that one of the primary ways to increase students' competence is to ensure that academic tasks are at the appropriate level of challenge (Schunk & Pajares, 2005). Tasks that are perceived to be too easy are likely to engender boredom, whereas tasks that are perceived to be too difficult are likely to lead to frustration and disengagement. Designing academic tasks at the optimal level of challenge for *all* learners can be especially challenging when one considers the great diversity of learning needs that exists in most classrooms. Needless to say, it is not particularly surprising that many teachers have difficulties meeting this challenge.

Consequently, one of the goals of the ALL-ED PD is to help teachers understand the importance of considering academic rigor when designing tasks. In line with other studies (Cooper, 2014), we define academic rigor in terms of the provision of challenging tasks (i.e., tasks that require high levels of attention, effort, and thinking) as well as through academic press for understanding (i.e., an emphasis on complexity and use of techniques to probe understanding;

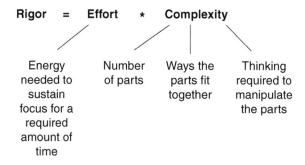

FIGURE 6.2 Rigor equation

Middleton & Midgley, 2002). In particular, teachers are taught a practical definition enabling them to measure and adjust the amount of rigor in a learning task. To provide a concrete tool for teachers, ALL-ED defines rigor through an equation: Rigor equals effort multiplied by complexity (see Figure 6.2). In this equation, effort equals the energy needed to sustain focus for the required duration. Complexity equals the number of parts, ways the parts can fit together, and type of thinking required to manipulate the parts.

For example, if the task was to create a timeline of six events, then the number of parts is six, the ways the parts fit together is one, sequential, and the thinking required may be comparison to determine the order of the events or logical, organizing the events by actions before results. To increase the rigor of this task, obviously more events to sort would require more sustained focus time. Rigor could be increased in other ways, for example, by asking students to order the events by time and then reorder them in another layout that reveals a theme relevant to the topic. Another option would be for some students to order the events by time and others to order the events by time and perspective of people impacted. By understanding how to adjust rigor using the same task, teachers are better equipped to ensure all students experience optimal challenge with given tasks daily.

Promoting Value

Research on the classroom contextual bases of motivation suggests that students are more likely to value those tasks that they find relevant in some way (Blumenfeld, 1992). Thus, another way ALL-ED helps to promote student motivation is to improve teachers' abilities to design relevant tasks. Indeed, research on ethnic minority students further demonstrates that one of the reasons many minority students feel disengaged from school may be because of the lack of culturally relevant tasks (Zusho, Daddino, & Garcia, in press). Thus, ALL-ED PD includes a traction planning tool (see Figure 6.3) designed to first focus teacher attention on the cultural, experience, and academic strengths that students and teachers bring

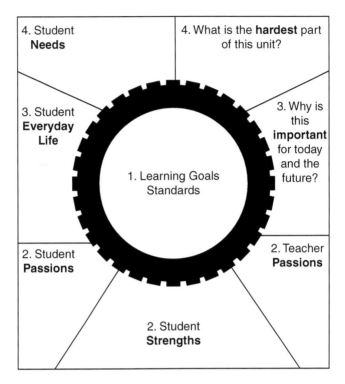

FIGURE 6.3 Traction planner with four key steps to gain relevance

to a unit of study. By rooting the new learning of a unit in strengths that learners already have, the students start with something that provides traction toward the new goals.

Promoting Belonging

Research consistently shows that students who perceive themselves to be a valued member of their learning community are more likely to display behaviors and engender feelings consistent with academic success. Research further reveals that feelings of belonging may be especially important for students of color, including ELLs (LeClair, Doll, Osborn, & Jones, 2009; Zusho et al., 2016). There are several ways the ALL-ED routines establish a culture of inclusion and respect. For example, the GPLRs mentioned earlier are designed to foster feelings of belonging and respect among students through the teacher establishing explicit norms and directions. These norms enable ELLs, especially newcomers, to participate in discussions such as, *"Confirm and Contribute."* When using *Rounds*, students can either *contribute* a new response or *confirm* a response of a previous student. To confirm a response, the student simply points to the student who has spoken before and that student will repeat the response,

Out of the Book and Into the Classroom **87**

thereby ensuring that again, *all* students are able to participate no matter what their level of prior knowledge. In addition, the procedure helps students notice patterns and surprises in responses that are unique among the group members.

Promoting SRL

Research on SRL consistently demonstrates that self-regulated learners, or students who reflect on their thinking, set appropriate goals and plan for learning, monitor progress toward those goals, and adjust or regulate thinking, motivation, and learning are more likely to achieve academic success (Pintrich, 2000). Self-regulated learners are those strategic, conscientious students who employ an arsenal of cognitive, motivational, and metacognitive strategies and proactively seek help when needed (Pintrich, 2000).

One of the guiding assumptions of ALL-ED is that SRL is the key to sustained, personalized learning—teachers will not be able to address the diversity that exists in the classroom, and students will not be able to learn effectively without being in the driver's seat of their own learning. To that end, ALL-ED recruits both students and teachers to set goals, monitor actions, and evaluate performance on an ongoing basis. Specifically, the ALL-ED PD promotes teachers' ability to increase SRL through the use of a variety of formative assessments.

For example, rubrics are a tool used for goal setting, monitoring, and providing actionable feedback. Rubrics assist students in self-assessment, an important part of self-regulation, by enabling students to think about the quality of their work in terms of specific goals, providing a readily available source of feedback (Andrade & Valtcheva, 2009). In addition to rubrics, ALL-ED PD encourages teachers to embed SRL processes in routine instructional practices such as asking students to complete a performance summary after taking a weekly test (see

Standard	Q #:	Points	Cumulative Fraction	%	Mastery Calculations		
A.N.4 Understand and use scientific notation to compute products and quotients of numbers	7	/2	/4		Yes!	Almost	Need to Practice
	12	/2					
	13	/2					
	15	/3					
A.A.12 Multiply and divide monomial expressions with a common base, using the properties of exponents	1	/2	/6		Yes!	Almost	Need to Practice
	8	/2					
	9	/2					
	2	/2					
	14	/2					
	4	/2					

FIGURE 6.4 Performance summary for algebra unit with mastery calculations

Figure 6.4). The performance summary helps students measure progress toward each learning standard and provides data that students use to plan realistic learning goals. In addition, students use daily homework reflection charts to consider patterns in their performance over several days related to study conditions.

ELLs and ALL-ED

The foregoing principles of ALL-ED overlap greatly with the overarching literature on effective learning and instruction (Hattie, 2009). Thus, ALL-ED could ostensibly be applied in any classroom. However, we believe that the routines featured in ALL-ED may be especially powerful in promoting the academic success of ELLs.

Currently, ELLs make up approximately 10% of the total U.S. student population, with the greatest concentrations in the West (Kena et al., 2014). ELLs as a group are considered to be at risk for underachievement; for example, compared with non–ELLs, ELLs significantly underperformed on both the mathematics and reading sections of the National Assessment of Educational Progress (NAEP; Heritage, Walqui, & Linquati, 2015).

Further challenging ELLs is the increasing prominence of college and career readiness expectations including the Common Core State Standards (CCSS) and Next Generation Science Standards (NGSS), which emphasize extensive and complex language use. For example, the CCSS in English language arts call for "regular practice with complex texts and their academic language" ("Key Shifts in English Language Arts," n.d.). Similarly, the NGSS advocates for students constructing complex and reasoned explanations and engaging in evidence-based arguments. As Heritage et al. (2015) note, these standards "present both a challenge and an opportunity for ELLs, who regularly must do 'double the work'— acquire content knowledge and analytical practices at the same time as they are learning English as an additional language" (p. 2).

Against this backdrop, the importance of the ALL-ED routines for ELLs should become evident. The GPLRs, for example, provide ELLs multiple opportunities to speak and use academic language (Bondie, Zusho, & Gaughran, 2014). Opportunities available to only a select few students in a more teacher-centered environment are now available to all students through the use of roles and rounds. Such practices are in line with the limited research on ELLs, which suggests that small-group collaboration is one effective way to promote the academic success of this group (Applebee, Langer, Nystrand, & Gamoran, 2003).

Considering the many academic challenges ELLs face in school, it is not surprising that ELLs sometimes report lower levels of self-efficacy when compared to non–ELLs (Taboada Barber & Gallagher, 2015). Routines such as *confirm and contribute* help further build the confidence of ELLs—as students develop expressive language skills, they can point and repeat a response and then add onto a response. This procedure ensures that all students participate and offer a response regardless of their proficiency with English, oral language skills, or knowledge of the discussion's topic.

Research also demonstrates that ELLs may struggle with self-regulation (Taboada Barber & Gallagher, 2015). When studying reading instruction with ELLs, Taboada Barbar and Gallagher (2015) noted that teacher practices of setting goals and offering feedback are critical for ELLS, who may not always be aware of effective strategies in reading. Consistent with this research, in the ALL-ED classroom, formative assessments such as rubrics and performance summaries provide ELLs with clear goals and feedback to improve their performance.

To summarize, the limited body of research on ELLs suggests that these students face additional challenges in school. Research also demonstrates that creating an inclusive, supportive, relevant yet academically rigorous classroom environment could potentially promote their motivation. In what follows, we present both quantitative and qualitative data on 45 New York City Public School high school teachers who serve ELLs and attended the ALL-ED PD during the 2013–15 academic years. Our overarching goal is to describe the ALL-ED PD and its preliminary impact on these teachers' instructional practices. The quantitative portion of the study was guided primarily by a quest to document the frequency of instructional practices related to ALL-ED, as well as to understand what effect, if any, the ALL-ED PD had on these teachers' use of the routines. The qualitative portion of the study provides more detailed accounts of how teachers used ALL-ED routines with ELLs.

Method

Description of Participants and Schools

The participants in this study were part of a network of 23 high schools located throughout New York City's five boroughs. The schools were primarily International High Schools serving students with low literacy both in their native language and in English. The students (ages 14 to 21) attending these schools are typically recent immigrants to the United States, representing about 47 countries and 32 different languages. As such, many are new to formal schooling and are being exposed to the content of the American curriculum for the first time. Where the case studies took place during the 2013–14 academic year, the 4-year graduation rate was 40% and the 6-year graduation rate was 66%. The teachers ranged in terms of their experience working with ELLs from novices who are in their first 5 years of teaching to accomplished master's-level teachers with more than 10 years of experience.

The teachers highlighted in this chapter all received the ALL-ED PD through the New York City Department of Education (NYC DoE). Forty-five teachers from 17 of the network's 23 schools participated in the ALL-ED PD. Teachers from all subject areas including English, math, science, social studies, special education, and electives (shop, drama, foreign language, etc.) attended the PD. The years of teaching experience of the participants ranged from 1 year to more than 30 years. However, most teachers had less than 6 years of experience. Common to all teachers were that 100% of their students were ELLs, although the ELLs ranged widely in terms of their level of English proficiency.

Description of the ALL-ED Professional Development

The ALL-ED PD consisted of three all-day workshops during the 2013–14 school year. The PD's content focused on GPLRs, self-regulation, and planning for specialized instruction. The following year, 2014–15, the PD was divided into ALL-ED 1 (similar to the previous year) and ALL-ED 2 for returning teachers who had participated in ALL-ED the previous year. The content for ALL-ED 2 focused more on SRL and planning curriculum that was more in line with CCSS. ALL-ED 1 continued to be offered across 3 days spread out over 3 months, and ALL-ED 2 was offered for 2 days with 1 month in between workshops.

Sources of Data

Quantitative Measures and Analyses

As part of the ALL-ED PD, all teachers completed a survey measuring the frequency of instructional practices related to the ALL-ED PD. More specifically, participants were invited to assess the extent to which their instruction emphasized and/or promoted rigor, SRL, GPLRs, relevance, access, structured choice, and mastery-oriented instructional practices. Teachers were also asked to respond to questions assessing their overall teacher efficacy. With the exception of the teacher efficacy scale, which was measured on a five-point scale where 1 = never to 5 = a great deal, all of the other items were assessed on a five-point scale where 1 = never to 5 = daily.

Rigor was assessed through a three-item scale (α = .72, e.g., "I don't let my students just do easy work, I make them think") measuring the extent to which teachers cognitively challenged students. These items were adapted from the academic press scale of the Patterns of Adaptive Learning Scales (PALS; Midgley et al., 2000). SRL was assessed through a seven-item scale (α = .83, e.g., "I ask all students to self-assess or try to determine which concepts they don't understand well throughout the unit"), adapted from the Regulation of Learning Questionnaire (RLQ) developed by McCardle and Hadwin (2015). The SRL scale measured teachers' support of goal setting, monitoring, and reflection, as well as use of formative assessments to guide instructional decisions. Relevance was measured using a three-item scale (α = .72, e.g., "I help my students apply what they're learning in my class to their life") and focused on whether academic tasks were tied to students' life experiences. GPLRs were assessed using a five-item scale (α = .71, e.g., "When working in groups, there are established routines for students to follow so that everyone knows what to do"), measuring the extent to which teachers utilized GPLRs related to ALL-ED. Access was measured through three items (α = .57, e.g., "I adjust my lesson plans to meet the needs of high-achieving students and low-achieving students simultaneously"), focused on the extent to which the teacher differentiated their lesson to meet the needs of all learners. Structured choice, in turn (three items, α = .60, e.g., "I ask all students to help me decide which activities are best for them") focused on a teacher's emphasis on providing students with learning options. The measure of mastery-oriented instructional practices was adapted from the PALS and assessed the extent to which a teacher focused on using instructional practices that emphasized growth and improvement (three items, α = .76, e.g., "I ask all students to help me decide which activities are best for them"). Finally, teacher efficacy was adapted from the Teacher Sense of Efficacy Scale, Short Form (Tschannen-Moran & Woolfolk-Hoy, 2001) and was assessed through an eight-item scale (α = .85, e.g., "How much can you do to adjust your lessons to the proper level of individual students?"). Data were analyzed using correlational methods.

Qualitative Methods and Analyses

Following the PD, three case studies were conducted to understand how the routines from the ALL-ED PD were used with ELLs. Data collected for the three case studies included seven classroom observations, curriculum materials, transcripts of conversations with teachers and students, and reflective memos. A grounded theory approach was used for coding data, generating a theoretical explanation through constant coding "grounded" in the data examined (Glaser & Strauss, 1967).

Results

Quantitative Results

As mentioned earlier, the major goal of the quantitative portion of the study was to document the instructional practices of the teachers attending the ALL-ED PD. Table 6.1 displays the means and standard deviations of the various instructional practices related to the ALL-ED PD for the total sample (N = 45), as well as broken down by those who attended ALL-ED 1 and those who attended ALL-ED 2. Overall, the results show that the various practices are not part of teachers' *daily* routine, considering that the means were mostly in the 3.00 range (recall that the scales were assessed on a 1 = never to 5 = daily scale). Frequencies were lowest for provision of choice, followed by self-regulated learning routines. The use of GPLRs was also relatively low.

92 Rhonda S. Bondie and Akane Zusho

TABLE 6.1 Descriptive statistics of instructional routines for total sample and by group

	Total Sample (N = 45)		ALL-ED 1 (n = 31)		ALL-ED 2 (n = 14)	
	M	SD	M	SD	M	SD
Rigor	3.88	.72	3.84	.79	3.98	.55
SRL	3.08	.70	3.10	.81	3.04	.38
Relevance	3.49	.88	3.37	.55	3.37	.93
GPLRs	3.12	.75	2.94	.71	3.54★	.71
Access	3.96	.72	3.91	.78	4.05	.54
Structured Choice	2.77	.79	2.67	.87	3.00	.55
Mastery	4.09	.79	3.99	.82	4.31	.70
Efficacy	3.97	.59	3.85	.62	4.23★	.42

Note. ★ *p* < .05.

To assess the impact of the PD, a multivariate analysis of variance (MANOVA) was conducted whereby the instructional routines and teacher efficacy were entered as dependent variables, and group (ALL-ED 1 and ALL-ED 2) was entered as the independent variable. The overall multivariate test for group was found to be statistically significant, $F(8, 36) = 2.42, p = .03$. Closer examination of the univariate tests revealed a significant main effect of group for GPLRs, as well as for teacher efficacy. In both cases, those teachers who attended ALL-ED 2 (i.e., had more experience with ALL-ED instructional routines) reported, on average, higher levels of use of GPLRs and more teacher efficacy (see Table 6.1).

Qualitative Results

The case studies sought to understand how teachers implement the routines learned in the ALL-ED PD to meet the needs of academically diverse ELLs. The case studies focused on a teacher team and two individual math teachers, one novice and one experienced.

First Case Study: Science Department Teacher Team

The first case study followed five teachers who comprised a high school science department providing life science, biology, chemistry, and physics courses. A common concern across all teachers was a lack of student engagement during whole-group instruction, specifically when teachers demonstrated problems on the board.

To address this problem, the teachers decided to change from "going over the problem with the whole class" to using the ALL-ED *Domino Share* GPLR for corrections. During the routine, after the 5 minutes of independent work, the teachers asked students to share their answer to the problem one at a time, going

Out of the Book and Into the Classroom   **93**

around in a circle at their table. The teachers described the process like the game of standing up dominos, and when one is pushed, each falls one after the other. The students each took turns each completing the same task, and if someone had a different answer then the group stopped to talk about whether there could be two correct answers or if something was wrong. At the end of the *Domino Share*, a reporter from the group shared out an answer representing the discussion of the group. Other group members listened to these responses, identifying contributions of vocabulary words, explanations, illustrations, and examples that increased the quality of a correct answer.

After 5 months, the result of the *Domino Share* was total student engagement. As one science teacher reported, "Students put pressure on each other to complete the problem independently before sharing with the group. Students don't want their friends to think that they didn't try to solve the problem." Another science teacher reported that "students bring questions to the group and get them answered much faster than if I took questions one by one." The routine helped students recognize their growth, "At first, I did not understand, but by the time we participated more . . . I saw people transform the way they report the problem . . . now I like it." Teachers confirmed student comments, noting that the benefits for "language development are big because some students who did not speak before are talking now, they are all communicating . . . they don't have any time to say, 'I am not talking today.' They have to. They have to use the vocabulary and [listen for] it."

The routine has changed the purpose of teacher-to-student interactions. Prior to the *Domino Share*, at the beginning of class the teachers always asked students to open their notebooks and start the assignment. Now, teachers spend time with each group asking and answering questions, often focused on challenging student thinking. Rarely are teachers managing behavior; instead, everyone is discussing the lesson's topic. The procedure ran smoothly within the first month of school, solving the problem of engagement at the beginning of class and enabling teachers to learn more about their students while ensuring rigorous thinking for ELLs.

Second Case Study: Novice Math Teacher

The second case study involved observing a novice-level math teacher over 2 years. The math teacher participated in both the ALL-ED 1 and ALL-ED 2 PDs and received coaching on a monthly basis from one of the researchers. The teacher created his own GPLRs and successfully implemented the routine three times per week with all of his classes. He reflected on how ELLs become independent when routine, practice, and expectations are clear:

> We have students who arrive with little English and we have to make it so they can participate and discuss. [GPLRs] take a lot of practice and as you . . . set-up structures and a time frame, then it becomes a routine and they are doing the work without someone asking them . . . It has to be organized first and the rest will take care of itself. Some of the things I want

to try are a script for them in the first few weeks to make them feel safe . . . [like having] a few training wheels.

To further clarify a progression of expectations for participation from novice to mastery and establish quality criteria for discussions, the teacher implemented a rubric so that students could self-assess their progress in the group discussion skills of speaking, listening, and thinking as well as measure the quality of their responses (connections, vocabulary, and volume). The teacher reported, "I made a checklist of group discussion expected outcomes . . . it is for students an eye opener providing a simple tool, indicative of where they are heading toward."

Classroom observations revealed that when "triad stations" were formed, the energy in the room increased dramatically. Students confirmed this feeling with enthusiastic responses when asked to describe how GPLRs work in their classroom. For example, one student stated, "[When teachers] are explaining something, we are tired, but when we do [group discussion routines], the hard work becomes easier. When we get in teams, [I want to] say something good for my team." Another recognized that "when I write, I just copy; when I listen, I remember more." When asked about their perceptions of the benefits of GPLRs for ELLs, students agreed with one student who stated, "I learned . . . how not to be scared about what I am presenting. It gives me confidence." Students agreed that GPLRs are "awesome, when we move into triad stations, the routine is not boring."

Third Case Study: Experienced Math Teacher

A second, experienced math teacher was observed regularly over the past 2 years. She was immediately able to integrate group-learning routines into her practice without any coaching. She reflected that the ALL-ED PD fit with her instructional beliefs. She observed that through GPLRs, "students are helping each other and becoming their own teachers, which is more powerful than having me lecture." When interviewed, her students confirmed the teacher's observations of how GPLRs empower ELLs and helps students value their own diversity. For example, common themes are represented in student statements such as, "not everybody has the same capability; more people understand much better when classmates explain . . . [This] makes you know your classmates better and what they are capable of." An additional common benefit of GPLRs included peer support. For example, students said, "If I am absent then I can't get the missed knowledge. But now, I don't have to go to the teacher . . . with [daily group discussion], my friends teach me quickly."

The experienced teacher reported making changes in the GPLRs to solve problems as they occurred in the classroom. For example, more talkative students and those with greater English skills were consistently volunteering to report the group's findings to the class. In addition, the principal noticed that boys were

Out of the Book and Into the Classroom **95**

volunteering to be the reporter more often than girls. The teacher described how she changed the routine to address this problem:

> This time I said I will choose the reporters and everyone got tense. I saw the seriousness they put into it. I picked the students who do not speak often and they did fabulous. Sometimes I let them pick and sometimes I say I will choose or I let a student from another group, choose a reporter in a different group . . . they like it, you can see the pride in their eyes.

Students confirmed the success of this solution, saying, "If we don't know who the group's reporter will be then everyone has to be prepared." The teacher summarized her reasoning for using GPLRs on a daily basis, often two or three times in a 60-minute period. She reflected, I use GPLRs to "let students be in charge of their own learning. They are hands on and participating. I am feeding them and transmitting knowledge, but they are in charge of their own learning. I learned everything from them. We learn from each other."

During the second year, GPLRs were observed on every classroom visit. The purpose of the GPLRs varied to achieve a specific instructional goal. For example, the researcher observed students struggling with independent practice following a direct-instruction mini-lesson. Many students had not started the problems and appeared confused. She asked those students who were finished and who could explain how they solved the problems to stand with their notebooks around the room. Then she assigned two students to each group leader. The group leader answered questions until both listeners could explain how to solve the problems. The teacher reported that everyone came in the next day with the assignment completed. This teacher reported using GPLRs to resolve issues of academic diversity such as confusion or lack of understanding, differences in background knowledge and experiences, ability to know and use vocabulary, and knowledge due to absences from school.

Discussion

Overall, the results of the quantitative portion of the study indicated that although teachers do not necessarily implement ALL-ED instructional routines every day, with increasing exposure to the ALL-ED PD, they are more likely to report greater use of GPLRs and teaching efficacy. Qualitative data confirmed that teachers were able to implement GPLRs and some SRL after participating in the ALL-ED PD. Implementation patterns such as the need to take time to practice the routine with students and to vary the routine to solve problems in student engagement and accountability were common among all teachers.

Table 6.2 illustrates how ALL-ED routines enabled teachers to provide regular opportunities that specifically addressed the learning needs of ELLs.

96 Rhonda S. Bondie and Akane Zusho

TABLE 6.2 Relationships among PD, Implementation, and ELLs

ALL-ED Routine	Observed in Classroom	ELL Instructional Need
GPLRs	Active participation Belonging	Use academic language Confidence
Planning	Academic rigor	Support safe engagement while challenging thinking
		Use evidence from student work to set achievable goals
Self-regulation	Use of formative assessment	Use feedback to learn from mistakes
		Plan/monitor visible action steps

Consistent outcomes of GPLRs included increased student engagement and teacher ability to address academic diversity. Specifically, ELLs benefitted from the need to use language purposefully to communicate in their small groups and peers as a resource for learning. Routine formative assessments fueled student use of self-regulation to further and value their progress. Taken together, the ALL-ED PD supports teachers in adopting instructional routines that specifically address the learning needs of academically diverse ELLs.

References

Andrade, H., & Valtcheva, A. (2009). Promoting learning and achievement through self-assessment. *Theory into Practice*, *48*(1), 12–19.

Applebee, A. N., Langer, J. A., Nystrand, M., & Gamoran, A. (2003). Discussion-based approaches to developing understanding: Classroom instruction and student performance in middle and high school English. *American Educational Research Journal*, *40*, 685–730.

Blumenfeld, P. C. (1992). Classroom learning and motivation: Clarifying and expanding goal theory. *Journal of Educational Psychology, 84*, 272–281. Retrieved from http://dx.doi.org/10.1037/0022–0663.84.3.272

Bondie, R., Zusho, A., & Gaughran, L. (2014). Fostering English learners' confidence. *Educational Leadership, 72*(3), 42–46.

Cooper, K. S. (2014). Eliciting engagement in the high school classroom: A mixed methods examination of teaching practices. *American Educational Research Journal, 51*, 363–402. doi:10.3102/0002831213507973

Eccles, J., & Wang, M. T. (2012). Part 1 commentary: So what is student engagement anyway? In S. L. Christenson, A. L. Reschly, & C. Wylie (Eds.), *Handbook of research on student engagement* (pp. 133–145). New York: Springer.

Finn, J. D. (1989). Withdrawing from school. *Review of Educational Research, 59*, 117–142.

Gay, G. (2010). *Culturally responsive teaching: Theory, research, and practice*. New York: Teachers College Press.

Glaser, B. G., & Strauss, A. L. (1967). *The discovery of grounded theory: Strategies for qualitative research*. Chicago: Aldine.

Hattie, J. (2009). *Visible learning: A synthesis of over 800 meta-analyses relating to achievement*. New York: Routledge.

Heritage, M., Walqui, A., & Linquati, R. (2015). *English language learners and the new standards: Developing language, content knowledge, and analytical practices in the classroom.* Cambridge, MA: Harvard University Press.

Kena, G., Aud, S., Johnson, F., Wang, X., Zhang, J., Rathbun, A., Wilkinson-Flicker, S., & Kristapovich, P. (2014). *The condition of education 2014* (NCES 2014–083). U.S. Department of Education, National Center for Education Statistics. Washington, DC. Retrieved May 18, 2015 from http://nces.ed.gov/pubsearch

Key Shifts in English Language Arts. (n.d.). Retrieved May 18, 2014 from http://www.corestandards.org/other-resources/key-shifts-in-english-language-arts/

Kuhn, D. (2015). Thinking together and alone. *Educational Researcher, 44,* 46–53.

Latz, A. O., Speirs Neumeister, K. L., Adams, C. M., & Pierce, R. L. (2009). Peer coaching to improve classroom differentiation: Perspectives from Project CLUE. *Roeper Review, 31,* 27–39.

LeClair, C., Doll, B., Osborn, A., & Jones, K. (2009). English language learners' and non-English language learners' perceptions of the classroom environment. *Psychology in the Schools, 46,* 568–577. doi:10.1002/pits.20398

Maehr, M. L., & Zusho, A. (2009). Achievement goal theory: The past, present, and future. In K. Wentzel & A. Wigfield (Eds.), *Handbook of motivation in school* (pp. 76–104). New York, NY: Routledge.

McCardle, L., & Hadwin, A. F. (2015). Using multiple, contextualized data sources to measure learners' perceptions of their self-regulated learning. *Metacognition and Learning, 10*(1), 43–75.

Middleton, M. J., & Midgley, C. (2002). Beyond motivation: Middle school students' perceptions of press for understanding in math. *Contemporary Educational Psychology, 27,* 373–391. doi:10.1006/ceps.2001.1101

Midgley, C., Maehr, M. L., Hruda, L. Z., Anderman, E., Anderman, L., Freeman, K. E., & Urdan, T. (2000). *Manual for the patterns of adaptive learning scales* [Measure]. Ann Arbor, MI: University of Michigan.

NYC Department of Education. (2014). *Office of English Language Learners 2013 demographics report.* Retrieved May 18, 2015 from http://schools.nyc.gov/NR/rdonlyres/FD5EB945–5C27–44F8-BE4B-E4C65D7176F8/0/2013DemographicReport_june2013_revised.pdf

Pintrich, P. R. (2000). The role of goal orientation in self-regulated learning. In M. Boekaerts, P. Pintrich, & M. Zeidner (Eds.), *Handbook of self-regulation* (pp. 451–502). San Diego: Academic Press.

Reschly, A. L., & Christenson, S. L. (2012). Jingle, jangle, and conceptual haziness: Evolution and future directions of the engagement construct. In S. L. Christenson, A. L. Reschly, & C. Wylie (Eds.), *Handbook of research on student engagement* (pp. 3–19). New York: Springer.

Schunk, D. H., & Pajares, F. P. (2005). Competence perceptions and academic functioning. In A. J. Elliot & C. S. Dweck (Eds.), *Handbook of competence and motivation* (pp. 85–104). New York: Guilford.

Skinner, E. A., & Pitzer, J. R. (2012). Developmental dynamics of student engagement, coping, and everyday resilience. In S. L. Christenson, A. L. Reschly, & C. Wylie (Eds.), *Handbook of research on student engagement* (pp. 21–44). New York: Springer.

Taboada Barber, A., & Gallagher, M. (2015). Supporting self-regulated reading for English language learners in middle schools. In T. Cleary (Ed.), *Self-regulated learning interventions with at-risk youth: Enhancing adaptability, performance, and well-being* (pp. 113–133). Washington, DC: American Psychological Association.

Tomlinson, C. A. (2014). *The differentiated classroom: Responding to the needs of all learners.* Alexandria, VA: Association for Supervision and Curriculum Development (ASCD).

Tschannen-Moran, M., & Woolfolk-Hoy, A. (2001). Teacher efficacy: Capturing and elusive construct. *Teaching and Teacher Education, 17*, 783–805.

Zusho, A., Daddino, J., & Garcia, C. (2016). Cultural contexts and motivation. In K. Wentzel & G. Ramani (Eds.), *Handbook of social influences on socio-emotional, motivation, and cognitive outcomes in school contexts* (pp. 273–292). New York, NY: Routledge.

7

SCHOOL ENGAGEMENT AND FUTURE ACADEMIC EXPECTATIONS AMONG U.S. HIGH SCHOOL STUDENTS

Variations by Ethnicity

Cynthia Hudley and Su-je Cho

Serious discussions about reforming American public schools have been underway for more than a half century. As our ideas about reorganizing public schools in the new century continue to develop, persistent problems such as school dropout and more general group disparities in academic achievement remind us of the importance of learner-centered principles of schooling and school reform (American Psychological Association, 1997). Such models attend not only to the individual needs of students but also to the ever-present and increasing diversity among students. Interactions at school between adults and peers are influential in children's social, emotional, and academic future outcomes. Thus, personal expectations in the school context must be accounted for if we wish to ensure that school reform will improve school experiences for all students.

Among the many variables that reference the specific needs of students, students' engagement and students' beliefs about their futures must not be underestimated. Students must feel motivated to engage in and persist with schooling if they are to take full advantage of whatever educational opportunities are available to them. Even if high-quality schooling is available, high levels of achievement will implicitly demand high levels of engagement on the part of students. High levels of engagement can be driven by students' beliefs about the future they desire for themselves and their families. Across a range of stakeholders including parents, educators, policy makers, and researchers, there is broad agreement that active participation in, persistence with, and enjoyment of academic tasks and positive beliefs about the future are necessary although not sufficient for maximizing student achievement and minimizing school dropout.

Student engagement and future academic expectations are important contributors to educational success. However, engagement and future expectations are constructed in social contexts, and the school setting is an important and very influential environment for student beliefs. In particular, student perceptions of the most proximal environment, classroom climate, are related to engagement and future expectations (Hudley & Daoud, 2008). We have found in prior research with the data we discuss here that these three constructs—(1) engagement, (2) expectations, and (3) perceived classroom climate—are definitely interrelated. Most importantly for this discussion of student engagement and expectations, these constructs vary by student ethnicity. Thus, an understanding of student perceptions and beliefs must be increasingly mindful of the diversity in the student population. The data presented in this chapter were able to include the diversity represented by Asian ethnic subgroups, an analysis that is often not attended to in motivational research.

Ethnic Variability

The ethnic diversity of the population subsumed under the racial label Asian-Pacific Islander (API) has been well described (Hune & Chan, 1997) but not always accounted for in education research. As a group, this racial label includes students whose heritage derives from East Asia (e.g., Chinese, Koreans), Southeast Asia (e.g., Cambodians, Vietnamese), the Philippines, Pacific Islands (e.g., Hawaiians, Samoans), and South Asia (e.g., Indians, Pakistanis). Given the remarkable ethnic diversity within this single racially identified group (e.g., nationality, culture, language, economic status, immigration history, to name but a few dimensions of diversity), subgroup analysis is a reasonable and potentially instructive strategy that is all too infrequently undertaken. For example, Cambodian students may have a family history of remarkable stress and economic instability linked to a relatively recent and challenging immigration or refugee experience and a cultural belief system that may take a fatalistic view of academic underachievement (see Chhuon, Hudley, Brenner, & Macias, 2010, for a discussion). In comparison, East Asian families more often have relatively stable communities in the United States, relatively higher economic attainment, and are ascribed a strong Confucian ethnic of hard work and effort in academics (Kitano & DiJiosia, 2002). Yet Asian students continue to be ascribed a monolithic "model minority" identity that assumes all Asian students are academically successful and all Asian families are financially successful. Fortunately, there is a growing consensus that data must be disaggregated in order to reflect the heterogeneity in the API population (Teranishi & Nguyen, 2011) and better meet the needs of all students.

Student Engagement

Engagement is a motivational construct that indexes the persistence and quality of students' involvement in learning activities. Student engagement in the project discussed in this chapter was operationalized in two components, behavioral engagement and affective engagement (Skinner & Belmont, 1993). Behavioral engagement represents what students do to remain involved in learning, including low rates of disciplinary problems (Ekstrom, Goertz, Pollack, & Rock, 1986) and absenteeism (Hudley, 1995) and high rates of task completion (Conchas, 2001; Hudley, 1995). Affective engagement represents attitudes or feelings about academic activities and achievement striving, somewhat similar to intrinsic motivation (Deci & Ryan, 1987; Hudley & Daoud, 2008).

The construct of engagement is potentially useful for helping us understand individual student outcomes that are strongly influenced by the school context. For example, research on peer victimization has found that student engagement in the classroom is related to higher academic achievement and serves as a buffer against the effects of victimization (Totura, Karver, & Gesten, 2014). A positive classroom climate also supports students' school engagement and academic achievement, while disengagement is a precursor to school dropout (Fall & Roberts, 2012). Student engagement also serves to mediate the positive relationship between classroom emotional climate and academic achievement (Reyes, Brackett, Rivers, White, & Salovey, 2012). Data from ethnic Korean high school students in Korea (Reeve & Lee, 2013) affirms the positive relationship among multiple dimensions of classroom engagement (i.e., behavioral, emotional, cognitive, and agentic) and student achievement. However, research to date has yet to examine the relationship among engagement, student beliefs, and expectations in data that include samples disaggregated by Asian ethnic subgroup in U.S. schools, which are typically very ethnically diverse settings.

Expectations

Classic theories of motivation posit that people engage in tasks that provide some expectancy of success (Weiner, 1991). For example, limited expectations of academic and career success prompt many adolescents to disengage from academic pursuits and leave high school early (Fall & Roberts, 2012; Franse & Siegel, 1987). Further, student engagement and future academic expectations are reciprocally linked among high school students (Hudley & Daoud, 2008). Future expectancies of academic success predict high school grades and coursework selections (Nauta & Epperson, 2003). Expectancies have also been strongly related to beliefs about the larger social climate (e.g., beliefs in justice and fairness) for African American students (Irving & Hudley, 2005). Research also has found that positive outcome expectancies predict successful school completion when measured as early as sixth grade (Eccles, Vida, & Barber, 2004). Thus, understanding relationships among students' engagement and their future expectations remains an important area of study. Again, there is little evidence, if any, that students' future expectancies have been studied in ethnically disaggregated samples of Asian students.

There is an assumption that Asian American students are a model minority, and they are typically discussed as an aggregated, monolithic racial group.

The model minority stereotype includes assumptions that students of Asian racial backgrounds excel in school and go on to very bright futures, including significant careers. However, some Asian students who do not match the stereotype may not adjust and achieve in school as well as expected and may not have future expectations that are as bright as posited by the model minority stereotype. For example, a significant percentage of Southeast Asian–heritage students (e.g., 40% of Hmong, 38% of Laotians, and 35% of Cambodians) do not graduate from high school (White House Initiative on Asian Americans and Pacific Islanders, 2009). Research has determined that perceived negative stereotypes can shape student perceptions and general expectations of others (Hudley & Graham, 2001) as well as of themselves (Steele, 2010). However, we still have only a relatively limited understanding of the role of positive stereotypes on personal expectations among high school students. How much expectations of one's personal future for Asian students, a strongly positively stereotyped group, vary by ethnicity is a substantially understudied question, a central goal of this research, and one to which we will return.

Perceived Climate

Student perceptions of teacher behaviors and classroom climate (emotional support from teachers and peers, instructional support and encouragement by teachers, classroom organization and stability) are related to engagement and to future academic expectations, and this relationship is particularly strong for ethnic minority adolescents. Perceived teacher behavior and classroom climate are also strongly interrelated, as teachers have enormous influence in setting the climate in the classroom (Hudley, 1995, 1997; Murdock, 1999). For the study presented here, we were especially interested in possible ethnic differences in perceived classroom climate, given the long-documented, troubling reality that teachers' views of students vary by student ethnicity (Gollnick, 1992). For example, research in multicultural education has historically found that teachers across all grade levels (Kalin, 1999; Katz, 1999) as well as preservice teachers (King, 1991), may perceive African American and Latino students as more behaviorally (i.e., discipline problems) and affectively (i.e., don't care about education) disengaged than other groups, regardless of objective similarities in behavior across groups. Disaggregated data specific to Asian students has similarly found that both students and teachers respond positively or negatively to perceived differences in behavior and attitudes by student ethnic subgroup, evidence that contradicts the monolithic model minority stereotype (Chhuon & Hudley, 2011; Conchas, 2006). This is particularly strong evidence of the need to deconstruct a racialized monolithic identity.

Classroom climate plays an important role in both school engagement and future expectations. For example, as noted previously, work with early adolescent students reveals that classroom climate is related to student grades, and that relationship is mediated by student engagement (Reyes et al., 2012). Data from an aggregated sample of API high school students in New Zealand similarly demonstrates a strong, positive relationship between classroom climate and student engagement (Anderson, Hamilton, & Hattie, 2004). As well, data collected with Canadian early adolescent students assessed classroom climate, including satisfaction with school, peer cohesiveness, friction among students, difficulty with assignments, and competitiveness among students (Lagacé-Séguin & d'Entremont, 2010). Analyses found that climate was related to future expectations. Difficulty with assignments and friction among students were negatively related. In addition, satisfaction with school and peer cohesiveness was positively related to future expectations. Taken together, these data highlight the importance of students' perception of climate for their future expectations and outcomes. More research is needed that examines the role of student perceptions with increased attention to the very important dimension of diversity.

Bandura's concept of reciprocal determinism (1978) is an interesting lens when thinking about the interrelationship of perceptions and climate. Reciprocal determinism captures the reality that a perceiver's biases and subsequent behavior may be evoked by a target's personal characteristics (e.g., speech style, clothing, perceived race). In turn, the perceiver's biases and behavior may shape a target's subsequent behavior. A target's negative reaction to perceived bias may prompt the target individual to respond in ways that maintain and confirm the initial biases of the perceiver. A student may respond negatively to a teacher perceived as unfair, for example, leading ultimately to disengagement and low student expectations. Examining how ethnicity is related to perceived climate, future academic expectations, and student engagement might be useful for understanding the mechanisms linking climate variables to student outcomes.

Examining Disaggregated Data

Early research on student academic perceptions revealed substantial variability by Asian ethnic subgroup. These early studies typically contrasted East Asian (e.g., Japanese, Chinese) subgroups (e.g., Bond & Cheung, 1983; Stevenson, Lee, & Stigler, 1986). However, one early study is notable for the breadth of subgroups included. Mizokawa and Ryckman (1990) examined effort and ability attributions for success and failure in two subject areas for six Asian American ethnic groups: Chinese, Japanese, Korean, Filipino, Vietnamese, and "other" Southeast Asians. Using a written survey of attributional beliefs, the authors found that attributions to effort for success varied substantially by ethnic group, with Korean students scoring the highest in attributions to effort and Vietnamese and other Southeast Asian students scoring the lowest in attributions to effort. These data, early on, contrasted sharply with the model minority stereotype that attributed East Asian Confucian cultural values of effort to all Asian subgroups.

One can also look at research that has increased substantially in the past decade examining several other domains of functioning among Asian ethnic subgroups (Kim, Wong, & Maffini, 2010). These findings also demonstrate significant ethnic variability. Research on health disparities and lifestyles revealed that Asian American subgroups (Chinese, Japanese, Korean, Filipino, and Vietnamese) differed significantly on a variety of health indicators, including weight, physical activity, and alcohol and tobacco use. These findings suggest that the Asian-identified racial group is not best served as a monolithic entity but instead may have unique profiles of risk and protective factors that will require quite diverse intervention and health maintenance strategies (Maxwell, Crespi, Alano, Sudan, & Bastani, 2012). Similarly, in helping students realize their full potential, Asian students may be best served by diverse strategies. To understand how best to support these students, it is necessary to examine unique differences evident in subgroup analyses.

Research on Southeast Asian and East Asian immigration histories similarly revealed very different goals for immigration for these two groups, with substantial implications for variability in successful adaptation and coping for Asian subgroups (Lui & Rollock, 2012). A recent study of disaggregated data (Pang, Han, & Pang, 2011) revealed substantial differences in academic achievement across middle school students from 13 distinct Asian ethnic groups and White students. Research with community college students from four Asian ethnic subgroups and White students (Orsuwan, 2011) revealed that satisfaction with college, perceived academic integration, and sense of belonging were moderated by ethnicity. Students from distinct Asian subgroups differed in how strongly their perceptions of the academic opportunities offered at their institution (i.e., academic integration) influenced positive attitudes toward that institution. The relationship was stronger for Japanese and particularly for Filipino students in comparison to Chinese and Hawaiian students. Differences in a sense of belonging on campus were similarly moderated by ethnicity. The effect of a sense of belonging and positive attitudes was significant only for Japanese students. Thus, data from a variety of fields (health, psychology, education) converge to support the importance of disaggregating data examining student adjustment.

The Current Study

The analyses we discuss here are part of a larger study that examines a large, multiethnic group of students' future academic expectations as a function of students' school engagement and perceptions of school climate. For this analysis, we disaggregated data from our several ethnic Asian participants and posed three specific hypotheses to take a more nuanced look at ethnic variability. We hypothesized that future academic expectations would differ by ethnicity, as student groups have been shown in past research to have varying expectations that education is a means to access the opportunity structure (Irving & Hudley, 2005). We also anticipated that perceptions of the school climate would be positively related to future expectations for all students, but we expected the pattern of relationships to vary by ethnicity. Similarly, we expected student engagement to be positively related to future expectations but again anticipated that the pattern of relationships would vary by ethnicity.

Sample

Participants ($N = 554$) were drawn from a sample of students attending public high schools in southern California (grades 10–12) for the 2008–2009 academic year. Our sample was 32% Chinese, 23% Korean, 13% Cambodian, 13% Latino, and 19% White; the gender balance was similar across ethnicity ($X^2[8] = 12.08$, ns). We decided to include our Latino and White participants in these analyses as a strategy for comparing the relative differences among our Asian subgroups with findings from other, more frequently studied groups. Further, our Latino students were 90% Mexican heritage, and our White participants were drawn almost entirely from students who had been born in southern California. Thus we were comfortable that we had not aggregated our two other groups or subsumed possible ethnic variability.

Measures

We collected self-report data during English classes in a single 30-minute session. All students were completely fluent in English. Students also provided demographic information (age, grade, gender, and ethnicity). We measured future academic expectations by asking students, "How possible is it that you will go to a 4-year college or university?" Perceived climate was assessed with two items ($\alpha = .79$) tapping perceived bias: "Non (ethnic group) students are treated better than (ethnic group) students in my classes" (reverse coded) and "All students receive equal treatment in my school."

Behavioral engagement combined two behaviors: if the student came to school "just because my friends are there" and how much the student preferred "to do easy assignments" ($\alpha = .73$); both responses were reverse coded so that higher values meant greater behavioral engagement. We measured affective engagement with two items ($\alpha = .75$) assessing attitudes toward achievement ("I enjoy learning more about something that I don't understand right away; It is interesting to learn new school subjects.").

Findings

An ANOVA tested the first research hypothesis, using future academic expectations as our outcome and ethnicity and grade level as grouping variables. We decided to include grade because there is every reason to logically conclude that in high school, future expectations are shaped by the increasing proximity of graduation. As expected, results revealed a significant interaction of ethnicity and grade level (F $[11, 514] = 2.23, p < .01, \eta^2 = .08$). Chinese students' expectations overall reached the highest levels and showed a linear increase from 10th to 12th grade. Cambodian students had the lowest overall expectations. These students' expectations varied the greatest by grade level, with a significant increase from 10th to 11th and 12th grade, while for Korean students, differences by grade were greatest for 12th graders. For all students except White students, expectations increased with grade level (see Figure 7.1).

Turning to perceived climate, an ANOVA revealed partial support for the second hypothesis, with a trend for the interaction of ethnicity and perceived climate on future expectations (F [12, 521] = 2.00, $p < .10$, $\eta^2 = .07$). Chinese students who perceive more bias have higher expectations. For Cambodians, Koreans, and Whites, higher perceived bias is related to lower future expectations. Perceived bias was not related to future expectations for Latinos (see Figure 7.2).

Two ANOVAS examined future academic expectations as a function of engagement. The analysis containing behavioral engagement and ethnicity as grouping variables revealed a trend for a significant interaction, as expected (F [12, 514] = 1.98, $p < .10$, $\eta^2 = .08$). For all Korean, Chinese, and White students, higher behavioral engagement was related to higher future expectations; the effect was especially strong for Chinese and White students. For Cambodian and Latino students, behavioral engagement was unrelated to future expectations (see Figure 7.3).

Turning to affective engagement, the analyses revealed only a main effect of engagement, with no moderating influences of ethnicity (F [9, 525] = 3.07, $p < .01$, $\eta^2 = .05$). For all students, as self-reported affective engagement increased, future expectations also increased.

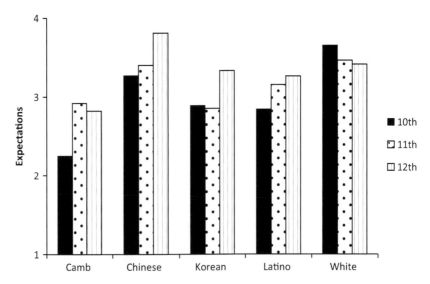

FIGURE 7.1 Future expectations by ethnicity and grade level

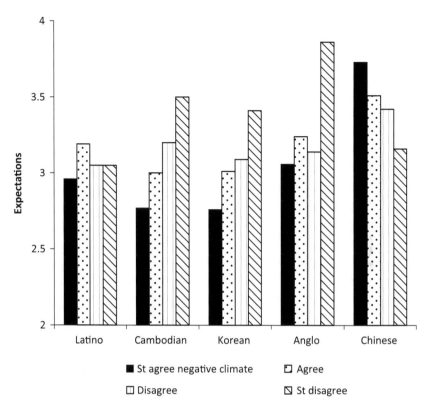

FIGURE 7.2 Future expectations by perceived climate and ethnicity

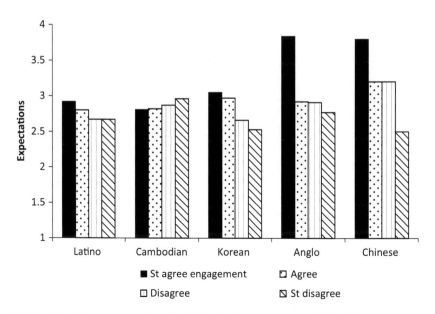

FIGURE 7.3 Future expectations by behavioral engagement and ethnicity

Discussion

These analyses support our first hypothesis; academic expectations varied by ethnicity for the three ethnic subgroups of Asian students in ways that differed somewhat in comparison to Latino and White students. Chinese students had the highest expectations overall and Cambodian students the lowest. This is consistent with research that disaggregates achievement data and concludes that East Asian students may be more successful due to residence in more established and stable communities in the United States and higher levels of families' education and economic resources in comparison to Southeast Asian students (Pang et al., 2011).

Further, expectations to participate and succeed in American higher education might be higher among Chinese and to a somewhat lesser extent among Korean students for very similar reasons. Again, families and communities that have more resources to invest in education and are represented by more highly visible role models who have benefitted from educational success might have substantial influence on students' expectations in high school. Resources and role models may be quite different for Southeast Asian students. Although our data cannot speak directly to family structure and income, there is evidence that Southeast Asian students are disadvantaged in both family wealth and family structure. For example, in an extreme groups comparison, the 2012 American Community Survey (U.S. Census, 2012) examined an East Asian group (Asian Indian) and a Southeast Asian group (Bangladeshi) on a variety of indicators. The groups differed sharply on median annual income ($97,000 vs. $47,000 respectively) and female-headed households in poverty (22% vs. 66%). Further, similar U.S. Census data (U.S. Census, 2011) reveals that in the aggregated Asian population, 49% of people 25 and older had completed at least a bachelor's degree, while for the Vietnamese subgroup only 25% had completed at least a bachelor's degree. Outcomes were even lower for other Southeast Asian groups (Cambodian—16%, Hmong—15%, Laotian—13%), suggesting that the average figure reflects much higher educational attainment for East Asian groups. The census data support our surmise that Southeast Asian students' expectations might be constrained by their family circumstances. In our data, note that the highest level of expectations for Cambodian students, a Southeast Asian ethnic group, does not reach the lowest level of expectations for Chinese and Korean students. Finally, the increase of expectations with grade level for most of our student groups may be a function of student engagement. These cross-sectional data cannot answer the question of whether students with relatively low expectations earlier in high school simply dropped out and therefore were not present in the samples from upper grades.

Perceptions of climate in the school and classroom had a somewhat counterintuitive influence on Chinese students, but, as expected, relationships differed by ethnic group. We speculate that Chinese students might experience a more negative climate as a challenge rather than a threat. Consistent with the biopsy-chosocial model of challenge and threat (Blascovich & Mendes, 2000), appraisals of challenge and threat arise in situations that are goal relevant and involve self-evaluation (e.g., academic success). A situation is perceived as a challenge when one perceives that s/he has sufficient resources to meet the demands of the situation; conversely, a perception of threat is induced when one perceives that s/he lacks sufficient resources to meet situational demands. Prior research has found that students differ in perceptions of the classroom climate as a challenge or a threat to their academic abilities, and these differences are related to student outcomes (Putwain & Deveny, 2009). It is reasonable that a perception of challenge or threat would be equally influential in shaping student expectations. If so, our data suggest that for Chinese students who perceive a school climate as negative, future expectations may be increased because the negative climate serves as a challenge. Students may perceive that they have the resources to succeed in the negative climate, and this self-confidence enhances their future expectations. This is a somewhat speculative interpretation that invites future research.

The finding that affective engagement did not differ by ethnicity was counter to the hypothesis but not difficult to interpret. Of all the variables measured, affective engagement is the closest assessment of a student's personal preferences for education. It is unsurprising and completely consistent with motivation theory that any student who enjoys and is successful at a given activity will expect to continue in that activity into the future.

Overall, these data are a bare first step toward unpacking monolithic racial designations that will allow research to better understand motivational variables. In these analyses, we have examined ethnic differences in one racial group. We began our intragroup analyses with Asian students because, as discussed in the introduction, Asian students are uniquely stereotyped as a model minority, and this positive stereotype is perhaps the most powerful stereotype attributed to any racialized group of students. This research contributes to an expanding literature about the disaggregated experiences of Asian students, who are a rapidly growing population in U.S. schools (Reeves & Bennett, 2004). These findings extend the literature by examining a set of motivational variables that have been shown to be influential in affecting student academic success. Focusing solely on the model minority stereotype might have led us to distinctly different conclusions about Asian students than those evident in these empirical data.

The model minority stereotype appears to identify Asians more positively than other ethnic minorities, though not equal to the dominant White racialized group (Chhuon & Hudley, 2011). However, the stereotype masks the not unremarkable proportion of Asian American students who are poor, not successful in school, involved in delinquent and antisocial behavior, and school dropouts. Thus, we contend the model minority stereotype and presumption of success for Asian students may cause extreme pressure on some ethnic subgroups who, as a result of this pervasive stereotype, are not well served by public schools, both K–12 and higher education (Wong & Halgin, 2006). For example, research that dates back over 20 years (Toupin & Son, 1991) demonstrated with an aggregated Asian sample of college undergraduates that, although Asian students were much more heavily enrolled in math and science fields (consistent with the stereotype), non-Asian matched students were more likely to graduate in 4 years and less likely to withdraw for medical reasons than their Asian peers (inconsistent with the stereotype). More recent research with similarly aggregated Asian samples (Cokley, McClain, Enciso, & Martinez, 2013) similarly found that Asian students self-reported significantly lower perceived competence than their Latino/a and African American peers. Further, these self-perceptions significantly predicted psychological distress. Our findings elaborate on this research that suggests Asian American students are experiencing psychological pressure by examining important achievement-related variables in a manner that attends to the unique ethnic characteristics of students subsumed under the racialized Asian or stereotyped model minority label.

We are committed to unpacking monolithic racial categories in future analyses of our data. We plan to examine variability in other groups that have similarly been studied in ways that mask in-group variability (e.g., Black students, Latino students). For example, research among Black students (e.g., Worrell, 2007) and Latino students (Hudley & Daoud, 2008) has been attuned to variability in academic achievement. Findings often refute the stereotypes of academic incompetence and lack of motivation that are applied universally to these groups of students. Research has also begun to deconstruct the racialized label Black when examining the school experiences of students of African descent in U.S. schools (Hudley, 2015). Recent data reveals clearly that immigration status, gender, and SES play influential roles in school adjustment and achievement for Black students in higher education. Thus we will continue our research program with more nuanced examinations of school-relevant variables among disaggregated data.

Finally, these data remind us of the importance of student expectations. Encouragement for high future expectations may be especially beneficial for those students who see little place for themselves in the opportunity structure. Schools, especially those serving urban and immigrant communities with highly diverse student populations, represent important settings where student expectations are formed. As such, schools have a major role to play in deconstructing the model minority myth and changing practices that are detrimental to Asian students who are not achieving consistent with the myth or who are high achievers but paying a steep psychological price due to the pressure of the stereotype. Schools must challenge the racial and ethnic stereotypes so prevalent in students' larger communities while fostering positive self-beliefs for all groups. We must continue to make school a community in which everyone (students included) believes that all students can and will succeed.

References

American Psychological Association, Work Group of the Board of Educational Affairs. (1997). *Learner-centered psychological principles: A framework for school reform and redesign.* Retrieved from http://www.apa.org/ed/governance/bea/learner-centered.pdf

Anderson, A., Hamilton, R., & Hattie, J. (2004). Classroom climate and motivated behaviour in secondary schools. *Learning Environments Research, 7,* 211–225.

Bandura, A. (1978). The self system in reciprocal determinism. *American Psychologist, 33,* 344–358.

Blascovich, J., & Mendes, W. B. (2000). Challenge and threat appraisals: The role of affective cues. In J. Forgas (Ed.), *Feeling and thinking: The role of affect in social cognition* (pp. 59–82). New York: Cambridge University Press.

Bond, M., & Cheung, T. (1983). College students' spontaneous self-concept: The effects of culture among respondents in Hong Kong, Japan, and the United States. *Journal of Cross-Cultural Psychology, 14,* 153–171.

Chhuon, V., & Hudley, C. (2011). Ethnic and panethnic Asian American identities: Contradictory perceptions of Cambodian students in urban schools. *Urban Review, 43,* 681–701.

Chhuon, V., Hudley, C., Brenner, M., & Macias, R. (2010). The multiple worlds of successful Cambodian American students. *Urban Education, 45,* 30–57.

Cokley, K., McClain, S., Enciso, A., & Martinez, M. (2013). An examination of the impact of minority status stress and impostor feelings on the mental health of diverse ethnic minority college students. *Journal of Multicultural Counseling and Development, 41,* 82–95.

Conchas, G. (2001). Structuring failure and success: Understanding the variability in Latino school engagement. *Harvard Educational Review, 71,* 475–504.

Conchas, G. (2006). *The color of success: Race and high-achieving urban youth.* New York: Teachers College Press.

Deci, E., & Ryan, R. (1987). The support of autonomy and the control of behavior. *Journal of Personality and Social Psychology, 53,* 1024–1037.

Eccles, J. S., Vida, M., & Barber, B. (2004). The relation of early adolescents' college plans and both academic ability and task-value beliefs to subsequent college enrollment. *Journal of Early Adolescence, 24,* 63–77.

Ekstrom, R. B., Goertz, M. E., Pollack, J. M., & Rock, D. A. (1986). Who drops out of high school and why? Findings from a national study. *Teachers College Record, 87,* 356–373.

Fall, A., & Roberts, G. (2012). High school dropouts: Interactions between social context, self-perceptions, school engagement, and student dropout. *Journal of Adolescence, 35,* 787–798.

Franse, S., & Siegel, A. (1987). A case for collaboratives: Turning around the Bronx public schools. *Urban Review, 19,* 129–135.

Gollnick, D. (1992). Understanding the dynamics of race, class, and gender. In M. E. Dilworth (Ed.), *Diversity in teacher education* (pp. 63–78). San Francisco, CA: Jossey-Bass.

Hudley, C. (1995). Assessing the impact of separate schooling for African-American male adolescents. *Journal of Early Adolescence, 15,* 38–57.

Hudley, C. (1997). Supporting achievement beliefs among ethnic minority adolescents: Two case examples. *Journal of Research on Adolescence, 7,* 133–152.

Hudley, C. (2015). *Adolescent identity and schooling: Diverse perspectives.* New York: Routledge.

Hudley, C., & Daoud, A. (2008). Cultures in contrast: Understanding the influence of school culture on student engagement. In C. Hudley & A. Gottfried (Eds.), *Academic motivation and the culture of school in childhood and adolescence* (pp. 187–217). New York: Oxford University Press.

Hudley, C., & Graham, S. (2001). Stereotypes of achievement striving among early adolescents. *Social Psychology of Education: An International Journal, 5*, 201–224.

Hune, S., & Chan, K. (1997). Asian Pacific American demographic and educational trends. In D. J. Carter & R. Wilson (Eds.), *Minorities in higher education: 1996–97 fifteen annual status report* (pp. 39–67). Washington, DC: American Council on Education.

Irving, M., & Hudley, C. (2005). Cultural mistrust, academic outcome expectations, and outcome values among African American adolescent men. *Urban Education, 40*, 476–496.

Kalin, W. (1999). How White teachers perceive the problem of racism in their schools: A case study in "liberal" Lakeview. *Teachers College Record, 100*, 724–750.

Katz, S. (1999). Teaching in tensions: Latino immigrant youth, their teachers, and the structures of schooling. *Teachers College Record, 100*, 809–840.

Kim, B., Wong, Y., & Maffini, C. (2010). Annual review of *Asian American Psychology*, 2009. *Asian American Journal of Psychology, 1*, 227–260.

King, J. (1991). Dysconscious racism: Ideology, identity, and the miseducation of teachers. *Journal of Negro Education, 60*, 133–146.

Kitano, M., & DiJiosia, M. (2002). Are Asian and Pacific Americans overrepresented in programs for the gifted? *Roeper Review, 24*, 76–80.

Lagacé-Séguin, D., & d'Entremont, M. (2010). A scientific exploration of positive psychology in adolescence: The role of hope as a buffer against the influences of psychosocial negativities. *International Journal of Adolescence and Youth, 16*, 69–95.

Lui, P., & Rollock, D. (2012). Acculturation and psychosocial adjustment among Southeast Asian and Chinese immigrants: The effects of domain-specific goals. *Asian American Journal of Psychology, 3*, 79–90.

Maxwell, A., Crespi, C., Alano, R., Sudan, M., & Bastani, R. (2012). Health risk behaviors among five Asian American subgroups in California: Identifying intervention priorities. *Journal of Immigrant and Minority Health, 14*, 890–894.

Mizokawa, D., & Ryckman, D. (1990). Attributions of academic success and failure: A comparison of six Asian-American ethnic groups. *Journal of Cross-Cultural Psychology, 21*, 434–451.

Murdock, T. (1999). The social context of risk: Status and motivational predictors of alienation in middle school. *Journal of Educational Psychology, 91*, 62–75.

Nauta, M., & Epperson, D. L. (2003). A longitudinal examination of the social-cognitive model applied to high school girls' choices of nontraditional college majors and aspirations. *Journal of Counseling Psychology, 50*, 448–457.

Orsuwan, M. (2011). Interaction between community college processes and Asian American and Pacific Islander subgroups. *Community College Journal of Research and Practice, 35*, 743–755.

Pang, V., Han, P., & Pang, J. (2011). Asian American and Pacific Islander students: Equity and the achievement gap. *Educational Researcher, 40*, 378–389.

Putwain, D., & Deveny, C. (2009). Predicting examination performance using an expanded integrated hierarchical model of test emotions and achievement goals. *Psychology Teaching Review, 15*, 18–31.

Reeve, J., & Lee, W. (2013). Students' classroom engagement produces longitudinal changes in classroom motivation. *Journal of Educational Psychology, 106*, 527–540.

Reeves, T., & Bennett, C. (2004). *We the people: Asians in the United States, Census 2000 Special Reports.* Washington, DC: U.S. Census Bureau.

Reyes, M., Brackett, M., Rivers, S., White, M., & Salovey, P. (2012). Classroom emotional climate, student engagement, and academic achievement. *Journal of Educational Psychology, 104*, 700–712.

Skinner, E., & Belmont, M. (1993). Motivation in the classroom: Reciprocal effects of teacher behavior and student engagement across the school year. *Journal of Educational Psychology, 85*, 571–581.

Steele, C. M. (2010). *Whistling Vivaldi: How stereotypes affect us and what we can do.* New York, NY: Norton & Co.

Stevenson, H., Lee, S., & Stigler, J. (1986). Mathematics achievement of Chinese, Japanese, and American children. *Science, 236*, 693–698.

Teranishi, R., & Nguyen, T. (2011). Asian Americans and Pacific Islanders: The changing demography of the United States and implications for education policy. *Asian American Policy Review, 22*, 17–27.

Totura, C., Karver, M., & Gesten, E. (2014). Psychological distress and student engagement as mediators of the relationship between peer victimization and achievement in middle school youth. *Journal of Youth and Adolescence, 43*, 40–52.

Toupin, E., & Son, L. (1991). Preliminary findings on Asian Americans: "The model minority" in a small private East Coast college. *Journal of Cross-Cultural Psychology, 22*, 403–417.

U.S. Census (2011). *American community survey single year estimates.* Retrieved from http://factfinder.census.gov/faces/nav/jsf/pages/searchresults.xhtml?refresh=t#none

U.S. Census (2012). *American community survey single year estimates.* Retrieved from http://factfinder.census.gov/faces/tableservices/jsf/pages/productview.xhtml?src=bkmk

Weiner, B. (1991). Metaphors in motivation and attribution. *American Psychologist, 46*, 921–930.

White House Initiative on Asian Americans and Pacific Islanders. (2009). *Critical issues facing Asian Americans and Pacific Islanders.* Retrieved from http://www2.ed.gov/about/inits/list/asian-americans-initiative/criticalissues.html

Wong, F., & Halgin, R. (2006). The "model minority": Bane or blessing for Asian Americans? *Journal of Multicultural Counseling and Development, 34*(1), 38–49.

Worrell, F. (2007). Ethnic identity, academic achievement, and global self-concept in four groups of academically talented adolescents. *Gifted Child Quarterly, 51*, 23–38.

PART III

Using Race-Focused Approaches to Examine Motivation in Educational Contexts

8

IDENTITY, MOTIVATION, AND RESILIENCE

The Example of Black College Students in Science, Technology, Engineering, and Mathematics

Tabbye M. Chavous, Samantha Drotar, Gloryvee Fonseca-Bolorin, Seanna Leath, Donald Lyons, and Faheemah Mustafaa

Despite the growing presence of Black professionals in science, technology, engineering, and mathematics (STEM) fields over the past 30 years, their numbers remain relatively small (Freeman & Taylor, 2008; Hill, Corbett, & Rose, 2010). A contributing structural factor is the quality of African Americans[1] precollege math and science experiences and preparation relative to non–underrepresented groups (Johnson & Watson, 2005). However, structural factors do not explain the entire picture, nor do they explain why Black college students' rates of pursuit of and persistence in STEM areas are lower than non–underrepresented groups', even when accounting for social class and academic preparation factors (Maton & Hrabowski, 2004). Our chapter goal is to outline psychological, motivational, and contextual factors associated with Black student achievement in predominantly White universities, particularly in STEM fields. We take a risk and resilience approach in considering within-group variation in motivation and persistence. We describe Black students' normative experience of racial stigma on campus (i.e., personal discrimination, negative campus racial climate) as a risk factor for decreases in academic identification and subsequent motivation and achievement, as well as the unique ways stigma may emerge within STEM contexts. At the same time, we consider person-level characteristics—including those related to students' racial and gender identities—that may serve to promote academic identification and motivation and help students maintain strong academic identity in the face of stigmatizing experiences. Finally, we consider how context-level characteristics—including institutional resources, opportunities, barriers, or constraints—relate to students' motivation and achievement in the face of stigma experiences.

118 Tabbye M. Chavous et al.

Conceptual Framework

Our chapter discussion is based on the premise that social, psychological, and structural dimensions of students' college contexts influence the academic attitudes, beliefs, values, and behaviors that ultimately lead to achievement and persistence (Chavous, 2005; Pascarella & Terenzini, 2005). Accordingly, we outline a conceptual model describing Black college student achievement in STEM fields (see Figure 8.1). The conceptual model focuses on both institution- and student-level factors that influence students' academic identity. Institution-level factors include contextual risk factors (stigma experiences) and resilience factors (academic and social supports). Student-level factors include demographic and academic background and resilience factors (racial and gender identity values and beliefs). The model also acknowledges broader institution-level factors such as institutional demographics, policies, and available support structures. Finally, the conceptual model proposes that institution-level and student-level factors have

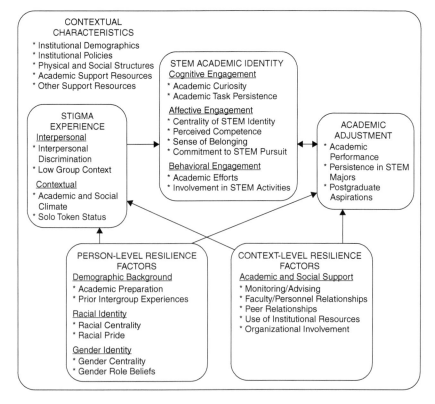

FIGURE 8.1 Conceptual model of associations among stigma, academic identity, and person-level and context-level factors in relation to STEM academic adjustment and persistence

The Experience and Impact of Stigma on STEM Academic Identification

One possible reason for African American college students' lower representation in STEM is that their academic contexts (e.g., classes, faculty interactions, formal and informal peer settings) are characterized by stigmatizing experiences (Maton & Hrabowski, 2004; Maton, Hrabowski, & Schmitt, 2000). These experiences occur at the interpersonal level, including: students' feelings of invisibility or hypervisibility due to their minority status on campus, personal discrimination, stereotyped treatment, harassment, and microaggressions such as disrespect and incivility. Such experiences are common among African American college students, especially in predominantly White universities, and serve to undermine academic engagement (e.g., Allen, 1992; Chavous, Harris, Rivas, Helaire, & Green, 2004; Solórzano, Ceja, & Yosso, 2000; Swim, Hyers, Cohen, Fitzgerald, & Bylsma, 2003). For instance, African American students reporting discrimination from faculty and White peers avoid interaction with them outside class and are less involved in social or leadership roles (Davis, 1995; Palmer, Davis, & Hilton, 2009).

Along with interpersonal experiences, stigma may occur at the contextual level through students' experiences of their campus climate. College climate is a psychologically meaningful representation of the college setting, entailing perceived norms and values; how individuals and groups are treated and interact with one another; and institutional-level supports or barriers (Bernstein & Salipante, 2015). A college's racial climate includes norms and values related to race, which may promote exclusion and perpetuate stereotypes, or in contrast, promote inclusion and work to dispel stereotypes (Chavous, 2005; Harper & Hurtado, 2007; Hurtado & Carter, 1997, Hurtado, Carter, & Kardia, 1998; Hurtado et al., 2011). Racial/ethnic minority students experiencing the college racial climate as hostile or unwelcoming show more social and academic withdrawal (Cabrera et al., 1999; Nora & Cabrera, 1996). Similarly, those perceiving the campus climate as devaluing diversity report lower sense of belonging (Ethier & Deaux, 1994), lower performance (Chavous et al., 2004), and higher stress (Mendoza-Denton, Downey, Purdie, Davis, & Pietrzak, 2002) than those who report a more positive racial climate (Gurin, Dey, Hurtado, & Gurin, 2002).

Interestingly, across these literatures, there has been relatively little analysis of Black students' stigma experiences within STEM fields. For instance, studies of stigma within mathematics have focused on gender and include primarily samples of White women and men (e.g., Schmader, 2002). The omission of ethnic minority participants in these studies is striking, given that math and science are subject domains in which racial stereotypes around ability are pervasive (Maton et al., 2000). Some of our prior work supports this contention. Chavous and colleagues

(2004) found that Black students in STEM–related majors reported more concerns around racially stereotyped treatment in classes than students in social science or humanities majors; findings were robust in predominantly White and predominantly Black college settings. Furthermore, on average, higher stereotype concerns were related to lower self-evaluations of academic competence.

Taken together, extant research suggests that one important mechanism through which stigma experiences influence STEM academic achievement and persistence is the impact on students' *academic identification* with STEM. Achievement motivation theories posit the importance of students' developing a strong academic identity—the importance and centrality of academic activities to one's self-concept—and view it as central to academic engagement, persistence, and performance (Eccles, 2009; Ko, Kachchaf, Hodari, & Ong, 2014; London, Rosenthal, Levy, & Lobel, 2011; Palmer, Maramba, & Dancy, 2011; Perez, Cromley, & Kaplan, 2014). Academic identification entails the individual adopting the role of student and learner; that is, the individual links her/his personal identity (including personal values, beliefs, and self-evaluations) to the academic domain (Wigfield & Wagner, 2005). The concept of academic identity derives from psychological frameworks of the self that presume individuals are constantly striving to maintain and enhance their self-concept (Dweck, 1999). As such, in order for individuals to engage and persist in academic tasks, their self-concept must be linked to those tasks. Academic contexts characterized by racial stigma may lead students to assess those academic contexts as incompatible with their personal identities; thus, they may "dis-identify" with or disconnect important aspects of their personal identity (e.g., self-esteem, self-concept, personal values) from the academic domain (Nussbaum & Steele, 2007). Subsequently, they are more likely to decrease efforts and underachieve and less likely to persist in those contexts. Steele (1992, 1997) proposed the concept of *academic dis-identification* as a psychological mechanism contributing to underachievement among Black students. Accordingly, academic dis-identification is a consequence of repeated exposure to identity threats in academic environments. In other words, the threats represented by the experience of racial stigma may jeopardize students' self-concept, particularly if their self-concept is grounded in their academic pursuits. Thus, to avoid the psychological consequences of persistent racial stigma, Black college students may renegotiate their self-concept so the basis of their self-esteem is independent of their academic experiences (Hope, Chavous, Jagers, & Sellers, 2013). Consequently, personal motivation and performance suffer. When academic performance is no longer tied to personal goals or self-concept, success is not intrinsically rewarding; neither is failure intrinsically aversive.

Stereotype threat research demonstrates that settings in which negative stereotypes are salient have deleterious impacts on academic task performance (e.g., Aronson & Inzlicht, 2004; Good, Aronson, & Harder, 2008; Houston, Vermillion, Doyle, & Ujitdehaage, 2014; Owens & Massey, 2010). Related research on solo status and tokenism (e.g., Crosby, King, & Savitsky, 2014; Sekaquaptewa,

Waldman, & Thompson, 2007) suggests that being a numerical and social minority member (as are most Black students at predominantly White universities) exacerbates this risk. Similarly, sociological literatures posit that students recognizing inequity or discrimination for their group may come to feel education has little usefulness for future occupational pursuits (e.g., Fordham & Ogbu, 1986; Rowley, 2000). Subsequently, they may minimize attributes and behaviors necessary for success in educational domains and develop personal identities around these areas.

The noted literatures have operationalized academic identification in numerous ways, from associations between self-concept and academic performance or academic values to situational task persistence (Chang, Eagan, Lin, & Hurtado, 2011; Cokley, 2003; Massey & Fischer, 2005). We view academic identification as a multidimensional construct, with cognitive, affective, and behavioral engagement dimensions (Wigfield & Wagner, 2005). This approach allows consideration of multiple ways that experienced stigma acts on students' connections with their academic contexts. Furthermore, while literature has examined academic identification more generally, we assert the importance of considering students' identification within their major areas. For instance, it is possible that Black students experiencing stigma in STEM settings might retain their connections to education and college more generally (academic values and self-concept); however, they might dis-identify with specific STEM domains. In doing so, they still may successfully attain a college degree (still a positive outcome), but they would be less likely to pursue STEM degrees or careers. Finally, among psychological research on stigma effects (e.g., stereotype threat effects), laboratory methodologies are most prevalent. While this work has yielded important insights, an important next step is to establish external validity by moving to broader student populations in their authentic academic contexts (Massey & Fischer, 2005) and examining experiences and effects of stigma over students' college transition and college years.

Racial Identity as a Resilience Factor in STEM Achievement

Despite evidence of obstacles or challenges common to Black college students, a substantial number do persist academically. Our focus is on considering personal resources persistent students possess and access that enable them to cope effectively in hostile or unsupportive academic environments. As Moore, Madison-Colmore, and Smith (2003) note, this does not mean that persistent students are unaffected by stigmatizing experiences. However, one possible difference between persistent and nonpersistent students is whether nonpersistent students allow stigma experiences to weaken their academic identification, impeding motivation to succeed. We highlight attributes related to students' racial and gender identities that can serve as resources to enhance academic identity and performance as well as help protect against the negative effects of experienced stigma.

122 Tabbye M. Chavous et al.

Racial Identity and Black Achievement

Racial identity entails individuals' beliefs about both the importance and meaning of race to their personal identities. The increasing work on this topic indicates that because of the salience of race in U.S. society, historically and currently, African Americans' experiences and beliefs around the meaning of their race in society have important consequences for their academic, social, and psychological development (Sellers, Chavous, & Cooke, 1998). The aforementioned literature on stigma effects posits—directly and indirectly—that having a stronger identification with a stigmatized or devalued group would relate to heightened risk for academic dis-identification relative to those with weaker group identification (Smalls, White, Chavous, & Sellers, 2007). One consideration, however, is that this literature often equates group membership with racial identity, with few studies explicitly measuring students' racial identity beliefs (Chavous, Rivas, Smalls, & Griffin, 2008; Chavous et al., 2003). In fact, research examining Black students' racial identity beliefs provides evidence that racial identity beliefs characterized by strong group identification, high racial pride, and heightened consciousness around racism can promote Black students' development of connections between their personal identities and the academic domain and, subsequently, facilitate positive academic adjustment (Butler-Barnes, Williams, & Chavous, 2011; Byrd & Chavous, 2009, 2011; Chavous et al., 2008, Richardson et al., 2014; Smalls et al., 2007). This research draws on conceptual perspectives rooted in psychology along with cultural and historical scholarship emphasizing value placed on educational success in many African American communities as a means to overcoming racial barriers and achieving social mobility. According to this perspective, those who identify more with being Black and with pride in African Americans' struggles to attain educational and occupational equality would be more likely to develop a sense of personal responsibility to succeed as a member of their group. From a motivational perspective, stronger racial identification would relate to higher intrinsic motivation to achieve, and thus higher academic identification, because academic success is linked to personally meaningful goals and values.

In addition to direct influences on achievement, Black students' racial identities can be *protective* against negative effects of experienced stigma on academic identification. Researchers studying precollege adolescents and college youth report that racial identity beliefs moderated relationships of racial discrimination with academic outcomes (performance, values, self-concept) and psychological health such that individuals with stronger racial identification (higher racial centrality) and awareness of societal racial bias (lower public regard) were less negatively affected by discrimination than were students with lower racial centrality and higher public regard (Chavous et al., 2008; Sellers, Caldwell, Schmeelk-Cone, & Zimmerman, 2003; Wong, Eccles, & Sameroff, 2003). Findings suggest that individuals draw on their connections with their racial group to counter devaluing experiences and maintain a strong academic identity (Spencer, Noll, & Stoltzfus, 2001). Additionally, in contrast to "colorblind" perspectives popular in education discourse, such research suggests higher consciousness around racism allows students to better cope with stigma experiences (Markus, Steele, & Steele, 2000). The research also supports college student development models such as that of Sedlacek and Brooks (1976), who have long argued that an understanding of racism relates to better college adjustment among minority students, but who had not tested this contention empirically.

Considering Race and Gender

In studying Black students' experiences in STEM, it is critical to consider race and gender. While women are still underrepresented in STEM, the increasing gender gap in academic performance and attainment among African Americans favors females, and Black women have made more gains in these areas than other groups of women. For instance, National Science Foundation statistics indicate that African American females account for 10.5% of the bachelor's degrees awarded in science and engineering in 2006. In contrast, African American males earned 6.1% of these bachelor's degrees during the same period.

The study of race and gender processes in education often occurs in isolation of one another. Studies of Black achievement often exclude consideration of gender processes. Similarly, scholars address how gender operates in educational settings, but often this work is based in frameworks developed around experiences of predominantly middle-class, White populations and excludes ethnically diverse study samples (Chavous & Cogburn, 2007). Less examined is how race interacts with gender to shape students' educational development. Thus, current paradigms may not describe Black students' experiences fully or accurately. Our consideration of gender in STEM achievement and persistence is rooted in African Americans' unique sociocultural and historical background.

Black Women in STEM

Because Black women are members of two stigmatized groups, they are sometimes framed as at enhanced risk for discrimination, often termed "double jeopardy" (King, 1988), especially in domains where academic stereotypes around race and gender are salient. Hanson (2004) documents Black girls' sustained interest in science during high school yet notes they often choose not to pursue postsecondary training for careers in these areas due to concerns about racism and sexism. Research among women of color in STEM careers suggest they are particularly likely to experience stigma such as disrespect and harassment—related to both race and gender—relative to males (Borum & Walker, 2012; Cromley et al., 2013; Hanson & Palmer-Johnson, 2000; Hughes, 2012; National Science Foundation, 2013; Reyes, 2011), and these experiences lead to job turnover and departure from STEM areas. However, there has been little examination of variation in Black undergraduate women's STEM experiences.

Although Black women may experience unique risks related to their group identities, scholarship also provides evidence that socialization around gender in many Black communities may provide young women with a unique set of resources relevant for interest and sustained efforts in STEM (Hanson, 2007). The cultural context of African American communities is one where historically, the reality of Black women's lives included a workforce presence, as well as heading or coheading families (Collins, 2000; Hanson, 2004). Furthermore, research has suggested more egalitarian roles in education domains among Black families relative to Whites (Hanson, 2004; Hill, 1999; Kane, 2000). Consequently, many Black women do not perceive work as conflicting with family roles but as an important dimension of family (Collins, 2000; Hanson, 2007). Studies of gender identification in math suggest strong gender identification as a risk factor for underachievement, as evidenced by experimental studies comparing task performance between women with stronger and weaker gender centrality in conditions in which gender stereotypes were salient (e.g., Bonnot & Croizet, 2007; Schmader, 2002). This research, however, did not examine women of color; thus it is unclear whether a strong gender identity places Black women at similar risk. Because the perceived incompatibility between STEM careers and family pursuits keeps many women from entering and pursuing STEM degrees and occupations, many Black women's socialization around gender may protect them from perceiving this incompatibility or conflict (Chavous & Cogburn, 2007; Hanson, 2004) and, instead, may promote identification with STEM areas.

Black Men in STEM

Women generally report more gender-based stigma than do males. However, scholarship on educational and social development of Black males suggests unique experiences around racial and gender stigma (Davis, 1995; Griffin, Jayakumar, Jones, & Allen, 2010; Moore et al., 2003; Palmer et al., 2009). Researchers assert that [White, middle-class] males have more social power than females in the classroom—they are more visible, responded to more positively by teachers and peers, and viewed as more intellectual compared to females (Beyer, 1999). However, stereotypes around race and gender in U.S. society often place Black males in a negative light compared to other males and females (e.g., stereotypes of Black males as aggressive, anti-intellectual, jocks, etc.; e.g., Chavous et al., 2004; Ruffins, 2013). Thus, in academic contexts in which racial stereotypes are salient, Black males may be ignored, not taken seriously intellectually, or viewed as threatening (Czopp, 2010; Smith, Allen, & Danley, 2007). Furthermore, African American family socialization literature suggests males receive more socialization around racial barriers and alertness to discrimination than do females due to recognition of societal views of Black males and families' subsequent efforts to prepare males for bias (e.g., Bowman & Howard, 1985; Coard & Sellers, 2005; Varner & Mandara, 2013). Thus, Black males may be particularly vulnerable to experiencing racial stigma.

Identity, Motivation, and Resilience **125**

In addition, due to historical cultural norms around male role socialization, Black male youth may be particularly likely to dis-identify with academic settings in which they experience unfair or biased treatment, manifesting as decreased interest and effort (Cokley, McClain, Jones, & Johnson, 2011). While responding to stigmatizing experiences this way may allow youth to maintain high self-esteem or self-respect, it may undermine achievement (Chavous et al., 2008). Interestingly, there is evidence that having an awareness of societal racism can buffer Black males against negative impacts of stigma experiences (Mandara, 2006). For instance, a strong and positive identification with being Black has been found to buffer the negative impacts of school-based discrimination on Black adolescent boys' academic identification (Chavous et al., 2008; Spencer et al., 2001). A strong racial group connection may be particularly relevant for Black male college students as a source of psychological support, given their severe underrepresentation in predominantly White settings relative to other males and to Black females (Chavous, Rivas, Green, & Helaire, 2002).

Taken together, there are unique academic risk factors for Black females and males. The persistent "gender gap" among African American students also suggests gender variation in resilience processes, or ways students effectively cope with and respond to experienced risk. The lack of systematic research testing mechanisms through which race and gender influence Black students in STEM contexts warrants more examination. Along with other individual factors known to promote academic success among college student (e.g., background preparation, subject matter mastery, strong study habits, willingness to use available university resources) (Maton et al., 2000; May & Chubin, 2003), our review suggests the importance of students' racial and gender identity as sources of resilience.

Contextual Factors Related to Resilience

For ethnic minority students in particular, college climates characterized by inclusion, positive intergroup interactions, high expectations, and equitable treatment relate to better academic performance as well as higher rates of academic persistence (Espinosa, 2011; Gurin et al., 2002; Hurtado & Carter, 1997; Hurtado et al., 1998; Massey & Fischer, 2005; May & Chubin, 2003; Rowley, Sellers, Chavous, & Smith, 1998; Schmader, Major, & Gramzow, 2001; Sellers et al., 1998). In addition to positive intergroup contact, research suggests the important role of intragroup supports, such as the presence of critical masses of highly able Black peers, which can enhance academic support and serve as a social support resource in dealing with racism (Gandara & Bial, 1999; Guiffrida & Douthit, 2010). Still other contextual factors related to minority student success include strong monitoring and advising systems, which can help anticipate, address, or counter negative academic or social experiences and provide students with valuable feedback about their personal strengths, weaknesses, and decision options (Chang, Sharkness, Hurtado, & Newman, 2014). Finally, multicultural organizations provide academic and personal support (Chavous, 2000).

126 Tabbye M. Chavous et al.

Surprisingly, there is relatively little research on contextual characteristics within specific academic units or of Black students' experiences within those units. The university campus represents a distinct and complex type of organizational setting, with different academic units having distinct climates created and perpetuated by social norms, physical structures, and policies that guide their functioning (Chavous, 2005; Hurtado et al., 1998). Thus, students may have unique experiences within STEM settings relative to those in other contexts within the broader university (Litzler, Samuelson, & Lorah, 2014). In addition, there has been less examination of psychological processes through which college context factors influence STEM outcomes. For instance, STEM contexts with norms, structures, and resources representing positive academic and social climates should lead to students' stronger academic identities within those contexts (Ramsey, Betz, & Sekaquaptewa, 2013). In addition, students more integrated in STEM communities may be less vulnerable to negative impacts of race or gender stigma on academic identity and motivation. The evaluation of multiple dimensions of students' experienced contexts will lead to (1) more comprehensive information regarding which contextual attributes predict outcomes of interest, (2) identification of college characteristics relevant to student perceptions and experiences, and (3) distinguishing characteristics that function similarly across institutions from those that function uniquely in specific contexts.

Summary and Conclusions

Our chapter discussion highlights the utility of considering individual, cultural, and contextual factors in understanding and studying Black achievement processes in STEM fields and higher education more broadly. We highlight ways that race, gender, and context coalesce to inform college experiences, leading to academic success or failure generally and retention or attrition in STEM fields, where Black students are especially underrepresented. Our review also highlights a need for more research on how both race and gender are lived by Black students in their day-to-day college lives and how intragroup differences, based on gender, as well as other aspects of their personal backgrounds and college contexts, inform their experiences. Finally, our discussion moves beyond a dominant focus on how Black students in STEM are "at risk" to how many effectively negotiate experiences that would be challenging to any student by drawing on personal, cultural, and institutional resources.

Note

1 In this chapter discussion, we use both the terms "Black" and "African Americans" to refer to the experiences of Black people in U.S. education and social contexts, and our discussion of Black racial identity is based on the historical and social context of race and African Americans in the U.S. context.

References

Allen, W. (1992). The color of success: African American college student outcomes at predominantly White and historically Black public colleges and universities. *Harvard Educational Review, 62*(1), 25–43.

Aronson, J., & Inzlicht, M. (2004). The ups and downs of attributional ambiguity stereotype vulnerability and the academic self-knowledge of African American college students. *Psychological Science, 15*(12), 829–836.

Bernstein, R., & Salipante, P. (2015). Comfort versus discomfort in interracial/interethnic interactions: Group practices on campus. *Equality, Diversity and Inclusion, 34*(5), 376–394.

Beyer, S. (1999). Gender differences in the accuracy of grade expectancies and evaluations. *Sex Roles, 41*(3–4), 279–296.

Bonnot, V., & Croizet, J. (2007). Stereotype internalization, math perceptions, and occupational choices of women with counter-stereotypical university majors. *Swiss Journal of Psychology, 66*(3), 169–178.

Borum, V., & Walker, E. (2012). What makes the difference? Black women's undergraduate and graduate experiences in mathematics. *The Journal of Negro Education, 81*(4), 366–378.

Bowman, P., & Howard, D. (1985). Race-related socialization, motivation, and academic achievement: A study of Black youth in three-generation families. *Journal of American Academy of Child Psychiatry, 24*, 134–141.

Butler-Barnes, S., Williams, T., & Chavous, T. (2011). Racial pride and religiosity among African American boys: Implications for academic motivation and achievement. *Journal of Youth and Adolescence, 41*(4), 486–498.

Byrd, C., & Chavous, T. (2009). Racial identity and academic achievement in the neighborhood context: A multilevel analysis. *Journal of Youth and Adolescence, 38*(4), 544–559.

Byrd, C., & Chavous, T. (2011). Racial identity, school racial climate, and school intrinsic motivation among African American youth: The importance of person-context congruence. *Journal of Research on Adolescence, 21*(4), 849–860.

Cabrera, A., Nora, A., Terenzini, P., Pascarella, E., Hagedorn, S., & Serra, L. (1999). Campus racial climate and the adjustment of students to college: A comparison between White students and African-American students. *Journal of Higher Education, 70*(2), 134–160.

Chang, M., Eagan, K., Lin, M., & Hurtado, S. (2011). Considering the impact of racial stigmas and science identity: Persistence among biomedical and behavioral science aspirants. *The Journal of Higher Education, 82*(5), 564–596.

Chang, M., Sharkness, J., Hurtado, S., & Newman, C. (2014). What matters in college for retaining aspiring scientists and engineers from underrepresented racial groups. *Journal of Research in Science Teaching, 51*(5), 555–580.

Chavous, T. (2000). The relationships among racial identity, perceived ethnic fit, and organizational involvement for African American students at a predominantly White university. *Journal of Black Psychology, 26*(1), 79–100.

Chavous, T. (2005). An intergroup contact-theory framework for evaluating the psychological impact of racial climate on predominantly White college campuses. *American Journal of Community Psychology, 36*(3), 239–257.

Chavous, T., Bernat, D., Schmeelke-Cone, K., Caldwell, C., Kohn-Wood, L. P., & Zimmerman, M. (2003). Racial identity and academic attainment among African American adolescents. *Child Development, 74*(4), 1076–1091.

Chavous, T., & Cogburn, C. (2007). Black girls and women in education. *Black Women, Gender, & Families, 1*(2), 24–51.

Chavous, T., Harris, A., Rivas, D., Helaire, L., & Green, L. (2004). Racial stereotypes and gender in context: An examination of African American college student adjustment. *Sex Roles, 51,* 1–16.

Chavous, T., Rivas, D., Green, L., & Helaire, L. (2002). The roles of student social and economic background, perceptions of ethnic fit, and racial identification in the academic adjustment of African American college students. *Journal of Black Psychology, 28*(3), 234–260.

Chavous, T., Rivas, D., Smalls, C., & Griffin, T. (2008). Gender matters: The influences of school racial discrimination experiences and racial identity on academic adjustment among African American adolescents. *Developmental Psychology, 44*(3), 637–654.

Coard, S., & Sellers, R. (2005). African American families as contexts for racial socialization. In V. C. McLoyd, N. E. Hill, & K. A. Dodge (Eds.), *African American family life* (pp. 264–284). New York: Guilford.

Cokley, K. (2003). What do we really know about the academic motivation of African American college students? Challenging the "anti-intellectual" myth. *Harvard Educational Review, 73,* 524–558.

Cokley, K., McClain, S., Jones, M., & Johnson, S. (2011). A preliminary investigation of academic disidentification, racial identity, and academic achievement among African American adolescents. *The High School Journal, 95*(2), 54–68.

Collins, P. H. (2000). *Black feminist thought: Knowledge, consciousness, and the politics of empowerment* (2nd ed.). New York: Routledge. (Original work published in 1999).

Cromley, J., Perez, T., Willis, T., Tanaka, J., Horvat, E., & Agbenyega, E. (2013). Changes in race and sex stereotype threat among diverse STEM students: Relation to grades and retention in the majors. *Contemporary Educational Psychology, 38,* 247–258.

Crosby, J., King, M., & Savitsky, K. (2014). The minority spotlight effect. *Social Psychological and Personality Science, 5*(7), 743–750.

Czopp, A. (2010). Studying is lame when he got game: Racial stereotypes and the discouragement of Black student-athletes from schoolwork. *Social Psychology of Education, 13*(4), 485–498.

Davis, J. E. (1995). College in Black and White: Campus environment and academic achievement of African American males. *Journal of Negro Education, 63*(4), 620–633.

Dweck, C. (1999). *Self-theories: Their role in motivation, personality, and development.* New York, NY: Psychology Press.

Eccles, J. (2009). Who am I and what am I going to do with my life? Personal and collective identities as motivators of action. *Educational Psychologist, 44*(2), 78–89.

Espinosa, L. (2011). Pipelines and pathways: Women of color in undergraduate stem majors and the college experiences that contribute to persistence. *Harvard Educational Review, 81*(2), 209–240.

Ethier, K., & Deaux, K. (1994). Negotiating social identity when contexts change: Maintaining identification and responding to threat. *Journal of Personality and Social Psychology, 67*(2), 243–251.

Fordham, S., & Ogbu, J. (1986). Black students' school success: Coping with the "burden of acting White." *Urban Review, 18,* 176–206.

Freeman, K., & Taylor, O. (2008). Introduction and overview. *The Journal of Negro Education, 77*(3), 184–189.

Gandara, P., & Bial, D. (1999). *Paving the way to higher education: K–12 intervention programs for underrepresented youth.* Washington, DC: National Postsecondary Education Cooperative.

Good, C., Aronson, J., & Harder, J. (2008). Problems in the pipeline: Stereotype threat and women's achievement in high-level math courses. *Journal of Applied Developmental Psychology, 29,* 17–28.

Griffin, K., Jayakumar, U., Jones, M., & Allen, W. (2010). Ebony in the ivory tower: Examining trends in the socioeconomic status, achievement, and self-concept of Black, male freshmen. *Equity & Excellence in Education, 43*(2), 232–248. doi:10.1080/1066568100 3704915.

Guiffrida, D., & Douthit, K. (2010). The Black student experience at predominantly White colleges: Implications for school and college counselors. *Journal of Counseling & Development, 88*(3), 311–318.

Gurin, P., Dey, E. L., Hurtado, S., & Gurin, G. (2002). Diversity and higher education: Theory and impact on educational outcomes. *Harvard Educational Review, 72*, 330–366.

Hanson, S. (2004). African American women in science: Experiences from high school through the post-secondary years and beyond. *NWSA Journal, 16*(1), 96–115.

Hanson, S. (2007). Success in science among young African American women. *Journal of Family Issues, 28*(1), 3–33.

Hanson, S., & Palmer-Johnson, E. (2000). Expecting the unexpected: A comparative study of African American women's experiences in science during the high school years. *Journal of Women and Minorities in Science and Engineering, 6*(4), 265–294.

Harper, S., & Hurtado, S. (2007). Nine themes in campus racial climates and implications for institutional transformation. *New Directions for Student Services, 120*, 7–24.

Hill, C., Corbett, C., & Rose, A. (2010). *Why so few? Women in science, technology, engineering, and mathematics.* Washington, DC: National Science Foundation.

Hill, R. (1999). *The strengths of African American families: Twenty-five years later.* Lanham, MD: University Press of America.

Hope, E., Chavous, T., Jagers, R., & Sellers, R. (2013). Connecting self-esteem and achievement: Diversity in academic identification and dis-identification patterns among Black college students. *American Educational Research Journal, 50*(5), 1122–1151.

Houston, K., Vermillion, M., Doyle, L., & Ujitdehaage, S. (2014). A study of stereotype threat and academic performance among underrepresented pre-medical and pre-dental students. *Journal of Investigative Medicine, 62*(1), 200–210.

Hughes, R. (2012). Gender conception and the chilly road to female undergraduates' persistence in science and engineering fields. *Journal of Women and Minorities in Science and Engineering, 18*(3), 215–234.

Hurtado, S., & Carter, D. F. (1997). Effects of college transition and perceptions of the campus racial climate on Latino college students' sense of belonging. *Sociology of Education, 70*, 324–345.

Hurtado, S., Carter, D. F., & Kardia, D. (1998). The climate for diversity: Key issues for institutional self-study. *New Directions for Institutional Research, 25*(2), 53–63.

Hurtado, S., Eagan, M., Tran, M., Newman, C., Chang, M., & Velasco, P. (2011). "We do science here": Underrepresented students' interactions with faculty in different college contexts. *Journal of Social Issues, 67*(3), 553–579.

Johnson, K., & Watson, E. (2005). A historical chronology of the plight of African Americans gaining recognition in engineering and technology. *Journal of Technology Studies, 31*(1/2), 81.

Kane, C. (2000). African American family dynamics as perceived by family members. *Journal of Black Studies, 30*(5), 691–702.

King, D. (1988). Multiple jeopardy, multiple consciousness: The context of a Black feminist ideology. *Signs, 14*(1), 42–72.

Ko, L., Kachchaf, R., Hodari, A., & Ong, M. (2014). Agency of women of color in physics and astronomy: Strategies for persistence and success. *Journal of Women and Minorities in Science and Engineering, 20*(2), 171–195.

Litzler, E., Samuelson, C., & Lorah, J. (2014). Breaking it down: Engineering student STEM confidence at the intersection of race/ethnicity and gender. *Research in Higher Education, 55*, 810–832.

London, B., Rosenthal, L., Levy, S., & Lobel, M. (2011). The influences of perceived identity compatibility and social support on women in nontraditional fields during the college transition. *Basic and Applied Social Psychology, 33*(4), 304–321.

Mandara, J. (2006). The impact of family functioning on African American males' academic achievement: A review and clarification of the empirical literature. *Teachers College Record, 108*, 206–223.

Markus, H., Steele, C., & Steele, D. (2000). Colorblindness as a barrier to inclusion: Assimilation and nonimmigrant minorities. *Daedalus, 129*(4), 233–259.

Massey, D., & Fischer, M. (2005). Stereotype threat and academic performance: New findings from a racially diverse sample of college freshman. *Du Bois Review: Social Science Research on Race, 2*(1), 45–67.

Maton, K., & Hrabowski, F. (2004). Increasing the number of African American PhDs in the sciences and engineering. *American Psychologist, 59*(6), 547–556.

Maton, K. I., Hrabowski, F. A., III, & Schmitt, C. L. (2000). African American college students excelling in the sciences: College and post college outcomes in the Meyerhoff Scholars Program. *Journal of Research in Science Teaching, 37*, 629–654.

May, G. S., & Chubin, D. E. (2003). A retrospective on undergraduate engineering success for underrepresented minority students. *Journal of Engineering Education, 92*, 1–13.

Mendoza-Denton, R., Downey, G., Purdie, V. J., Davis, A., & Pietrzak, J. (2002). Sensitivity to status-based rejection: Implications for African American student experience. *Journal of Personality and Social Psychology, 83*(4), 896–918.

Moore, J., Madison-Colmore, O., & Smith, D. (2003). The prove-them-wrong syndrome: Voices from unheard African American males in engineering disciplines. *The Journal of Men's Studies, 12*(1), 61–73.

National Science Foundation. (2013). *Women, minorities, and persons with disabilities in science and engineering.* Arlington, VA: National Center for Science and Engineering Statistics.

Nora, A., & Cabrera, A. F. (1996). The role of perceptions of prejudice and discrimination on the adjustment of minority students to college. *Journal of Higher Education, 67*, 119–148.

Nussbaum, D., & Steele, C. (2007). Situational disengagement and persistence in the face of adversity. *Journal of Experimental Social Psychology, 43*(1), 127–134.

Owens, J., & Massey, D. (2010). Stereotype threat and college academic performance: A latent variables approach. *Social Science Research, 40*(1), 150–166.

Palmer, R., Davis, R., & Hilton, A. (2009). Exploring challenges that threaten to impede the academic success of academically underprepared black males at an HBCU. *Journal of College Student Development, 50*(4), 429–445. doi:10.1353/csd.0.0078

Palmer, R., Maramba, D., & Dancy, T. (2011). A qualitative investigation of factors promoting the retention and persistence of students of color in STEM. *The Journal of Negro Education, 80*(4), 491–504.

Pascarella, E., & Terenzini, P. (2005). *How college affects students A third decade of research* (2nd ed., Vol 2). San Francisco, CA: Jossey-Bass.

Perez, T., Cromley, J., & Kaplan, A. (2014). The role of identity development, values, and costs in college STEM retention. *Journal of Educational Psychology, 106*(1), 315–329.

Ramsey, L., Betz, D., & Sekaquaptewa, D. (2013). The effects of an academic environment intervention on science identification among women in STEM. *Social Psychology of Education, 16*, 377–397. doi:10.1007/S11218–013–9218–6

Reyes, M. (2011). Unique challenges for women of color in STEM transferring from community colleges to universities. *Harvard Educational Review, 81*(2), 241–262.

Richardson, B., Macon, T., Mustafaa, F., Bogan, E., Cole-Lewis, Y., & Chavous, T. (2014). Associations of racial discrimination and parental discrimination coping messages with African American adolescent racial identity. *Journal of Youth and Adolescence, 44*(6), 1301–1317.

Rowley, S., Sellers, R. M., Chavous, T. M., & Smith, M. A. (1998). The relationship between racial identity and self-esteem in African American college and high school students. *Journal of Personality and Social Psychology, 74*(3), 715–724.

Rowley, S. J. (2000). Profiles of African American college students' educational utility and performance: A cluster analysis. *Journal of Black Psychology, 26*(1), 3–26.

Ruffins, P. (2013). Challenging stereotypes. *Diverse Issues in Higher Education, 29*(26), 10–11.

Schmader, T. (2002). Gender identification moderates stereotype threat effects on women's math performance *Journal of Experimental Social Psychology, 38*, 194–201.

Schmader, T., Major, B., & Gramzow, R. H. (2001). Coping with ethnic stereotypes in the academic domain: Perceived injustice and psychological disengagement. *Journal of Social Issues, 57*(1), 93–111.

Sedlacek, W. E., & Brooks, G. C. (1976). *Racism in American education: A model for change.* Chicago: Nelson-Hall.

Sekaquaptewa, D., Waldman, A., & Thompson, M. (2007). Solo status and self-construal. *Cultural Diversity and Ethnic Minority Psychology, 13*(4), 321–327.

Sellers, R. M., Caldwell, C. H., Schmeelk-Cone, K. H., & Zimmerman, M. A. (2003). Racial identity, racial discrimination, perceived stress, and psychological distress among African American young adults. *Journal of Health and Social Behavior, 44*(3), 302–317.

Sellers, R. M., Chavous, T. M., & Cooke, D. Y. (1998). Racial ideology and racial centrality as predictors of African American college students' academic performance. *Journal of Black Psychology, 24*(1), 8–27.

Smalls, C., White, R., & Chavous, T., & Sellers, R. (2007). Racial ideological beliefs and racial discrimination experiences as predictors of academic engagement among African American adolescents. *Journal of Black Psychology, 33*(3), 299–330.

Smith, W., Allen, W., & Danley, L. (2007). Assume the position . . . you fit the description. *American Behavioral Scientist, 51*(4), 551–578. doi:10.1177/0002764207307742

Solórzano, D., Ceja, M., & Yosso, T. (2000). Critical race theory, racial microaggressions, and campus racial climate: The experiences of African American college students. *The Journal of Negro Education, 69*(1/2), 60–73.

Spencer, M. B., Noll, E., & Stoltzfus, J. (2001). Identity and school adjustment: Revisiting the "acting White" assumption. *Educational Psychologist, 36*(1), Special issue: The schooling of ethnic minority children and youth, 21–30.

Steele, C. M. (1992). Race and the schooling of Black Americans. *The Atlantic Monthly, 269*, 68–78.

Steele, C. M. (1997). A threat in the air: How stereotypes shape intellectual identity and performance. *American Psychologist, 52*, 613–629.

Swim, J., Hyers, L., Cohen, L., Fitzgerald, D., & Bylsma, W. (2003). African American college students' experiences with everyday racism: Characteristics of and responses to these incidents. *Journal of Black Psychology, 29*(2), 38–67.

Varner, F., & Mandara, J. (2013). Discrimination concerns and expectations as explanations for gendered socialization in African American families. *Child Development, 84*(3), 875–890.

132 Tabbye M. Chavous et al.

Wigfield, A., & Wagner, A. (2005). Competence, motivation, and identity development during adolescence. In A. Elliot & C. Dweck (Eds.), *Handbook of competence and motivation* (pp. 222–239). New York: The Guilford Press.

Wong, C. A., Eccles, J. S., & Sameroff, A. (2003). The influence of ethnic discrimination and ethnic identification on African American adolescents' school and socioemotional adjustment. *Journal of Personality, 71*(6), 1197–1232.

9[1]

ASSET-BASED PEDAGOGIES AND LATINO STUDENTS' ACHIEVEMENT AND IDENTITY

Francesca López

Teacher expectancy research has added to our understanding about the ways teachers communicate their expectations to students (see Brophy & Good, 1970) as well as how students perceive differential teacher behavior (e.g., Weinstein, Marshall, Sharp, & Botkin, 1987) and its effect on students' own perceptions of ability (e.g., Harris, Rosenthal, & Snodgrass, 1986). Indeed, the established presence of research on teacher expectations in teacher preparation programs (e.g., Barnes, 1987) and licensure standards (e.g., Council of Chief State School Officers, 2011) is a testament to its influence. Despite the marked presence of teacher expectancy in teacher training, however, traditionally marginalized students—students who face particularly onerous obstacles associated with poverty and prejudice— continue to be underrepresented in a vast array of achievement outcomes (e.g., achievement test scores, high school completion, college matriculation). Scholars have argued that disparities will persist if we do not attend to the reasons teachers' expectations are often confounded with students' cultural background (Ladson-Billings, 1999; Villegas & Lucas, 2002).

To attend to differential student treatment rooted in biases, scholars have argued that there are unique beliefs that are essential to the effective teaching of traditionally marginalized students. These beliefs reflect teachers' *critical awareness*— their understanding of the historical context of traditionally marginalized students, the discrepancy between what is typically validated as knowledge in classrooms and the challenges to those assumptions, and the ways the curriculum in schools serves to replicate the power structure in society (e.g., Apple, 2004; Banks, 1993; Bowles & Gintis, 1976; Darder, 2012; Dewey, 1916; Ladson-Billings, 2004). In addition to these beliefs, scholars have argued that teachers must engage in distinctive behaviors that support traditionally marginalized students' culture, often collectively referred to as asset-based pedagogies[2] (ABP)—though scholars have

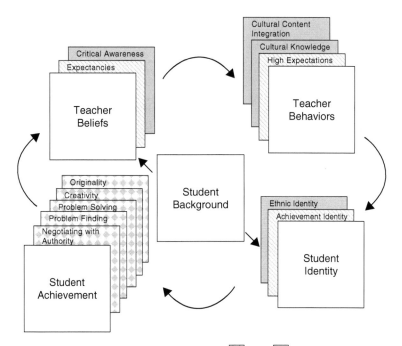

FIGURE 9.1 Asset-based pedagogy framework. ▨ and ☐ denote constructs represented in classroom dynamics research; ■ denote ABP constructs; and ▦ denote outcomes represented in both bodies of work. In the framework, students' background reflects demographics (e.g., gender, socioeconomic status, and ethnicity) that are bound by social norms and expectations. As such, they influence both teacher and student perceptions directly and student achievement and teacher behaviors indirectly.

also raised concerns about the paucity of empirical evidence linking ABP to students' outcomes (Goldenberg, Rueda, & August, 2008; Sleeter, 2012).

In this chapter, I describe a framework (see Figure 9.1) that can address the paucity of evidence on classroom dynamics research focused on traditionally marginalized youth by considering critical awareness and ABP. I illustrate the application of the framework with a summary of my own research and highlight implications of the framework to educational psychology, as well as necessary considerations for future research.

Asset-Based Pedagogy: A Framework for Programmatic Inquiry

The framework I present here reflects prior models that capture the interrelationships among students' backgrounds, teachers' beliefs, and students' outcomes (e.g., Jussim, Eccles, & Madon, 1996) as well as extant work that has established

Asset-Based Pedagogy and Latino Students **135**

evidence about how teacher beliefs and behaviors inform students' identities and their achievement (e.g., Brophy, 1986; Brophy & Good, 1970; Harris et al., 1986). It builds on prior work, however, by considering scholarship-based ABP that, while prominent in the teacher education literature, is largely missing in educational psychology. ABP, at times known under the more broadly encompassing term *multicultural education* (Banks, 1993), views students' culture as a strength, countering the more widespread view that inordinate achievement disparities stem from deficiencies in the child and/or child's culture.

Early attempts to address achievement disparities for poor youth, most of whom were students of color, were rooted in *deficit orientations* that reflect superiority of a group's practices, expectations, and experiences (see Banks, 1993). This perspective emerged prominently with Lyndon B. Johnson's War on Poverty initiative, which provided the first special funding in U.S. history for compensatory programs (Title I) aimed at addressing the "culture of poverty" (Kantor, 1991, p. 65) believed to be inherent among poor youth. Perspectives that challenged deficit orientations evolved to be known as *difference orientations* that reflected the need to consider dissimilarities between the school culture and that of traditionally marginalized students. Among these approaches were *culturally appropriate* (Au & Jordan, 1981), *culturally congruent* (Au & Mason, 1983), *culturally compatible* (Erickson & Mohatt, 1982), and *culturally responsive education* (Cazden & Leggett, 1981). Difference orientations that claim deficiencies are not assumed to be *in the child* but *in the child's culture*, however, remain oriented in deficiencies. In contrast to these earlier perspectives (although difference perspectives are still prevalent), ABP orientations that have evolved over decades underscore viewing students' differences as *assets*, contesting the ways differences are too often reduced to deficiencies. Recent conceptualizations of these approaches are known as *critical bicultural pedagogy* (Darder, 1991), *equity pedagogy* (Banks, 1993), *culturally relevant pedagogy* (Ladson-Billings, 1995a, 1995b), *culturally responsive teaching* (Gay, 2000), *cultural connectedness* (Irizarry, 2007), *culturally sustaining pedagogies* (Paris, 2012), and *critical culturally sustaining revitalizing pedagogy* (McCarty & Lee, 2014), among others. These conceptualizations have focused on different populations of traditionally marginalized student populations, underscoring the applicability of ABP across settings. As expressed by Banks (1993), "Race, ethnicity, class, gender, and exceptionality—and their interaction—are each important factors in multicultural education" (p. 5). In the sections that follow, I detail the various components of ABP (see Figure 9.1) against classroom dynamics research focused on (1) teacher beliefs, (2) teacher behaviors, and (3) student identity in promoting student achievement outcomes.

Teacher Beliefs

Teacher Expectancy

Although "distinguishing knowledge from belief is a daunting undertaking" (Pajares, 1992, p. 309), teacher expectancies have been defined as "inferences (based on prior experiences or information) about the level of student performance that is likely to occur in the future" (Good & Nichols, 2001, p. 113). Accordingly, they reflect the interplay among affect, evaluation, and knowledge. The accumulation of evidence on the potentially deleterious ways in which teacher expectancies can influence students' outcomes is often traced back to Merton's (1948) self-fulfilling prophecy: "a *false* definition of the situation evoking a new behavior which makes the originally false conception come *true*" (p. 195). What began with the observation of potential contamination of interpersonal expectations in a psychology experiment evolved to *Pygmalion Effects in the Classroom* (Rosenthal, 1994). In their pivotal experimental study, Rosenthal and Jacobson (1968) found that children in an experimental group whose teachers had been led to believe they would demonstrate greater gains at the end of the school year indeed had greater achievement gains than those in the control group. Although the study was criticized for methodological flaws (see Jussim & Harber, 2005), a generation of teacher expectancy research ensued.

In their review of decades of research on teacher expectancy effects (excluding those that did not focus exclusively on teacher expectancies), Jussim and Harber (2005) concluded that although the "condemnation of teachers for their supposed role in creating injustices" was not warranted by the available evidence (p. 131), "students who belong to a stigmatized group may be particularly vulnerable to self-fulfilling prophecies" (p. 143). At the time of their review a decade ago, however, only two studies that met their inclusion criteria had examined teacher expectancy effects among stigmatized students. Of these, only one examined the role of race/ethnicity and social class: the study conducted by Jussim et al. (1996) found teacher expectancy effects for stigmatized groups were considered "large by any standard" (p. 143). However, in their examination of whether these effects could be attributed to teachers' biases, the researchers found that "teachers perceived differences between different groups that closely corresponded to those groups' actual differences in prior grades and achievement tests" (p. 143). In other words, the researchers inferred that because stigmatized students' performance was consistent with teacher beliefs, no bias existed; the expectancies were accurate. However, since Jussim and Harber's (2005) review, scholars have established that teachers' expectations are often confounded with students' cultural background (McKown & Weinstein, 2003; Tenenbaum & Ruck, 2007). Consequently, it is insufficient to merely examine whether teachers' expectations of students' performance are aligned with students' prior performance; researchers must consider what is at times known as *critical awareness.*

Critical Awareness

Critical awareness can be described as teachers' understanding of the historical context of traditionally marginalized students, the discrepancy between what is typically validated as knowledge in classrooms and the challenges to those assumptions, and the ways the curriculum in schools serves to replicate the power structure in society (e.g., Banks, 1993; Bowles & Gintis, 1976; Darder, 2012; Dewey, 1916; Ladson-Billings, 2004). Accordingly, critical awareness is viewed as essential knowledge that enables teachers to engage in emancipatory pedagogy that empowers students (Banks, 1993; Darder, 2012; Gay, 2010; Ladson-Billings, 1995a). Despite the importance of establishing evidence on the ways beliefs influence behaviors (Pajares, 1992), the scholarship on the preparation of teachers for traditionally marginalized students continues to focus extensively on ways to influence teacher beliefs related to critical awareness (e.g., Anderson & Stillman, 2013; Hollins & Torres-Guzman, 2005; Morrison, Robbins, & Rose, 2008) and measure those beliefs (e.g., Pohan & Aguilar, 2001). Although there is evidence that critical awareness appears to be associated with traditionally marginalized students' achievement (Brown & Chu, 2012), there is still a need to establish how particular beliefs are related to behaviors to address the current limitations of the ABP literature. In the sections that follow, I describe prior research that moved beyond expectancies by examining teacher behaviors and their relationship to student outcomes, research often known under the domain of *teacher effectiveness.*

Teacher Behaviors

Teacher Effectiveness

Whereas teacher expectancy research focused on whether teacher beliefs influenced student outcomes, the teacher effectiveness research that was generated between the 1960s and the early 2000s focused on how processes in classrooms—teacher behaviors—were related to student outcomes (for reviews, see Brophy, 1986; Brophy & Good, 1970; Good, 2014). Although early research was murky because "no specific teacher behavior had been linked clearly to student achievement" (Brophy, 1986, p. 1069), researchers attended to the limitations raised (see Dunkin & Biddle, 1974). What followed was a vast body of work that detailed teacher behaviors such as how they provide information, how they elicit information, and the pacing of instruction, along with numerous other behaviors, and how these behaviors were associated with student achievement (for a detailed review, see Brophy & Good, 1984). The teacher effectiveness research is particularly noteworthy because of its role in establishing that teacher behaviors are related to student outcomes (addressing pessimism that questioned whether teachers had any effect at all), examining how teachers' beliefs were related to their behaviors, as well as generating research using observation coding systems that operationalized behaviors (Brophy, 1986).

To date, although researchers have examined teachers' differential expectations based on students' membership in a stigmatized group, teacher effectiveness research has yet to address this need despite evidence that teachers can and do

138 Francesca López

have biases that play out in different ways (McKown, 2013). Moreover, evidence suggests that general teacher behaviors do not generalize across student populations (López, 2011), underscoring the need to examine unique behaviors that are necessary in classrooms with traditionally marginalized students.

Asset-Based Pedagogy

To gauge how beliefs are related to student outcomes, they must be operationalized in such a way to be able to capture discrete, albeit interrelated, beliefs—as well as their respective behaviors—reflected in the ABP literature. Collectively, the various conceptualizations of CRT represented in the extant literature reflect four requisite teacher behaviors: high expectations, cultural knowledge, cultural content integration, and language.

High Expectations

Whereas teacher effectiveness work has contributed to our understanding of how teachers' expectancies play out in the classroom, high expectations in ABP reflects critical awareness that counteracts the ways teachers' expectations are otherwise confounded with students' cultural background (e.g., McKown & Weinstein, 2003; Tenenbaum & Ruck, 2007). That is, by possessing critical awareness, teachers engage in behaviors consistent with high expectations in which "students [are] not permitted to choose failure in their classrooms" (Ladson-Billings, 1995a, p. 479). Scholars who demand equity via access to a rigorous curriculum have pointed to the ways in which traditionally marginalized youth are inordinately exposed to subpar curricula and materials (Moll, 1992, p. 20).

The focus on low-level skills is perhaps more widespread now than ever given the narrowing of the curriculum that has resulted from an emphasis of test taking in schools (Baker et al., 2010). For traditionally marginalized students, the narrowing of the curriculum to produce higher achievement on high-stakes assessments tends to be particularly deleterious (Berliner, 2011; Golann, 2015).

The emphasis on high-stakes assessments has resulted in the proliferation of "no excuses" approaches for traditionally marginalized students that emphasize heightened behavioral control (Golann, 2015). As already described, however, behavioral control reflects a deficiency orientation that is not typically applied to students from more privileged backgrounds. As such, high expectations in the ABP tradition mirror the expectations for students from more privileged backgrounds: a rigorous curriculum, opportunities to take initiative, being able to assert their needs, and learning to negotiate with authority (Golann, 2015, p. 105). In turn, this consideration requires assessment of outcomes that mirror the kinds of outcomes high expectations are meant to promote (see Good, 2014). That is, while addressing early critiques in research that did not link teacher behaviors to outcomes, it was found that it is necessary to consider achievement as an outcome, as

Asset-Based Pedagogy and Latino Students **139**

well as other outcomes of learning (see Brophy & Good, 1984). Among these are "problem solving, creativity, originality, and problem finding" (Good, 2014, p. 2).

Cultural Knowledge

Cultural knowledge tends to be represented in *constructivist views of learning*, where "learners use their prior knowledge and beliefs … to make sense of the new input" (Villegas & Lucas, 2002, p. 25). Accordingly, it encompasses teachers' knowledge about how to access and validate students' prior knowledge in genuine ways that consider students' cultures as assets (Banks, 1993; Gay 2000, 2010; Ladson-Billings, 1994, 1995a, 1995b; Lee, 1993, 1995, 2007; Moll & González, 2004). ABP scholarship details numerous ways to access students' cultural knowledge. This includes incorporating students' home experiences into classroom instruction (González, Moll, & Amanti, 2005, p. 10); "[using] student culture as a vehicle for learning" (Ladson-Billings, 1995b, p. 161); and making "connections between language use in the community and language use in a tradition of literary texts" (Lee, 1995, p. 612).

Cultural Content Integration

Whereas cultural knowledge reflects the consideration of knowledge students already possess, cultural content integration is about the provision of culture that is not typically validated in the formal curriculum. ABP arose out of the need to address disparities that are rooted in inequitable treatment based on belonging to a particular group (Banks, 1993). To counter the socially entrenched experiences among traditionally marginalized students, including that of a hegemonic curriculum, ABP literature requires that teachers incorporate students' culture into the curriculum to affirm "the legitimacy of cultural heritages of different ethnic groups, both as legacies that affect students' dispositions, attitudes, and approaches to learning and as worthy content to be taught in the formal curriculum" (Gay, 2000, p. 29). Accordingly, cultural content integration requires that teachers possess critical awareness so they may determine "what information should be included in the curriculum, how it should be integrated into the existing curriculum, and its location within the curriculum" (Banks, 1993, p. 8).

Language

Within both the cultural knowledge and content integration dimension is *language* because of its role in students' culture and identity. This view is evident in González's (2001) examination of the identities of Latino children and their mothers in her seminal book, *I Am My Language*:

> [T]o speak of language is to speak of our "selves." Language is at the heart, literally and metaphorically, of who we are, how we present ourselves, and

how others see us. . . .The ineffable link of language to emotion, to the very core of our being, is one of the ties that bind children to a sense of heritage. (p. xix)

This view is shared by Darder (2012), who asserts, "It is critical that educators recognize the role language plays as one of the most powerful transmitters of culture, and as such, its central role to both intellectual formation and the survival of subordinate cultural populations" (p. 36). As a powerful transmitter of culture, cultivating a native or heritage language is not reserved for students who speak a language other than that of the dominant group in society; ABP reflects that the cultivation of students' native (or heritage) language is central to identity regardless of the language in which they have become fluent.

Student Identity

Achievement Identity

Identity, broadly speaking, is defined by the answer to the question "Who am I?" (Eccles, 2009; McCaslin, 2009). As a facet of identity, self-beliefs have been central to the examination of achievement outcomes because they reflect "the assumption that individuals' perceptions of themselves and their capabilities are vital forces in their success or failure in achievement settings" (Schunk & Pajares, 2005, p. 85). Although there are many self-constructs that have been found to be related to student achievement (see Schunk & Pajares, 2005), they include self-efficacy (Bandura, 1986), self-concept (Marsh & Shavelson, 1985), and expectancy value (Eccles et al., 1983). These self-constructs are all believed to develop through students' interpretation of their personal experiences, but few studies have examined the ways in which teachers' expectations are related to students' self-constructs. Instead, studies have focused on the extent to which students can infer teachers' beliefs and behaviors and the directionality of the relationship (for a review, see Rubie-Davies, 2006). For example, researchers have found that students are adept at inferring teachers' expectations (e.g., Weinstein et al., 1987) and that teachers' expectations tend to be more influential to students' outcomes than the reverse (e.g., Muijis & Reynolds, 2002; Rubie-Davies, 2006). Despite this evidence, few studies have focused on the interrelationship between teachers' expectancies and students' identity formation. The evidence that is available suggests teachers' beliefs (Rubie-Davies, 2006) and teachers' behaviors (Chen, Thompson, Kromrey, & Chang, 2011; Harris et al., 1986) markedly shape students' academic self-concepts.

Ethnic Identity

The limitations raised regarding the paucity of empirical evidence on ABP are not limited to achievement outcomes; Ladson-Billings (1995a) asserts, "A next step for positing effective pedagogical practice is a theoretical model that not only addresses student achievement but also helps students to accept and affirm their cultural identity" (p. 469). That is, the assumption about the role of ABP in promoting achievement tends to hinge on students' identities in a manner consistent with Marsh and Shavelson's (1985) assertion that self-concept is "formed through experience with and interpretations of one's environment" (p. 107). Accordingly, the centrality of students' cultural identities in ABP underscores the need to explicitly incorporate them in empirical frameworks that aim to establish a link between ABP and student achievement.

There is ample empirical evidence supporting the importance of strong ethnic identities for traditionally marginalized youth (Altschul, Oyserman, & Bybee, 2008; Brown & Chu, 2012; Umaña-Taylor, Wong, Gonzales, & Dumka, 2012). Researchers have found that discrimination is associated with lower academic achievement (DeGarmo & Martinez, 2006); however, when traditionally marginalized youth who are aware of racism have strong ethnic identities and view achievement as consistent with the goals of their group, they have better achievement outcomes (Altschul, Oyserman, & Bybee, 2006). Although seemingly counterintuitive, awareness of racism among traditionally marginalized youth provides an important buffer to negative societal stereotypes (Altschul et al., 2006). For example, a traditionally marginalized student who is aware of racism may infer differential treatment as a product of discrimination, whereas being unaware may lead to inferences of deficiencies within him- or herself. This awareness is consistent with Ladson-Billings's (1995b) assertion that "students must develop a critical consciousness through which they challenge the status quo of the current social order" (p. 160). Researchers have also found that dual ethnic identities (a sense of belonging to both one's cultural group and the majority group) promote resilience beyond affirmation toward one's cultural group alone (Oyserman, Kemmelmeier, Fryberg, Brosh, & Hart-Johnson, 2003), highlighting the nuances associated with multiple facets of identity. Despite its established importance to traditionally marginalized students' identity, the examination of how ethnic identity is formed in the context of schools remains pervasively understudied. To attend to this need, it is incorporated into the framework that has previously only examined students' academic self-concepts.

Application of the Framework[3]

In this section, I describe results from the first year of an ongoing study in southern Arizona in which I applied the framework presented here (López, 2016). The study is taking place across several elementary and middle schools in an urban district that is 63% Latino and where approximately 46% of the Latino student population in the district qualifies for free or reduced lunch. The first year of the study included 244 Latino students and their teachers ($n = 16$) across Grades 3 through 5 in three schools; year 2 includes 550 students and 39 teachers in six schools.

142 Francesca López

Context

Arizona policies reflect a long history of discriminatory and segregative practices that tend to target Latinos (Jiménez-Castellanos, Combs, Martínez, & Gómez, 2013). For example, despite empirical support for the use of Spanish in instruction for Latino students who speak Spanish as their first language, Proposition 203 replaced bilingual education with Structured English Immersion in 2001 (see López, 2012). More recently, the state of Arizona banned a Mexican American Studies program with HB 2281.[4] The program continues to be deemed illegal despite empirical evidence that the courses were associated with improved educational outcomes for Latino youth (see Cabrera, Milem, Jaquette, & Marx, 2014). Given the number of restrictive policies enacted over the past 15 years (Jiménez-Castellanos et al., 2013), it should be no surprise that Arizona leads the nation in the proportion of students who drop out of high school (NCES, 2013). Among them, close to 30% of Latino youth fail to complete high school within 4 years (NCES, 2013). When Latino youth are classified as English learners, the dropout rate soars to 75% (U.S. Department of Education, 2012).

The Study

To address limitations raised in the review of ABP research I presented earlier, I applied the framework presented here in a mixed-methods study to examine the extent to which each of the dimensions of teacher-reported ABP beliefs and behaviors are associated with Latino students' identities, as well as their achievement outcomes in reading.[5] Three schools participated in the first year of the study. One school did not explicitly focus on ABP; the other two participating schools are dual-language magnet schools.[6] Although both dual-language schools offer cultural extracurricular activities, only one explicitly emphasizes a strong focus on multicultural education and social justice in the curriculum.

In addition to conducting classroom observations that generated lengthy field notes, as well as interviews with both students and teachers, quantitative methods were applied. Student-level variables included reading achievement measures aligned with the state's academic standards (beginning-of-the-year scores were used to control for prior achievement), reading scholastic competence, ethnic affirmation,[7] and perceived discrimination. Teacher-level variables included teacher-reported beliefs (López, 2016) reflecting high expectations, critical awareness,[8] cultural knowledge, cultural content integration, and language. Teachers were also surveyed about their behaviors (López, 2016), which included cultural knowledge, cultural content integration, and language. Consistent with expectations, the school with the social justice and multicultural education mission had the highest level of ABP beliefs and behaviors, followed by the other dual-language school. The school without an explicit ABP mission had the lowest levels.

Correspondence Between Beliefs and Behaviors

Correlations between teacher-reported beliefs and behaviors demonstrated that some beliefs are more consistent with behaviors than others; however, closer inspection reveals that contexts can promote or constrain teachers' behaviors regardless of teachers' beliefs. Teachers' beliefs about the use of Spanish in instruction (e.g., "Whenever possible, students who do not speak English as their native language should receive instruction that will nurture their native language as well as develop English proficiency.") are largely consistent with their reported behaviors ($r = .61$); however, most of the teachers participating in year 1 of the study were certified as bilingual teachers ($n = 11$) and taught in schools that used a dual-language approach (i.e., instruction is carried out in both English and Spanish). Teachers' reported beliefs and their corresponding behaviors regarding cultural content integration were negatively, albeit weakly, related to one another. The dimension representing cultural content integration beliefs, however, was quite high ($M = 4.83$, $SD = .18$ on a 1–5 scale) compared to the behaviors ($M = 2.94$, $SD = .61$ on a 1–5 scale). In part, this finding might be explained by the fact that the schools that participated in the study must adhere to restrictive Arizona policies that require a focus on students' *individuality*, which can restrict opportunities to integrate cultural content into the curriculum. A lesson that transpired during a classroom observation highlights this. Students in a fourth-grade classroom were provided with a handout for a contest sponsored by the local university in which students were asked to draw a picture representing Hispanic heritage. The teacher explained to students,

> We are going to do an activity where you will draw what Hispanic heritage means to you. There are no wrong answers; it is about what it means to *you*, as an *individual*.

To model students' responses to the activity, the teacher explained her own background (e.g., she grew up in Mexico) and the meaning it had for her. She then asked students to give examples to share with the class, but rather than build on what students were reporting, every answer was affirmed regardless of whether it actually had anything to do with Hispanic culture. As students engaged in the task, the teacher commented to me, "We are not allowed to talk about ourselves as part of a group. It has to be about each individual." Thus, even when teachers have high levels of beliefs about the importance of cultural content integration, policies can limit the extent to which they can engage said practices.

Another discrepant relationship was found between cultural knowledge beliefs, which were also quite high ($M = 4.53$, $SD = .67$ on a 1–5 scale), and behaviors ($M = 2.38$, $SD = .81$ on a 1–5 scale), which were not. In this study, most teachers had high levels of beliefs as reflected by the level of agreement to statements such as "Getting to know parents is necessary to be able to access students' prior knowledge" and "Teachers should learn about students' home lives

144 Francesca López

and incorporate this knowledge into instruction." However, it is important to consider the time required of teachers who use cultural knowledge approaches with the growing demands placed on them (Simbula, 2010). That is, as much as teachers may believe in the benefits of strategies that incorporate their home lives into school, they must reconcile the increasing responsibilities placed on them (this was also reflected in the teacher interviews, which I elaborate on later). Thus, the discordance between beliefs and behaviors in the cultural knowledge dimension is possibly an artifact of the restrictive setting rather than teachers' failure to do what they report they believe they should.

ABP and Student Outcomes

To address the research questions in the study, I ran two separate hierarchical linear models that examined the relationship between (a) teacher-reported ABP beliefs and students' reading achievement and (b) teacher-reported ABP behaviors and students' reading achievement. I included prior reading achievement as a covariate; each point earned at the beginning of the year was associated with approximately .02 SD increase in reading achievement at the end of the year (for a potential total increase of 1 SD on end-of-year reading achievement for students with the highest prior achievement).

Consistent with the assertions in extant literature that teachers' critical awareness is paramount in addressing the needs of traditionally marginalized students, the dimension was associated with largest effects on students' reading achievement, with up to 1.70 SD higher reading outcomes at the end of the school year after controlling for prior achievement. In terms of discrete ABP beliefs, the role of instruction in Spanish was associated with up to .85 SD higher reading outcomes. What is especially noteworthy about the role of Spanish instruction on students' achievement is that a majority of the students were not labeled English learners. Cultural knowledge was also associated with higher reading achievement—up to .60 SD when teachers held the highest levels of cultural knowledge beliefs.

As previously mentioned, cultural knowledge and cultural content integration behaviors were not reflective of teachers' beliefs of the dimensions. These dimensions were also not found to be related to student outcomes—but they appear to be an artifact related to constraints placed on teachers by policies. Teachers who reported the highest level of behaviors in terms of Spanish were significant, albeit very small (about a .03 SD increase). The small effect, however, may have been an artifact of restricted range given that most teachers provided instruction in two languages.

Student Identity

On average, students with the highest levels of reading competence had .33 SD higher outcomes in reading achievement; students with the highest level of ethnic affirmation had .20 SD higher outcomes in reading achievement. Thus, consistent with prior studies I reviewed earlier, students' identity was positively related to

Asset-Based Pedagogy and Latino Students **145**

their achievement outcomes. Moreover, students in the school with the highest levels of ABP had the highest levels of both ethnic affirmation and reading competence. Students in the school with the highest levels of ABP, however, had higher levels of perceived discrimination (Cohen's $d = .18$) compared to the other dual-language school—although this finding is consistent with prior work finding a positive effect associated with both the awareness of discrimination and higher levels of academic identity (Altschul et al., 2006). It should be noted that the school with the highest levels of ABP engages in discussions about discrimination and ways to promote equity, while supporting students with an explicit focus on honoring students' heritage and others' heritage as well (and accordingly, students at that school also had the highest levels of "other" ethnic identity that contributes to a bicultural identity). As such, the pedagogy reflects a critical awareness described by Ladson-Billings (1995b) that was confirmed by the student interviews. One student stated, "People come to the school and teach us about things that other people don't learn." Another said, "It's really connected around here. And it really brings out like the culture of anybody who's here."

The cultural focus of the school and its link to students' identities was also salient. When asked what their parents say about their school or how their school is different from other schools or what their favorite thing about their school is, students in the high–ABP school often discussed the bilingual emphasis at their school. Several students discussed their parents' desire for them to speak better Spanish and learn about their culture as the primary motivating factor in their school placement. Many students communicated that both they and their parents valued bilingualism as a tool for academic success and long-term career success.

Operationalizing High Expectations

The questions used to reflect teachers' beliefs about high expectations (e.g., "Latino students can close achievement gaps if teachers provide them with rigorous instruction") were unable to capture a relationship between high expectations and students' achievement outcomes, whereas critical awareness was. Moreover, there was a significant negative correlation between high expectations and critical awareness ($r = .20$). Although there were potential issues associated with a restricted range (i.e., no one "strongly disagreed," and only one teacher "somewhat disagreed" with the statements associated with high expectations beliefs aligned to a rigorous curriculum), findings suggest that high expectations are more accurately reflected by critical awareness for traditionally marginalized students. Indeed, there was ample evidence from teacher interviews regarding an awareness of the need to deliver rigor to students consistent with ABP. For example, one teacher expressed the following:

> As far as material resources, our textbooks are outdated and now that we're trying to implement the Common Core curriculum, our textbooks are not aligned. So that's really detrimental to the learning environment.

146 Francesca López

Another teacher stated,

> I am worried about my class size and the current trend in education to be
> so focused on test scores and data, so that we feel more like statisticians than
> educators sometimes. And so, unfortunately, that takes our focus away from
> the kids when so much is being required in terms of data.

In addition to impediments in being able to deliver a rigorous curriculum, *all*
teachers expressed frustration with the inordinate amount of time they were
required to spend on testing students, as well as assessing themselves on the teacher
evaluation framework that had been implemented that year. From the interviews,
it appeared teachers were aware of the need for rigor (which was substantiated
by the beliefs survey), but the interviews uncover the structural impediments in
providing rigor. Indeed, most of the teacher interviews reflected that they simply
make do with what they have to deliver the best instruction they can—and students appear to notice. An example of student response reveals this trend:

> Our school has more help than other schools. We have better teachers that
> actually like help us in our school work when we need it and we can go to
> like a counselor that we have here and stuff if we need help or we can stay
> after school, come in the morning, or grab lunch to get even more extra
> credit or help.

Thus, although there may be face validity in asking teachers about whether they
agree that rigorous instruction can address achievement disparities, teachers'
beliefs about students' capabilities for high levels of achievement may be more
accurately assessed by examining beliefs related to sociohistorical impediments
to their success.

Taken together, the findings presented here suggest that application of the
framework has salient implications for classroom dynamics theories and educational psychology research, although the limitations to the study underscore the
need for more research. Accordingly, I now turn to a discussion of these implications, which include a concerted focus in establishing the operationalization of
ABP behaviors in future work.

Conclusion

In this chapter, I have argued that ABP can be defined and assessed by the use of
evidence-driven data collected with both qualitative and quantitative methods.
For some time, scholars have argued (using various terminology and theories)
that differences students bring to schools can be seen as assets. Although the historical voices calling for what I refer to as ABP have provided a rich conceptual
basis that provides a compelling picture for its need, what it is and its effects on
students have been largely missing from its collective paradigm. I have tried to

Asset-Based Pedagogy and Latino Students **147**

articulate a better definition (i.e., a more measureable independent variable) and to mark a path between teacher beliefs and actions and student beliefs, actions, and outcomes. This is admittedly a fledgling attempt at integrating a complex and diverse literature into a focused program of study that explores ABP as it unfolds in actual classroom instruction. Clearly ABP can appear in many forms, and there can likely be too much of it as well as too little. The reported study presents a way to operationalize ABP and to study its effects in a particular context, though more work is clearly needed to refine the theories about the ways students' identities are shaped in the context of classrooms.

Notes

1 Portions of this chapter appear in López, F. (forthcoming). Altering the trajectory of the self-fulfilling prophesy: Asset-based pedagogy and classroom dynamics. *Journal of Teacher Education.*
2 To capture the breadth of asset-based educational practices, I use the term *asset-based pedagogies* (ABP) but retain authors' terminology when quoting their work.
3 The study reflects findings from López (2016) unless otherwise noted.
4 HB 2281 (2010) reads, "A school district or charter school in this state shall not include in its program of instruction any courses or classes that . . . advocate ethnic solidarity instead of the treatment of pupils as individuals" (Section 15–112). Now A.R.S. § 15–112.
5 Consistent with the facets of design research presented earlier, prior studies had contributed to the refinement of the framework and operationalization of the constructs (López, 2016).
6 The schools' magnet status was prompted by a desegregation case, wherein funds are received to promote integration within the district.
7 Ethnic exploration, although a subscale in the multigroup ethnic identity measure (Phinney, 1992), was not used due to developmental considerations of the participating students.
8 Coefficient alpha for all dimensions ranged from .70 to .97.

References

Altschul, I., Oyserman, D., & Bybee, D. (2006). Racial-ethnic identity in mid-adolescence: Content and change as predictors of academic achievement. *Child Development, 77,* 1155–1169.
Altschul, I., Oyserman, D., & Bybee, D. (2008). Racial-ethnic self-schemas and segmented assimilation: Identity and the academic achievement of Hispanic youth. *Social Psychology Quarterly, 71,* 302–320.
Anderson, L. M., & Stillman, J. A. (2013). Student teaching's contribution to preservice teacher development: A review of research focused on the preparation of teachers for urban and high-needs contexts. *Review of Educational Research, 83,* 3–69.
Apple, M. W. (2004). *Ideology and curriculum* (3rd ed.). London and Boston: Routledge.
A.R.S. § 15–112 (Formerly HB 2281). Retrieved http://www.azleg.gov/legtext/49leg/2r/bills/hb2281p.pdf
Au, K., & Jordan, C. (1981). Teaching reading to Hawaiian children: Finding a culturally appropriate solution. In H. Trueba, G. Guthrie, & K. Au (Eds.), *Culture and the bilingual classroom: Studies in classroom ethnography* (pp. 69–86). Rowley, MA: Newbury House.

148 Francesca López

Au, K.H.P., & Mason, J. M. (1983). Cultural congruence in classroom participation structures: Achieving a balance of rights. *Discourse Processes, 6*, 145–167.

Baker, E. L., Barton, P. E., Darling-Hammond, L., Haertel, E., Ladd, H. F., Linn, R. L., . . . & Shepard, L. A. (2010). *Problems with the use of student test scores to evaluate teachers.* EPI Briefing Paper# 278. Washington, DC: Economic Policy Institute.

Bandura, A. (1986). *Social foundations of thought and action: A social-cognitive view.* Englewood Cliffs, NJ: Prentice-Hall.

Banks, J. A. (1993). Multicultural education: Historical development, dimensions, and practice. *Review of Research in Education, 19*, 3–49.

Barnes, C. P. (1987). *The profile of the beginning teacher.* Report of the CSU Committee to Study the Teacher Preparation Curriculum. Retrieved from http://eric. ed.gov/?id=ED282863

Berliner, D. (2011). Rational responses to high stakes testing: The case of curriculum narrowing and the harm that follows. *Cambridge Journal of Education, 41*, 287–302.

Bowles, S., & Gintis, H. (1976). *Schooling in capitalist America: Educational reform and the contradictions of economic life.* New York: Basic Books.

Brophy, J. (1986). Teacher influences on student achievement. *American Psychologist, 41*, 1069–1077.

Brophy, J., & Good, T. L. (1970). Teachers' communication of differential expectations for children's classroom performance: Some behavioral data. *Journal of Educational Psychology, 61*, 355–374.

Brophy, J., & Good, T. L. (1984). *Teacher behavior and student achievement.* Occasional Paper No. 73. Retrieved from http://eric.ed.gov/?id=ED251422

Brown, C. S., & Chu, H. (2012). Discrimination, ethnic identity, and academic outcomes of Mexican immigrant children: The importance of school context. *Child Development, 83*, 1477–1485.

Cabrera, N. L., Milem, J. F., Jaquette, O., & Marx, R. W. (2014). Missing the (student achievement) forest for all the (political) trees: Empiricism and the Mexican American studies controversy in Tucson. *American Educational Research Journal, 51*, 1084–1118.

Cazden, C., & Leggett, E. (1981). Culturally responsive education: Recommendations for achieving Lau remedies II. In H. Trueba, G. Guthrie, & K. Au (Eds.), *Culture and the bilingual classroom: Studies in classroom ethnography* (pp. 69–86). Rowley, MA: Newbury.

Chen, Y. H., Thompson, M. S., Kromrey, J. D., & Chang, G. H. (2011). Relations of student perceptions of teacher oral feedback with teacher expectancies and student self-concept. *The Journal of Experimental Education, 79*, 452–477.

Council of Chief State School Officers. (2011). *InTASC model core teaching standards: A resource for state dialogue.* Retrieved from http://www.ccsso.org/documents/2011/ intasc_model_core_teaching_standards_2011.pdf

Darder, A. (1991). *Culture and power in the classroom: A critical foundation for bicultural education.* Westport, CT: Bergin & Garvey.

Darder, A. (2012). *Culture and power in the classroom: A critical foundation for the education of bicultural students.* Boulder, CO: Paradigm Press.

DeGarmo, D. S., & Martinez, C. R. (2006). A culturally informed model of academic well-being for Latino youth: The importance of discriminatory experiences and social support. *Family Relations, 55*, 267–278.

Dewey, J. (1916). *Democracy and education.* New York: The Macmillan Company.

Dunkin, M. J., & Biddle, B. J. (1974). *The study of teaching.* New York: Holt, Rinehart & Winston.

Eccles, J. (2009). Who am I and what am I going to do with my life? Personal and collective identities as motivators of action. *Educational Psychologist, 44*, 78–89.

Eccles (Parsons), J., Adler, T. F., Futterman, R., Goff, S. B., Kaczala, C. M., Meece, J. L., & Midgley, C. (1983). Expectancies, values, and academic behaviors. In J.T. Spence (Ed.), *Achievement and achievement motivation* (pp. 75–146). San Francisco, CA: W. H. Freeman.

Erickson, F., & Mohatt, G. (1982). Cultural organization and participation structures in two classrooms of Indian students. In G. Spindler (Ed.), *Doing the ethnography of schooling* (pp. 131–174). New York: Holt, Rinehart & Winston.

Gay, G. (2000, 2010). *Culturally responsive teaching: Theory, research, and practice.* New York: Teachers College Press.

Golann, J. (2015). The paradox of success at a no-excuses school. *Sociology of Education, 88,* 103–119.

Goldenberg, C., Rueda, R. S., & August, D. (2008). Sociocultural contexts and literacy development. In D. August & T. Shanahan (Eds.), *Developing reading and writing in second language learners: Lessons from the report of the national literacy panel on language minority children and youth* (pp. 95–130). Washington, DC: Center for Applied Linguistics and Newark, DE: International Reading Association.

González, N. (2001). *I am my language: Discourses of women and children in the borderlands.* Tucson, AZ: University of Arizona Press.

González, N., Moll, L., & Amanti, C. (2005). *Funds of knowledge: Theorizing practices in households, communities, and classrooms.* Mahwah, NJ: Lawrence Erlbaum Associates.

Good, T. (2014). What do we know about how teachers influence student performance on standardized tests: And why do we know so little about other student outcomes? *Teachers College Record, 116,* 1–23.

Good, T. L., & Nichols, S. L. (2001). Expectancy effects in the classroom: A special focus on improving the reading performance of minority students in first-grade classrooms. *Educational Psychologist, 36*(2), 113–126.

Harris, M. J., Rosenthal, R., & Snodgrass, S. E. (1986). The effects of teacher expectations, gender, and behavior on pupil academic performance and self-concept. *The Journal of Educational Research, 79*(3), 173–179.

Hollins, E., & Torres-Guzman, M. E. (2005). Research on preparing teachers for diverse populations. In M. Cochran-Smith & K. Zeichner (Eds.), *Studying teacher education: The report of the AERA panel on research and teacher education* (pp. 477–548). Mahwah, NJ: Lawrence Erlbaum Associates.

Irizarry, J. G. (2007). Ethnic and urban intersections in the classroom: Latino students, hybrid identities, and culturally responsive pedagogy. *Multicultural Perspectives, 9,* 21–28.

Jiménez-Castellanos, O., Combs, M. C., Martínez, D., & Gómez, L. (2013). *English language learners: What's at stake for Arizona?* Latino Public Policy Center, Morrison Institute for Public Policy, Arizona Indicators, Arizona State University. Retrieved from http:// arizonaindicators.org/sites/default/files/content/publications/ELL_stake.pdf

Jussim, L., Eccles, J., & Madon, S. (1996). Social perception, social stereotypes, and teacher expectations: Accuracy and the quest for the powerful self-fulfilling prophecy. *Advances in Experimental Social Psychology, 28,* 281–388.

Jussim, L., & Harber, K. D. (2005). Teacher expectations and self-fulfilling prophecies: Knowns and unknowns, resolved and unresolved controversies. *Personality and Social Psychology Review, 9,* 131–155.

Kantor, H. (1991). Education, social reform, and the state: ESEA and federal education policy in the 1960s. *American Journal of Education, 100,* 47–83.

Ladson-Billings, G. (1994). *The dreamkeepers.* San Francisco, CA: Jossey-Bass.

Ladson-Billings, G. (1995a). Toward a theory of culturally relevant pedagogy. *American Educational Research Journal, 47,* 465–491.

150 Francesca López

Ladson-Billings, G. (1995b). But that's just good teaching! The case for culturally relevant pedagogy. *Theory into Practice, 34*, 159–165.

Ladson-Billings, G. J. (1999). Preparing teachers for diverse student populations: A critical race theory perspective. *Review of Research in Education, 24*, 211–247.

Ladson-Billings, G. (2004). New directions in multicultural education. *Handbook of Research on Multicultural Education, 2*, 50–65.

Lee, C. D. (1993). *Signifying as a scaffold for literary interpretation: The pedagogical implications of an African American discourse genre (Research report series)*. Urbana, IL: National Council of Teachers of English.

Lee, C. D. (1995). A culturally based cognitive apprenticeship: Teaching African American high school students' skills in literary interpretation. *Reading Research Quarterly, 30*, 608–631.

Lee, C. D. (2007). *Culture, literacy, and learning: Taking bloom in the midst of the whirlwind*. New York: Teachers College Press.

López, F. (2011). The nongeneralizability of classroom dynamics as predictors of achievement for Hispanic students in upper elementary grades. *Hispanic Journal of Behavioral Sciences, 33*, 350–376.

López, F. (2012). Moderators of language acquisition models and reading achievement for English language learners: The role of emotional warmth and instructional support. *Teachers College Record, 114*(8), 1–30.

López, F. (2016). Teacher reports of culturally responsive teaching and Latino students' reading achievement in Arizona. *Teachers College Record, 118*(5), http://tcrecord.org, ID Number: 19369

Marsh, H. W., & Shavelson, R. (1985). Self-concept: Its multifaceted, hierarchical structure. *Educational Psychologist, 20*, 107–123.

McCarty, T. L., & Lee, T. S. (2014). Critical culturally sustaining/revitalizing pedagogy and Indigenous education sovereignty. *Harvard Educational Review, 84*, 101–124.

McCaslin, M. (2009). Co-regulation of student motivation and emergent identity. *Educational Psychologist, 44*, 137–146.

McKown, C. (2013). Social equity theory and racial-ethnic achievement gaps. *Child Development, 84*, 1120–1136.

McKown, C., & Weinstein, R. S. (2003). The development and consequences of stereotype consciousness in middle childhood. *Child Development, 74*, 498–515.

Merton, R. K. (1948). The self-fulfilling prophecy. *The Antioch Review, 8*, 193–210.

Moll, L. (1992). Bilingual classroom studies and community analysis: Some recent trends. *Educational Researcher, 21*, 20–24.

Moll, L. C., & González, N. (2004). Engaging life: A funds of knowledge approach to multicultural education. *Handbook of Research on Multicultural Education, 2*, 699–715.

Morrison, K. A., Robbins, H. H., & Rose, D. G. (2008). Operationalizing culturally relevant pedagogy: A synthesis of classroom-based research. *Equity & Excellence in Education, 41*, 433–452.

Muijis, D., & Reynolds, D. (2002). Teachers' beliefs and behaviors: What really matters?. *The Journal of Classroom Interaction, 2*, 3–15.

NCES. (2013). *Public school graduates and dropouts from the common core of data: School year 2009–2010*. U.S. Department of Education, NCES 2013–309rev. Retrieved from http://nces.ed.gov/pubs2013/2013309rev.pdf

Oyserman, D., Kemmelmeier, M., Fryberg, S., Brosh, H., & Hart-Johnson, T. (2003). Racial-ethnic self-schemas. *Social Psychology Quarterly, 66*, 333–347.

Pajares, M. F. (1992). Teachers' beliefs and educational research: Cleaning up a messy construct. *Review of Educational Research, 62*, 307–332.

Paris, D. (2012). Culturally sustaining pedagogy: A needed change in stance, terminology, and practice. *Educational Researcher, 41*, 93–97.

Phinney, J. (1992). The multigroup ethnic identity measure: A new scale for use with adolescents and young adults from diverse groups. *Journal of Adolescent Research, 7*, 156–176.

Pohan, C. A., & Aguilar, T. E. (2001). Measuring educators' beliefs about diversity in personal and professional contexts. *American Educational Research Journal, 38*, 159–182.

Rosenthal, R. (1994). Interpersonal expectancy effects: A 30-year perspective. *Current Directions in Psychological Science, 3*, 176–179.

Rosenthal, R., & Jacobson, L. (1968). Pygmalion in the classroom. *The Urban Review, 3*, 16–20.

Rubie-Davies, C. M. (2006). Teacher expectations and student self-perceptions: Exploring relationships. *Psychology in the Schools, 43*(5), 537–552.

Schunk, D. H, & Pajares, F. (2005). Competence perceptions and academic functioning. In A. J. Elliot & C. S. Dweck (Eds.), *Handbook of competence and motivation* (pp. 85–104). New York: Guilford Press.

Simbula, S. (2010). Daily fluctuations in teachers' well-being: A diary study using the Job Demands–Resources model. *Anxiety, Stress, & Coping, 23*, 563–584.

Sleeter, C. E. (2012). Confronting the marginalization of culturally responsive pedagogy. *Urban Education, 47*, 562–584.

Tenenbaum, H. R., & Ruck, M. D. (2007). Are teachers' expectations different for racial minority than for European American students? A meta-analysis. *Journal of Educational Psychology, 99*, 253–273.

Umaña-Taylor, A. J., Wong, J. J., Gonzales, N. A., & Dumka, L. E. (2012). Ethnic identity and gender as moderators of the association between discrimination and academic adjustment among Mexican-origin adolescents. *Journal of Adolescence, 35*(4), 773–786.

U.S. Department of Education. (2012). *Ed Data Express: Data about elementary and secondary schools in the US.* Retrieved from http://eddataexpress.ed.gov/

Villegas, A. M., & Lucas, T. (2002). Preparing culturally responsive teachers: Rethinking the curriculum. *Journal of Teacher Education, 53*, 20–32.

Weinstein, R., Marshall, H., Sharp, L., & Botkin, M. (1987). Pygmalion and the student: Age and classroom differences in children's awareness of teacher expectations. *Child Development, 58*, 1079–1093.

10

ROLE OF CULTURE AND PROXIMAL MINORITY/MAJORITY STATUS IN ADOLESCENT IDENTITY NEGOTIATIONS

Revathy Kumar, Stuart A. Karabenick, and Jeffery H. Warnke

Culturally diverse public schools function as contact zones in which minority and immigrant adolescents resolve differences between the cultural values and valued behaviors of their home community and the culture they confront at school (Kumar, 2006; Sarroub, 2010). The potential remediating function of such contact zones is especially important when cultural differences are exacerbated by racism, discrimination, and violence directed toward their home community (Haddad, 2011), often as a consequence of social, historical, and political events. This chapter draws on studies of adolescents of Arab descent (ArD)[1] and Chaldeans[2] attending neighborhood schools in ethnic and nonethnic enclaves. We discuss the role of proximal cultural and interpersonal contexts of schools, peers, and neighborhoods and the broader historical and socio-cultural context that influence adolescents' daily phenomenological experiences, their identity negotiations, behavioral motivations, and school adjustment. By integrating research conducted in culturally and economically diverse middle schools in two school districts with a high percentage of students from Middle Eastern nations, we demonstrate that addressing issues related to the study of the social and academic well-being of culturally diverse students requires an interdisciplinary approach that draws on different theoretical perspectives and utilizes multiple research methodologies.

We begin by providing a brief review of the theoretical perspectives that frame the research then describe the Arab and Chaldean populations in two districts represented by the participating adolescents from these communities, followed by a description of the neighborhoods in which they live and the schools they attend. Next we discuss research findings that demonstrate the contextually situated interpretations of culture and social identity and its impact on adolescents' self-perceptions, academic and social motivations, and psychological well-being. We conclude with a brief discussion of implications for school policies and teacher practices.

Theoretical Perspectives for the Study of Cultural Diversity in Schools

We draw on social identity theory (Tajfel & Turner, 1986), identity-focused ecological theories (Bronfenbrenner, 1979; Beale-Spencer, 1999), and intergroup contact theory (Allport, 1954; Pettigrew, 1998) to understand how adolescents' identity negotiations are informed by their experiences in school. We utilize achievement goal theory to capture characteristics of learning environments that can ameliorate or exacerbate feelings of home/school dissonance and school belonging and influence students' motivation to learn (Kumar, 2006; Maehr & Zusho, 2009).

Social Identity Theory

The term *social identity*, as defined by Tajfel (1981), refers to "that part of the individual's self-concept which derives from his knowledge of his membership to the social group (or groups) together with the value and emotional significance attached to that group membership" (p. 255). This theory proposes that individuals strive for positive social identity via both social categorization and comparisons between in- and out-group members (Hogg, 2003). Social identity is multifaceted, with the salience of any particular facet or facets dependent on social contexts and everyday life experiences. It is tied to the meaning individuals associate with various group identities such as their nationality, religion, and gender and by institutionalized definitions associated with those identities (Lamont & Molnar, 2002). Social identity may contribute to a sense of belonging among adolescents in a dominant cultural group, whereas by contrast, the social identity of those from immigrant and minority communities who are held in low regard by the dominant culture may contribute to fears of isolation and alienation. This is particularly true when social identity in the school context is highly salient (Ethier & Deaux, 1994) and boundaries between a minority social group and dominant out-groups are perceived as impermeable and stable (Bettencourt, Dorr, Charlton, & Hume, 2001).

Group Threat Theory

When members of the mainstream group perceive an increase in the subordinate group's size threatening their own group's dominant status in society, their negative attitudes toward and reactions to the members of the subordinate group increase (Hjerm, 2007). According to Hjerm (2007), the size and visibility of the subordinate group and perceptions of impermeable and rigid boundaries between groups contributes to dominant group members' feeling threatened.

Phenomenological Variant of the Ecological Systems Theory (PVEST)

Central to research about cultural minority adolescents are considerations of macro-level historical, economic, and political realities in conjunction with their day-to-day experiences within the community and school contexts in molding their social identity. PVEST theory (Beale-Spencer, 1999), an extension of Bronfenbrenner's (1979) ecological systems model, integrates considerations of macro- and micro-level developmental contexts, with due regard to the individual's developmental needs. It enables highlighting the phenomenological contextualization of adolescents' identity negotiation and development while emphasizing the bidirectional relationship between the individual and the environment. The nature of adolescents' identity negotiations lays the adverse or productive foundations for their educational and vocational aspirations.

Intergroup Contact Hypothesis

Research demonstrates that contact can ameliorate intergroup prejudice and promote inclusion if certain *prerequisite* conditions for intergroup interactions are met (Allport, 1954). As originally specified by Allport (1954), these conditions include equal status among groups in the contact situation, intergroup cooperation, pursuit of common goals, and a broader social climate that supports intergroup contact. Two other factors identified as crucial for effective intergroup contact include personal acquaintance between members (Amir, 1976) and the development of intergroup friendships (Pettigrew, 1998). Under these conditions, intergroup contact can reduce intergroup bias. Though the contact hypothesis outlines the prerequisites necessary for positive intergroup contact, it does not prescribe steps for transforming school cultures so that they meet these conditions.

Achievement Goal Theory

Research emerging from the achievement goal theory framework specifies conditions likely to create supportive learning environments, promote learning, and encourage cooperation and positive intergroup interactions. Specifically, Maehr and Midgley (1996) delineate how mastery-focused goals (an emphasis on learning and individual improvement) and performance-focused goals (an emphasis on ability and interpersonal comparisons) in classrooms and schools influence the extent to which students perceive learning environments as validating, empowering, and inclusive. Research indicates that mastery-focused classrooms and schools are associated with positive student outcomes, whereas less adaptive student outcomes are more likely in classrooms and schools that are more performance focused (Anderman & Maehr, 1994; Meece, Anderman, & Anderman, 2006).

Students who perceive that their learning environment emphasizes performance goals experience heightened self-consciousness and poor self-image (Eccles & Midgley, 1989). Evidence also indicates that performance-focused conditions can cause students to question their ability or the ability of their social group, thereby evoking schemas, or stereotypes, about the group (Steele, 1997) and, especially under performance-evaluative conditions, exacerbating feelings of disengagement and home–school cultural dissonance (Kumar, 2006). By contrast, a mastery-focused emphasis on the benefits of learning as a shared experience, in which other learners are considered important resources for assistance and information rather than competitors to be avoided (Karabenick & Newman, 2006), leads to more adaptive learning outcomes. Conditions such as equal status between groups and the absence of interpersonal competition tend to promote positive intergroup contact (Dixon, Durrheim, & Tredoux, 2005), which mastery-focused learning environments are designed to. Thus, mastery-focused academic environments have the potential to more closely approximate contact hypothesis prerequisites for promoting positive intergroup relationships among students from mainstream and minority cultural groups.

Summary

A variety of theoretical perspectives are relevant for understanding issues of culture and intergroup relations in diverse schools and communities. The value of these frameworks depends in part on their application in specific contexts with the intercultural conditions for which the theories are relevant. With that in mind, we describe the experiences of ethnically Middle Eastern students in culturally diverse schools and, where relevant, draw comparisons with their cultural/ethnic majority peers. We begin by describing these populations, then the neighborhood and school contexts that are the contact zones for adolescents in these groups.

Arab American and Chaldean Students in American Schools

Arabs are a heterogeneous group, with roots in different nations, religions, and subcultures, practices, and customs (Naber, 2000; Read, 2008). While Islam is the dominant religion, there are significant numbers of Arab Christians in Egypt, Lebanon, Syria, Palestine, Jordan, and Iraq. Arabs in America are identified, though seldom recognized, as White (Cainkar, 2008) and remain suspended "between zones of whiteness, otherness, and color" (Shryock, 2008, p. 112). Arab Americans were a relatively invisible group within the United States (Naber, 2000) until the 9/11 terrorist attacks catapulted them to "hyper-visibility," creating a racialized Arab/Middle Eastern/Muslim social category (Sirin & Fine, 2008) and further conflating the concepts *Arab* and *Muslim* (Naber, 2008). This hypervisibility has raised awareness among Arab immigrants and American-born Arabs of their "Arabness" and has contributed to an emerging pan-Arab identity (Shaheen, 2001).

Chaldean Christians in the United States emigrated from villages in Kurdish-controlled Northern Iraq (USCIS, 2000) in the wake of international sanctions against Iraq in early 1990 and the recent U.S.–Iraq war that followed 9/11. Though they are Christians and attempt to distance themselves from Muslim immigrants, Chaldean Americans and Arab/Muslim Americans are linked together in the public mind. Over the past decade many Chaldean Christian immigrants around Detroit have moved into areas where the ethnic composition is predominantly White and of Polish descent. As discussed below, these changes in neighborhood demographics have had a disquieting effect on established residents.

Neighborhood Characteristics and the School Context

Twelve middle-schools[3] in two economically diverse southeastern Michigan districts (k = 7 in D1 and k = 5 in D2) at high risk for intercultural conflict participated in the project. The seven schools in D1 are characterized by a long-established Arab ethnic enclave in a portion of the city. The immigration patterns in this ethnic enclave mirror the larger trends for Arab Americans in the United States, with a significant and continuously established Lebanese American population that has been a historical fixture of the community for a significant period. Loudon, Stanton, Underwood, and Worley, the ethnic enclave schools, have an Arab/Arab American majority enrollment, whereas schools located outside the ethnic enclave include Bruner, Jones, and Porter and have majority White, non-Arab/Arab American enrollment. The contiguous non–ethnic enclave neighborhoods have significantly higher median household incomes and lower rates of poverty.

District 2 has an open enrollment policy, and school populations do not necessarily pull from the neighborhoods in the schools' proximity. Also, the ethnic enclave is a newer phenomenon as migration patterns continue to shift the local demographics. D2 is constructed from two cities (North and South); South was historically a Polish American enclave. During the first U.S. war in Iraq, migration by Chaldeans to this area of the metropolis emerged. The second war in Iraq commenced another wave of immigration by Chaldeans to this area. Bowson and Cutler were situated in the most diverse neighborhoods in terms of racial composition, which was reflected in the school enrollment figures in which Bowson had the most African American students (13%). Lowell and Suder had majority Chaldean student enrollment with a significant White/European American minority.

Research Methodologies for the Study of Arab American and Chaldean Adolescents' Identity Negotiation and School Experiences

Complementary research methodologies were required to capture the complex and often complicated macro-level realities and micro-level interactions that mold the multifaceted and often fluid identities of ArD and Chaldean adolescents and their everyday experiences in school. The following section draws on the research findings obtained from focus group interviews with ArD, Chaldean, and White adolescents to understand their identity concerns, experiences of cultural dissonance and sense of belonging in various contexts, educational aspirations, and academic expectations. Next, we discuss the results of a quantitative study of teacher beliefs and instructional practices from survey and Implicit Association Test (IAT) data obtained from teachers in the same participating schools. Finally, we synthesize the results of these studies, obtained from different sources and using different research methodologies, to discuss the policy and practice implications.

Focus Group Interviews

Focus groups provided opportunities to observe and investigate peer interactions, as their spontaneous discussion about sensitive issues helped uncover the experiences of these understudied groups. This approach allowed us to understand, at a relatively detailed level, the reasons for their experiences of inclusion and/or exclusion in their schools and peer contexts, academic aspirations, cultural beliefs and values, and ultimately how these experiences, emotions, and values informed their identity negotiations and interpretations of their multifaceted social identity.

Sample Selection and Interview Process

Participants were systematically selected based on a random sampling of eighth-grade students stratified by ethnicity, gender, and primary language spoken at home as indicated in school records. Those within each group were of the same ethnic background and further stratified by gender, except in cases where gender stratification was not a viable option. Ethnic groups consisted of African American, White, and Asian. Further stratification of Whites by language spoken at home (English, Arabic, Chaldean, Albanian, etc.) helped distinguish the Chaldean and Arabic students from European American White students. The next layer of stratification was by students' primary language and number of years in the United States. This layer enabled us to identify recent immigrant students within the ArD and Chaldean groups, as evidence indicates that over time immigrant children (including first, second, and third generation) to the United States prefer to speak English over their native language. Final stratification by gender ensured that both males and females within each group were given equal voice. On average,

10 students were then randomly selected from each subgroup to participate. Within each school, the number of focus group sessions and whether the groups were stratified by gender depended on the number of students who received parental permission for participation. In all, we conducted 62 focus group interviews across the 12 schools. Focus group size ranged from four to eight, in accordance with Morgan's (1996) suggestion that groups averaging five to seven participants are optimal for high-level involvement and interaction. Research assistants who underwent an intensive 4-month training period conducted the focus group interviews.

Adolescents' Identity Negotiations and Schooling

In this section, we highlight the salient results emerging from three studies (Kumar, Seay, & Karabenick, 2011, 2014; Kumar, Warnke, & Karabenick, 2014) and provide illustrative examples from focus group interviews with Chaldean adolescents. In general, the findings demonstrate that personal vulnerabilities and strengths combine in complex ways with proximal and distal environmental adversities and affordances to shape the nature and quality of adolescents' adjustment, mental health, academic motivation, and achievement and, ultimately, their personal and social identities.

The Sliding Identity and the Complexity of Cultural Considerations: National, Religious, Gender, and American Identity

Regardless of how long they have lived in the United States or their citizenship status, ArD and Chaldean adolescents must contend with the identity the dominant society assigns them. Chaldeans are not Arabs yet are frequently labeled as such. For the Chaldean participants, being labeled Arab was a major source of dissonance and concern, as demonstrated in the following exchange among Chaldean females in Lowell (D2):

SARA: There's like some kids, like the White kids are so like racist against Chaldeans.
SANA: Yea they hate Chaldeans.
SANA: He's like "I hate you, you stupid Arab." And I get offended when I'm [called] an Arab cause I'm not an Arab.
SARA: I know, we're not Arabic we're Chaldean.
ZAINAB: Me either. They don't like if they like [think] like you look Chaldean or whatever like Arabic they're like "oh that's an Arab." It's like "I'm not Arab."

Chaldean participants also frequently made it a point to state that they were Christians and not Muslims.

Minority Status in Identity Negotiations **159**

The need to reject the pan-Arab label was also evident among ArD participants (Kumar et al., 2014). Even within the focus group interview context, some ArD adolescents rejected the pan-Arab identity to assume a more integrated Arab American identity. Other male ArD adolescents adopted a more separatist Arab or national (e.g., Lebanese, Yemeni, Iraqi) identity or attempted to assume an American identity. Exchanges among focus group participants at Bruner, where intergroup and intercultural contact is common, individuals' self-identification spanned the continuum of assimilation, ranging from desire to assimilate as an American to a strong Arab identity that eschewed American status.

OMAR: No. Well we're Arab American.
WASIM: I mean we're all Americans.
AHMAD: No. I'm not . . . don't even put American next to my name . . . it makes me 100 percent Arab.

For both ArD and Chaldean adolescents, self-perceptions were moderated by social interactions (e.g., school personnel and peers) and symbolic and sometimes explicit messages sent by such social structures as the school (e.g., school policies/ practices). ArD male and female adolescents demonstrated a context-dependent sliding identity along the national (Yemini, Lebanese, Iraqi) and religious (Suni, Shia, Christian) Arab–Arab American–American continuum (Deaux, 2006). ArD males also demonstrated that gender relationships manifested themselves at the intersection of social categories of nationality, ethnicity, and religion. Across several interviews, and in line with other research with individuals of Arab origin (Haddad, 2004), ArD males talked about cultural norms and religious teachings that delineate values and behaviors associated with gender-appropriate roles. Haddad (2011) argues that in the post–9/11 world, issues of gender and race are commingled with discussions of inter- and intra-religious pluralism among Muslim intellectuals. Analyses of the interviews indicate that concerns regarding the melding of masculine identity within the framework of religious and cultural values are as much a concern for ArD male adolescents as they are for adults. ArD male identity is also shaped by the prevailing perceptions in the United States of Arab males as aggressive and Arab females as submissive. However, as revealed in these interactions, recorded during interviews at Bruner, Louden, and Porter respectively, despite shared influences and experiences, there is variability among the ArD male adolescents' interpretations of religion, nationality, and male–female counterroles and the importance and salience of these factors in shaping their masculine identity.

Bruner:

OMAR: Yea, he's a Sunni.
AHMAD: You're Sunni?

160 Revathy Kumar et al.

WASIM: I don't, I don't find that a difference between people. I don't . . . It doesn't matter if you are Sunni or Shia.
AHMAD: Yea it does.
SARA: No it doesn't.

Porter:

HADDAD: It doesn't matter. It don't make a difference *(annoyed)*.
KHALID: Yea it does.
HADDAD: No it doesn't. Muslims are Muslims.
TAREQ: No it doesn't.
KHALID: Political it does.
HADDAD: Okay to you it does, to us it don't. You can't say that *(annoyed)*.
TAREQ: We're all brothers and sisters.

Louden:

AHMAD: Girls are treated with like respect. Like we don't lay our hand on a girl, nobody will, but . . . I feel like girls need more respect than guys because they have, they like take things harder. If we say something to them it will stick with them. It won't fall out as easy . . .
OMAR: Like some people would like do the completely opposite of that . . . They wouldn't respect a girl like that, we would.

As seen from the exchanges above, forging a coherent sense of self that encompasses multiple social identities can be particularly challenging for ArD and Chaldean adolescents who live in cultural contact zones polarized by religion, nationality, gender, and political and cultural ideologies. Unlike adolescents from other groups, ArD and Chaldean adolescents appear acutely aware of the current political tensions between the United States and countries in the Middle East and the consequent racism, discrimination, and violence that are directed toward their community. This was apparent even as they negotiated their daily lives, resolving differences in cultural values among their home, school, and peer contexts (Kumar, 2006). These macro-level realities and micro-level interactions shaped and molded the multifaceted identities of ArD and Chaldean adolescents.

Schooling in Ethnic Versus Nonethnic Enclaves

Many immigrant cultural minorities gravitate to ethnic enclaves in their host country because it provides some measure of familiarity and comfort in an otherwise alien and strange land. Analysis of focus group interviews highlighted the relative advantages and disadvantages for ArD adolescents of resettlement in ethnic enclaves upon immigrating to the United States. New immigrant participants

(3 years or less in the United States) in ethnic enclave schools (Stanton, Loudon, Worley, and Underwood) expressed comfort and a strong sense of belonging to the school and the Muslim, Arab American community. Their daily lives were not marred by constant exposure to discrimination or prejudice. Ethnic enclave neighborhood and school contexts provided immigrant ArD adolescents such transitional affordances as familiar values, language, dress, and opportunity to develop friendships with other young people with similar experiences. The enthusiasm and excitement we encountered particularly among new immigrant ArD participants in Loudon school attests to the protective and stabilizing effect of living in an ethnic enclave and attending a school that positively acknowledges students' cultural background. These findings mirror the experiences of other cultural minority immigrant groups residing in ethnic enclaves (Suarez-Orozco & Suarez-Orozco, 2002).

That social identity is a function of the structural, social, cultural, historical, and phenomenological contexts of development, in particular the school demographic context was also evident in our study with ArD male adolescents, where we compared the experiences of ArD males who attended schools in ethnic versus non–ethnic enclave schools. ArD adolescent males' experiences, their coping strategies, and the development of varied identities—as some combination of national, religious, Arab, and American—appeared to be a function of their proximal context, specifically of their school. Thus focus group discussions with ArD adolescents in the four ethnic enclave schools in D1 had a different character than did discussions with ArD adolescents in schools composed of predominantly European American adolescents. In ethnic enclave schools, ArD male participants felt safe despite their minority status in the broader community. They neither reported experiencing cultural dissonance (Arunkumar [Kumar], Midgley, & Urdan, 1999) nor felt a heightened group consciousness. In contrast, ArD males in non–ethnic enclave schools experienced a heightened level of consciousness regarding their "Arabness," engaged in denial and reactive coping when faced with discrimination, and were more likely to make a deliberate effort to assimilate into an unhyphenated American identity.

Status Hierarchy in Ethnic Enclave Schools

Analysis of interviews also revealed findings unique to ArD adolescents and demonstrated the heterogeneity among ArD adolescents based on their heritage national identities that mirror the religious and national divisions that exist in the Arab world. The different groups within the enclave often have their own distinctive community organizations. As other studies have also demonstrated (Haddad, 2011), rather than their Arabness, it is the national and ancestral identity as Lebanese, Iraqi, or Yemini that may take precedence. This, we found, was a source of contention due to the hierarchical power differences that exist among Arab immigrants based on country of origin and socioeconomic status (Suleiman, 1999).

162 Revathy Kumar et al.

In Loudon (D1), for example, a Lebanese participant described the Yemini students as "smelly." Girls in Underwood reported that boys self-segregated along national lines and bullied out-group members:

> Yeah, the boys are, you know ... He's Iraqi, we don't talk to ... he's ... the Iraqis don't talk to the Lebanese, the Lebanese don't talk to Iraqis, the Yemenis don't talk to Lebanese.

There was a clearly established status hierarchy within the ethnic enclave community with Lebanese at the top of the totem pole, Yeminis at the bottom, and Iraqis in between. These findings lend support to our assertion that the enactment of culture is contextually grounded. Ethnic enclaves have the potential to function either as a risk or a protective factor in influencing ArD adolescents' adjustment and well-being.

School Cultural Responsiveness

Analyses of the interviews revealed that ethnic enclave schools were often better positioned to meet the needs of ArD students than were non–ethnic enclave schools. Such was the case in Stanton, where a predominant Yemeni presence provided a measure of security for the new Yemeni immigrants. As one female participant in Stanton noted, "we're all Yemenis," and another responded, "Yemenis rock." Thus, the consonance between their heritage culture and immigrant community in the United States created a haven for immigrant ArD adolescents in their transition from home to host country. Furthermore, principals, faculty, and staff in ethnic enclave schools demonstrated sensitivity to the cultural needs of their student body. This was particularly true of Loudon and Stanton in D1 that had the highest percentage of ArD students. Across all four ethnic enclave schools in D1, as noted by immigrant ArD participants and confirmed by school staff, communication with parents was conducted in Arabic if necessary.

However, interviews with ArD and Chaldean adolescents in ethnic enclave schools revealed that attending an ethnic enclave school did not guarantee that all teachers were culturally sensitive to students' needs. Feelings of marginalization that accompanied perceptions of some teachers' cultural insensitivity, their prejudices and discrimination against people of ArD and Chaldean descent, and the lack of curricular cultural visibility were evident in adolescents' conversations in both ethnic and non–ethnic enclave schools.

Societal Dominant/Subordinate Status and School Numerical Majority/Minority Status

Research attempting to address issues of intergroup relationships and prejudice focuses almost exclusively on the adjustment and adaptation of minority and immigrant youth. Less recognized, however, is the effect on mainstream White adolescents' cognitive and affective responses to the changed social contexts and their intergroup behaviors within these contexts. Our analysis of 10 focus group interviews conducted with White adolescents across the five schools in D2 (Kumar & Maehr, 2010) revealed relationships between White majority/minority status in school and the saliency and centrality of White identity, awareness of their disadvantaged position in school, feelings of exclusion and dissonance, exhibition of in-group favoritism, and out-group bias. In contrast to White majority schools—those in the White ethnic enclaves where "Whiteness" was invisible and taken for granted—White identity was foregrounded in schools where Whites were in the minority. In these schools, White students displayed many of the characteristics commonly manifested by other minorities, demonstrating that status in society interacts with group numbers within the proximal context to shape prejudice and discriminative behavior (Sachdev & Bourhis, 1991). White students in these schools felt socially excluded, that they did not belong, perceived that friendships depended on ethnicity and race, and reported incidents of verbal and physical abuse. For instance, they reported that Chaldeans called them names such as "white trash." Even in Bowson, where Whites were a majority with a significant Chaldean minority, Whites were very aware of group stratification. In Lowell, Suders, and Bowson, White adolescents perceived their Chaldean counterparts as a potentially threatening minority group and feared angering or getting into a fight with them because "Chaldeans are like a swarm of bees." Actual and subjective minority status among White adolescents also spawned concerns about friendships and differential treatment by teachers perceived as favoring Chaldeans.

In contrast, White participants in White-majority schools such as James, spent their days surrounded by White peers, with their privilege intact and no alternative ethnicity to provide a cultural contrast. They did not report experiencing negative intergroup interactions. Instead, they described school as fun and cool, with harmony and permeability among home, school, and community (Kumar, 2006). Similar to majority population group members in general, incidents of disharmony and disunity were attributed to minority-group students (e.g., African Americans).

By and large, White middle school adolescents were not aware of the distinction between Arabs and Chaldeans. White adolescents' stereotyping of Chaldeans as aggressive, loud, undisciplined students who frequently get suspended may, in part, be attributed to the commonly held societal stereotype of the "violent Arab." In Lowell and Bowson, White adolescents' comments and responses also suggest that their negative reactions were sometimes due to the greater perceived affluence of some Chaldean students relative to White students.

Numerical minority status, whether actual or subjective, created an emotionally charged White ethnic identity closely tied to beliefs about American patriotism. Defined in opposition to Chaldean identity, this White ethnic identity included differential valuing of in- and out-group characteristics (Hogg, 2003), with dispositional attributions linked to negative out-group characteristics (e.g., Pettigrew, 1998). When compounded with stereotypes and prejudicial attitudes, perceived threat created xenophobic responses by White students who were either a minority or even a slight majority.

Teachers' Beliefs and Attitudes and the Learning Environment

School demographics, school policies, and teacher practices in and out of the classroom were critical in shaping cultural minority (ArD and Chaldean) and mainstream White adolescents' experiences in school. Evidence regarding the existence of possible teacher influences emerged from our study of White teachers ($n = 241$; 72% female) who participated in the project (Kumar, Karabenick, & Burgoon, 2015). Teachers responded to both a web-based survey and the IAT that examined their implicit attitudes toward White relative to ArD/Chaldean and African American students. Based on the analysis of the IAT data (Greenwald, Nosek, & Banaji, 2003), teachers held more implicitly positive attitudes toward White over ArD and Chaldean students. Further, teachers who held more implicitly favorable attitudes toward White relative to ArD and Chaldean adolescents were less likely to promote mutual respect among students and were consequently less responsible for engaging in culturally adaptive practices and for resolving intergroup conflict among students. Ultimately, these teachers were less likely to engage in mastery-focused instructional practices. Interestingly, explicit negative belief regarding minority and poor students was directly related to endorsing performance-focused instructional practices.

Conclusion

Evidence from ArD and Chaldean adolescents revealed the process of constructing and deconstructing their social identities—asking such fundamental questions as "Who am I?" and "Where do I belong?" Some that we interviewed felt overburdened by social pressures, and the specter of alienation loomed large as they faced discrimination and rejection not only from mainstream peers but also from more well-established immigrant adolescents. ArD males in particular had to cope with being stereotyped as violent and aggressive. Chaldean adolescents felt invisible, their roots unrecognized, and labeled in ways that did not mesh with their self-defined and authentic social identity. Interestingly, even mainstream White students felt overwhelmed by their White identity in schools where they were a numerical minority.

Analyses of interviews with new and established ArD and Chaldean immigrant adolescents juxtaposed with analysis of interviews with White adolescents demonstrate that adolescents' social identity and adjustment is molded, as the PVEST model (Beale-Spencer, 1999) suggests, by the confluence of macro-level historical, economic, and political realities with their day-to-day experiences within the

Minority Status in Identity Negotiations **165**

community, school, and classroom contexts. These findings highlight the need for taking into consideration the proximal, distal, and psychological contexts in studies of potentially marginalized minority groups. General demographic conditions notwithstanding, the proximal conditions in the contact zones that students encounter daily play a major role in their identity negotiations and general well-being.

Optimal conditions for positive intergroup relationships (e.g., ensuring equal status among groups in school, creating shared common goals, and providing supportive institutional authority) were often unmet in the school context. The evidence reinforces how schools can be a positive force in minority and immigrant adolescents. However, such positive influences can be stymied when teachers' biases—conscious and unconscious—inhibit establishing mastery-focused learning environments in which positive intergroup relationships can flourish and in which all students are engaged in the learning process (Kumar et al., 2015). Therefore, it is critically important for the education and well-being of all students "to make schools into better communities of caring and support for young people" (Hargreaves, Earl, & Ryan, 1996, p. 77).

Notes

1 The term *Arab descent* refers to established and new immigrants to North America from Arabic-speaking countries of the Middle East and their descendants. The Arabic-speaking countries include among others Algeria, Bahrain, Egypt, Iraq, Jordan, Kuwait, Lebanon, Libya, Mauritania, Morocco, Oman, the Palestinians, Qatar, Saudi Arabia, Sudan, Syria, Tunisia, United Arab Emirates, and Yemen (http://www.unesco.org/new/en/unesco/worldwide/arab-states/).
2 Chaldean are Christians from villages in Kurdish-controlled northern Iraq (USCIS, 2000).
3 Pseudonyms for schools in District 1: Bruner, Jones, Porter, Loudon, Stanton, Underwood, Worley. Pseudonyms for schools in District 2: Bowson, Cutler, James, Lowell, Suders.

References

Allport, G. W. (1954). *The nature of prejudice*. Reading, MA: Addison-Wesley.

Amir, Y. (1976). The role of intergroup contact in change of prejudice and race relations. In P. A. Katz (Ed.), *Towards the elimination of racism* (pp. 245–280). New York: Pergamon.

Anderman, E. M., & Maehr, M. L. (1994). Motivation and schooling in the middle grades. *Review of Educational Research, 64*, 287–309.

Arunkumar [Kumar] R., Midgley, C., & Urdan, T. (1999). Perceiving high or low home-school dissonance: Longitudinal effects on adolescent emotional and academic well-being. *Journal of Research on Adolescence, 9*, 441–466.

Beale-Spencer, M. (1999). Social and cultural influences on school adjustment: The application of an identity-focused cultural ecological perspective. *Educational Psychologist, 34*, 43–57.

Bettencourt, B. A., Dorr, N., Charlton, K., & Hume, D. L. (2001). Status difference and in-group bias: A meta-analytic examination of the effects of status stability, status legitimacy, and group permeability. *Psychological Bulletin, 127*, 520–542.

Bronfenbrenner, U. (1979). *The ecology of human development: Experiments by nature and design.* Cambridge, MA: Harvard University Press.

Cainkar, L. (2008). Thinking outside the box: Arabs and race in the United States. In A. Jamal & N. Naber (Eds.), *Race and Arab Americans before and after 9/11: From invisible citizens to visible subjects* (pp. 46–80). Syracuse, NY: Syracuse University Press.

Deaux, K. (2006). *To be an immigrant.* New York: Russell Sage Foundation.

Dixon, J., Durrheim, K., & Tredoux, C. (2005). Beyond optimal contact strategy: A reality check for contact hypothesis. *American Psychologist, 60*(7), 697–711.

Eccles, J. S., & Midgley, C. (1989). Stage/environment fit: Developmentally appropriate classrooms for early adolescents. In R. E. Ames & C. Ames (Eds.), *Research on motivation in education* (pp. 139–181). New York: Academic Press.

Ethier, K.A., & Deaux, K. (1994). Negotiating social identity when contexts change. Maintaining identification and responding to threat. *Journal of Personality and Social Psychology, 67*(2), 243–251.

Greenwald, A. G., Nosek, B. A., & Banaji, M. R. (2003). Understanding and using the Implicit Association Test: I. An improved scoring algorithm. *Journal of Personality and Social Psychology, 85*(2), 197–216.

Haddad, Y.Y. (2004). *The shaping of Arab and Muslim identity in the United States.* Waco, TX: Baylor University Press.

Haddad, Y.Y. (2011). *Becoming American?: The forging of Arab and Muslim identity in pluralist America.* Waco, TX: Baylor University Press.

Hargreaves, A., Earl, L., & Ryan, J. (1996). *Schooling for change: Reinventing education for early adolescents.* New York, NY: Routledge Falmer.

Hjerm, M. (2007). Do numbers really count?: Group threat theory revisited. *Journal of Ethnic and Migration Studies, 33,* 1253–1275.

Hogg, M.A. (2003). Social identity. In M. R. Leary & J. P. Tangney (Eds.), *Handbook of self and identity* (pp. 462–479). New York: The Guilford Press.

Karabenick, S.A., & Newman, R. S. (Eds.). (2006). *Academic help seeking: Goals, groups, and contexts.* Mahwah, NJ: Lawrence Erlbaum Associates.

Kumar, R. (2006). Students' experiences of home-school dissonance: The role of school academic culture and perceptions of classroom goal structures. *Contemporary Educational Psychology, 31,* 253–279.

Kumar, R., Karabenick, S.A., & Burgoon, J. (2015). Teachers' implicit and explicit attitudes toward culturally diverse students and classroom instructional practices. *Journal of Educational Psychology.* Advance online publication. doi:http://dx.doi.org/10.1037/a0037471

Kumar, R., & Maehr, M. L. (2010). Schooling, cultural diversity and student motivation. In J. L. Meece & J. S. Eccles (Eds.), *Handbook of schools, schooling and human development* (pp. 308–323). New York: Routledge.

Kumar, R., Seay, N., & Karabenick, S. A. (2011). Shades of White: Identity status, stereotypes, prejudice, and xenophobia. *Educational Studies: A Journal of the American Educational Studies Association, 47*(4), 347–378.

Kumar, R., Seay, N., & Karabenick, S. A. (2014). Immigrant Arab adolescents in ethnic enclaves: Physical and phenomenological contexts of identity negotiation. *Cultural Diversity and Ethnic Minority Psychology.* Advance online publication. doi:http://dx.doi.org/10.1037/a0037748

Kumar, R., Warnke, J. H., & Karabenick, S.A. (2014): Arab-American male identity negotiations: Caught in the crossroads of ethnicity, religion, nationality and current contexts. *Social Identities: Journal for the Study of Race, Nation and Culture, 20,* 22–41. doi:10.1080/13504630.2013.864464

Lamont, M., & Molnar, V. (2002). The study of boundaries in the social science. *Annual Review of Sociology, 28*, 167–195.

Maehr, M. L., & Midgley, C. (1996). *Transforming school cultures*. Boulder, CO: Westview, Harper Collins.

Maehr, M. L., & Zusho, A. (2009). Achievement goal theory: The past, present, and future. In K. R. Wenzel & A. Wigfield (Eds.), *Handbook of motivation at school* (pp. 77–104). New York, NY: Routledge/Taylor & Francis Group.

Meece, J. L., Anderman, E. M., & Anderman, L. H. (2006). Classroom goal structure, student motivation, and academic achievement. *Annual Review of Psychology, 57*, 487–503.

Morgan, D. L. (1996). Focus groups. *Annual Review of Sociology, 22*, 129–152.

Naber, N. (2000). Ambiguous insiders: An investigation of Arab American invisibility. *Ethnic and Racial Studies, 23*, 37–61.

Naber, N. (2008). "Look, Mohammed the terrorist is coming!" Cultural racism, nation-based racism, and the intersectionality of oppressions after 9/11. In A. Jamal & N. Naber (Eds.), *Race and Arab Americans before and after 9/11: From invisible citizens to visible subjects* (pp. 276–304). Syracuse, NY: Syracuse University Press.

Pettigrew, T. F. (1998). Intergroup contact theory. *Annual Review of Psychology, 49*, 65–85.

Read, J. G. (2008). Discrimination and identity formation in post 9/11 era: A comparison of Muslim and Christian Arab Americans. In A. Jamal & N. Naber (Eds.), *Race and Arab Americans before and after 9/11: From invisible citizens to visible subjects* (pp. 305–317). Syracuse, NY: Syracuse University Press.

Sachdev, I., & Bourhis, R. Y. (1991). Power and status differentials in minority and majority group relations. *European Journal of Social Psychology, 21*, 1–24.

Sarroub, L. (2010). Discontinuities and differences among Muslim Arab-Americans. In M. L. Dantas & P. C. Manyak (Eds.), *Home-school connections in a multicultural society: Learning from and with culturally and linguistically diverse families* (pp. 76–93). New York: Routledge.

Shaheen, J. G. (2001). *Reel bad Arabs: How Hollywood vilifies people*. New York: Olive Branch Press.

Shryock, A. (2008). The moral analogies of race: Arab American identity, color politics, and the limits of racialized citizenship. In A. Jamal & N. Naber (Eds.), *Race and Arab Americans before and after 9/11: From invisible citizens to visible subjects* (pp. 81–113). Syracuse, NY: Syracuse University Press.

Sirin, S. R., & Fine, M. (2008). *Muslim American youth: Understanding hyphenated identities through multiple methods*. New York: New York University Press.

Steele, C. M. (1997). A threat in the air: How stereotypes shape intellectual identity and performance. *American Psychologist, 52*, 613–629.

Suarez-Orozco, C., & Suarez-Orozco, M. (2002). *Children of immigrants*. Cambridge, MA: Harvard University Press.

Suleiman, M. W. (1999). *Arabs in America: Building a new future*. Philadelphia, PA: Temple University Press.

Tajfel, H. (1981). *Human groups and social categories: Studies in social psychology*. Cambridge, UK: Cambridge University Press.

Tajfel, H., & Turner, J. (1986). The social identity theory of intergroup behavior. In S. Worchel & W. G. Austin (Eds.), *The psychology of intergroup relations* (pp. 7–24). Chicago: Nelson-Hall.

United States Citizenship and Immigration Services (USCIS). (2000). *Iraq: Chaldean Christians*, IRQ00001.ZLA. Retrieved March 13, 2010 from http://www.unhcr.org/refworld/docid/3dee0b564.html

11

MOTIVATION AND ACHIEVEMENT OF HISPANIC COLLEGE STUDENTS IN THE UNITED STATES

Tim Urdan and Veronica Herr

The history of the Hispanic[1] population in the United States is interesting and complex. This population is composed of people from many different countries (e.g., Mexico, Cuba, Puerto Rico, Dominican Republic, Guatemala, El Salvador, Honduras, etc.), and these countries differ in their histories, traditions, values, and relationship with the United States. In addition, the Hispanic population in the United States includes immigrants who have arrived in the United States this year, families whose roots in the United States date back to before the establishment of the country, and everything in between. It includes families who speak almost no English and families who have spoken only English for generations. The Hispanic population in the United States includes individuals who identify themselves as fully assimilated members of the dominant American culture as well as those who feel little or no connection to these cultural values or identity.

The complex history of the Hispanic population within the United States has created a complex developmental task for Hispanic students in the United States: to forge a coherent identity that coordinates one's ethnic identity with his or her conceptions of what it means to be a student in school. The identity integration task is influenced by a number of factors that grow out of the history of the Hispanic population in the United States. How long has the student's family lived in the United States? What is the economic status of the student's family? Does the student attend a school in which he is in the ethnic majority or the ethnic minority? What are the stereotypes about the academic abilities of the student's ethnic group, and how aware of these stereotypes is the student? What does the student's family say or do to encourage him or her to maintain a connection with the cultural heritage and values of the family? What do the student's friends and school do to reinforce or contradict the values of the student's family? These factors and many more influence how the student thinks about him- or herself as a student and as a member of an ethnic group and how s/he is able to coordinate these two important components of his/her identity.

In this chapter we provide information about the demographics of the Hispanic population in the United States, with a particular focus on the college student population. Next, we define and discuss the issues of acculturation and ethnic identity as they pertain to the Hispanic population. We then discuss how issues of ethnic identity and acculturation are associated with the academic motivation and achievement of Hispanic students, including a description of some of our recent work in this area. We conclude the chapter with an examination of what schools are doing or could be doing to reduce the tension that some Hispanic students experience as they coordinate their ethnic and academic identities.

Demographics

In the Population

According to data from the U.S. Census Bureau (U.S. Department of Commerce, 2013), 17% of the population in the United States as of 2013 was Hispanic, and this percentage is expected to increase to 28% by 2050. Within the K–12 student population, 21.5% are Hispanic (Pew Hispanic Center, 2009). In some states the percentage of Hispanics in the population is quite a bit higher than the national averages. For example, more than 50% of all youth between the ages of 16 and 25 in New Mexico are Latino, 42% in California, and 40% in Texas. It is important to remember that Latinos in the United States are a very diverse group who differ in country of origin, generational status, and state of residence in the United States, among other factors. For example, currently 62% of all Hispanics in the United States were born in the United States (i.e., native born), compared to 38% who were born outside of the United States and immigrated (i.e., foreign born).

Latino Students and College

From 1996 to 2012, Hispanic youth enrollment in college (including both 2-year and 4-year colleges) increased 240%, a rate much faster than the growth for White (12%) and African American (72%) youth (Krogstad & Fry, 2014). In fact, in 2012 the percentage of high school graduates who enrolled in college the fall after graduation was higher for Hispanic students (69%) than for White students (67%). From 2000 to 2011, the percentage of 16- to 24-year-old Hispanic youth who were high school dropouts shrank from 28% to 14%. Despite these tremendous advances in college enrollment in recent years, Hispanic students are less likely than their White peers to enroll in 4-year colleges (56% and 72%, respectively) and are less likely to receive bachelor's degrees, less likely to attend a selective college, and less likely to attend college full time (Fry & Taylor, 2013). Although Hispanics aged 16 and older are more likely than the rest of the U.S. population to say it is important to attend college (88% to 74%), it appears that completing a 4-year college degree is more difficult for Hispanic students than for White students.

Research indicates that Latinos' decisions about college enrollment are strongly affected by three factors: cost, the need to work and make money, and a lack of adequate academic preparation for college (Fry, 2004). These are the three concerns mentioned most frequently by White and African American students as well, so the importance of money and academic preparation are not unique to the Hispanic population. Because Hispanic youth are more likely to suffer economic disadvantage and attend lower-performing schools than are White students (Pew Hispanic Center, 2009), these concerns with money and academic preparation are perhaps more salient among Hispanic students. In the same study, 40% of Hispanic students also mentioned that racism was a barrier to attending, or staying in, college.

One area where Latino and White students differ dramatically is what they think about when deciding *where* to attend college. The proximity to home and family was an important factor mentioned by one third of Latino participants and only one sixth of White students. The importance many Latino students place on staying near family affects whether they apply to college, where they apply to college, and whether to stay in or leave college. Proximity to family, along with affordability and the need to work, is what drives many Latino students to enroll in community colleges (Perez, 2010). Because of the greater number of community colleges and their flexibility, it is easier for students to live at home while attending them.

Factors Affecting Hispanic College Student Retention

Latino students are also more likely to leave college after they are enrolled, further reducing their college graduation rates. Ishitani (2003) found that lower family income, being from a smaller hometown, and being the first member of one's family to attend college all predict lower rates of retention in college. Unfortunately, these three factors are all higher among Hispanic college students than among White college students. In a review of research, Lascher (2008) found little evidence that Latino student retention in college is negatively affected either by characteristics of the Latino culture or by college climate characteristics (i.e., institutional racism) that push Latino students out of college. Instead, Lascher argues that the evidence clearly indicates that Latino students, compared to their White peers, tend to be lower income, have more financial stress while in college, and have weaker academic preparation before arriving in college. These factors steer many Latino students into community colleges, and the transfer rate from community college to 4-year college is quite low.

Research examining the college enrollment and retention processes of Hispanic students clearly indicates that economic pressures and academic preparation play central roles. There is also a long history of research examining the associations among ethnic identity, acculturation processes, stereotypes, and academic

Achievement of Hispanic College Students **171**

motivation and achievement. In the next sections of this chapter, we examine this research as it relates to Latino students.

Acculturation and Ethnic Identity: An Overview

Acculturation refers to the process through which immigrant families become aware of and adopt as their own the dominant beliefs, values, and behaviors of the host country. Often, this process is most clearly witnessed as families stay in the host country over successive generations. Whereas immigrant parents (first generation) are often slow to learn the dominant language of the host culture, their children (second generation) usually grow up speaking both the native language of the parents as well as the dominant language of the host culture. For Latino families living in the United States, the children of immigrant parents often learn Spanish as their first language but are fluent in English upon entering school. Research has consistently demonstrated that students with higher levels of acculturation, including fluency in English, parental assistance with schoolwork, and an orientation toward college, tend to achieve at higher levels than their less acculturated peers (Fry, 2004; Pew Hispanic Center, 2009; Plunkett & Bámaca-Gómez, 2003; Waldinger & Feliciano, 2004).

But there is also evidence that there are costs of acculturation for Latino youth in the United States. For example, second-generation Latino youth have higher academic aspirations and lower dropout rates than either first- or *third*-generation Latinos (Pew Hispanic Center, 2009). In addition, there is evidence that the Latino children of immigrant parents have more positive academic motivational profiles and achieve at higher levels than do Latino children of United States–born parents (Fuligni & Tseng, 1999; Schleicher, 2006). The positive motivational, achievement, and behavioral profiles of the children of immigrants, relative to the children of native-born parents, has led some researchers to hypothesize an "immigrant paradox" (Coll et al., 2009; Suarez-Orozco & Suarez-Orozco, 1995). According to this hypothesis, there may be something about the process of acculturation that places Latino youth at risk of developing maladaptive behaviors and attitudes. The process of acculturation creates stress for some Latino families and individuals as they try to maintain a connection to the families' native beliefs and behaviors while adopting some of the beliefs and behaviors of the dominant culture in the United States (Cervantes & Castro, 1985; Padilla, 2006). Differences in language use, norms about gender roles, dating behavior, and clothing styles between these two cultures are a frequent source of conflict between immigrant parents and their children.

Ethnic Identity

The process of acculturation is closely tied to issues of cultural and ethnic identity. Ethnic identity refers to how individuals think about and define themselves in terms of their connection to their ethnic heritage. It is multidimensional and includes how important one's ethnicity is to one's overall sense of self (centrality), how one feels about their ethnic group (private regard), and one's perceptions about how one's ethnic group is perceived by members of the larger society (public regard; Chavous et al., 2003). Although there are subtle differences among ethnic, racial, and cultural identity, for the purposes of this chapter we will use the term *ethnic identity* and assume that it incorporates elements of race, ethnicity, and culture. In this manner, students from the same racial group (e.g., Hispanic) may differ in their ethnic identity due to differences in the families' countries of origin (e.g., Guatemala vs. Mexico) and to other factors, such as how many generations the family has lived in the United States (Hudley & Irving, 2012). Although everyone has an ethnic identity, ethnicity tends to be a more salient and central part of overall identity for members of ethnic minorities than for Whites in the United States (Cross & Vandiver, 2001).

Adolescents who are members of ethnic minority groups are confronted with a complex identity problem: how to coordinate aspects of their families' ethnic culture with aspects of the dominant culture in the society in which they live (Berry, Phinney, Sam, & Vedder, 2006; Phinney & Devich-Navarro, 1997). For example, a Latino adolescent must figure out what it means to him/her to be Hispanic and how that part of his/her identity fits within the cultural norms of the larger society in which s/he lives. These judgments will be influenced by a number of social factors, including information from his/her family about what it means to belong to his/her ethnic group, messages from his/her peers, and how s/he is treated and portrayed by various people (e.g., teachers, police, store clerks, etc.) and media (e.g., television, magazines, music) in society (Gitlin, Buendia, Crosland, & Doumbia, 2003).

Several scholars have examined how adolescents and early adults have tried to combine different cultural and ethnic identities (Berry, 2005; Phinney & Devich-Navarro, 1997). Most models have identified several patterns of ethnic identity formation that include some combination of the following:

- Full assimilation, in which the ethnic minority individual identifies fully with the dominant culture in society;
- Full separation, in which the ethnic minority individual identifies fully with his or her ethnic group and not at all with the dominant culture in society;
- Bicultural identity, in which the ethnic minority individual either views him- or herself as having an identity that blends his or her ethnic culture with the dominant societal culture or "switches" between the two cultures in different situations; and
- Marginalized, in which the ethnic minority individual does not feel like he or she identifies with either the ethnic culture or the dominant culture in society.

These four patterns of ethnic identity formation among ethnic minorities in the United States are closely related to different patterns of acculturation whereby individuals and families from nonmajority cultures become fully assimilated into the dominant culture, remain fully separate from it, adopt some beliefs and behaviors of the dominant culture but maintain strong connections to their native culture, or feel somewhat distant and unaccepted from both cultures. Latino students in the United States, who are simultaneously members of their families' native culture and the dominant U.S. culture, can experience stress when they feel like they are not fully accepted by or do not belong to either their own ethnic group or the dominant cultural group in society (i.e., marginalized). On the other hand, there can be benefits for those who are able to maintain a strong connection to their native culture while also taking advantage of the affordances made possible by adapting to the cultural norms and values in societal institutions like schools (e.g., bicultural identity; Ogbu, 1992; Suarez-Orozco & Suarez-Orozco, 1995). The balancing act of trying to fit into contexts that emphasize different cultural values can be quite challenging and can influence the academic motivation and achievement of Latino students.

The Association Between Ethnic Identity and Academic Motivation

Research examining the association between ethnic identity and academic motivation has revealed that the relationship is quite complex. Some researchers have found that for ethnic minority students in the United States, a belief that one's ethnic background is a central and valuable part of their identity (i.e., ethnic identity) is positively associated with academic motivational beliefs (Fuligni, Witgow, & Garcia, 2005; Phinney, Cantu, & Kurtz, 1997). Others, however, have found that the effect of a strong ethnic identity on academic motivation depends on the social status and academic values of the specific ethnic group (Guyll, Madon, Prieto, & Scherr, 2010; Schneider & Ward, 2003). For example, Portes and Fernández-Kelly (2008) found that second-generation youth (i.e., children born in the United States to parents who were immigrants) were both more successful in school and able to maintain a strong ethnic identity when their parents were highly educated and when they lived in multiethnic neighborhoods. Similarly, research with low-income Latino adolescents revealed that students who developed an ethnic identification with both the larger society and their home culture had relatively high academic achievement (Altschul, Oyserman, & Bybee, 2008). In general, research indicates that maintaining some connection with one's native culture and having positive regard for one's ethnic group are associated with positive educational outcomes for a variety of ethnic groups, but these associations depend on other factors such as the socioeconomic status of the family, socialization practices of the parents, and the home obligations of the adolescent students (Fuligni & Tseng, 1999).

In the United States, negative stereotypes about the academic abilities of Latino students are prevalent (Gitlin et al., 2003). In addition, high-achieving Latino students in college-track classes in high school or who attend selective 4-year colleges often find themselves in the minority in those academic settings (Guyll et al., 2010). One result of these negative stereotypes and the relative scarcity of Latinos in the higher-achieving tracks is that some Latino youth may develop an ethnic identity that is incompatible with an academic identity that is high achieving. If Latino students develop a belief that academic success is primarily associated with the dominant culture (i.e., White students) and not with Latino culture, an ethnic identity that includes the belief that being Latino is a central part of one's identity may create a disconnect between ethnic identity and positive academic self-concept for many Latino students. Ironically, it may be higher-achieving Latino students who are most likely to develop such a disconnect, as it is these students who are most likely to have the experience of being the minority in their high-achieving classrooms and schools.

Research evidence supporting this hypothesis comes from several sources. In their study of ninth-grade students, Fuligni and his colleagues (2005) found that ethnic identity was positively associated with several motivational beliefs (e.g., intrinsic value of school, academic value, utility of education) but was not correlated with academic self-concept. These results were found with a multiethnic sample that included Latino students, but the researchers did not examine Latino students separately in this analysis. In a study of Latino college students, Armenta (2010) found that when negative academic stereotypes about Latinos were made salient, Latinos with stronger ethnic identification performed worse on a math exam than did Latinos with weaker ethnic identification. Consistent with these results, Guyll and his colleagues (2010) speculate that Latinos with stronger ethnic identification are more susceptible to stereotype threat effects because their membership in the stereotyped ethnic group is a more salient feature of their self-concept. As Steele and Aronson (1995) noted, stereotype threat is most likely to be activated in contexts in which the stereotyped group is in the minority and is highly invested in the activity, such as high-achieving Latino students attending a predominantly White university.

Subconscious Processes

Most of the extant research examining ethnic identity and its association with psychological adjustment, including academic motivation, has relied on self-report data. As much of the research on the effects of stereotype threat has revealed, it may be that the processes underlying the association between ethnic identity and academic identity occur beneath the level of consciousness. Nonconscious processes in the form of implicit associations can influence motivation and behavior. Implicit associations refer to connections that people make between certain stimuli or concepts even when they are not aware that they are making such an association or that the implicit association is affecting behavior. Scores of studies have examined implicit associations to assess everything from voting tendencies (Bassili, 1995) to stereotype threat (Armenta, 2010; Lee & Ottati, 1995;

Steele & Aronson, 1995) to racism (Fazio & Dunton, 1997). This research has documented that self-report data are often at odds with implicit associations. For example, people who profess to harbor no ill will toward members of ethnicities different from their own nonetheless have patterns of implicit associations that reveal negative perceptions of other ethnic groups (Fazio & Dunton, 1997).

Research using self-report data has documented that when students, particularly ethnic minority students, have a strong sense of ethnic identity, they tend to have stronger academic motivation and higher educational aspirations (Fuligni et al., 2005; Gibson, 1988). But research that has not relied on self-report data suggests that ethnic identity may not be positively associated with academic outcomes (Armenta, 2010; Guyll et al., 2010). For example, even if a Hispanic student has a strong connection to and pride in his/her Hispanic heritage and culture, his/her implicit association between academic success and Hispanic culture may have been weakened by stereotypes at the societal level, messages from his/her peers, and role models in his/her neighborhood. In turn, this weak implicit association between academic success and Hispanic culture may affect his/her academic motivation and educational aspirations in a manner that is beneath his/her level of conscious awareness. These implicit associations may cause some Hispanic students to be less inclined to develop and pursue academic and professional goals that require a high level of academic success. As research on nonconscious influences of motivation and behavior have demonstrated, these associations can be beneath the level of conscious awareness and still affect motivated behaviors such as choice, engagement, and persistence (Steele & Aronson, 1995). We have examined associations among ethnic identity, implicit associations, and academic motivation in samples of Hispanic and White college students, and we discuss this research in the next section of this chapter.

Summary of Our Research Examining the Association Between Ethnic Identity and Academic Motivation

Given the findings of previous research and theory (e.g., Armenta, 2010; Guyll et al., 2010, Steele & Aronson, 1995), we hypothesized that Latino students attending a selective liberal arts university with a majority White student body may report a disconnect between their ethnic identity and their academic self-concept. We also suspected that despite a strong sense of ethnic pride, these Latino students might display a stereotypical pattern of implicit associations that linked success more strongly with being White and failure more strongly with being Hispanic.

We have conducted two studies to examine whether our hypotheses were supported and, if so, whether we could do anything to reverse these trends. In the first study, we collected survey data from Latino ($n = 77$) and White ($n = 57$) undergraduates to assess their reports of their ethnic identity centrality, valuing of their ethnic group, academic self-concept, valuing of school, and awareness of stereotypes about the academic abilities of their ethnic group (Urdan, 2013). These data indicated that there were no differences between the two samples in their average levels of academic self-concept or valuing of school. The Latino sample reported higher average levels of ethnic identity centrality and valuing of belonging to one's ethnic group than did White students, results we attributed to the higher salience of ethnicity in the overall identity of ethnic minority students, especially when attending majority-White schools. The Latino students in this sample were quite aware of the negative stereotypes about the academic abilities of their ethnic group.

Steele (1997) argued that the continual threat of fulfilling negative stereotypes about one's group (i.e., ethnic group, gender) can eventually lead one to dis-identify with a previously valued domain. For example, female college students who value math may begin to devalue being good at math as a part of their own identity as they are repeatedly confronted with the threat of fulfilling the negative stereotype about girls' and women's inferiority in math. We hypothesized that a similar process of disidentification may happen with Latino students in a mostly White college. Instead of disidentifying with academics, however, we speculated that many Latino students might disconnect their ethnic identities from their academic identities. In other words, we thought that the Hispanic students in our sample, who felt a strong connection to their ethnic identity and highly valued academic achievement but were aware of the negative stereotypes about their ethnic group might view their academic accomplishments as separate from their ethnic identity. Although these academically successful students were the living contradiction to the negative stereotypes about the academic abilities of Latino students, we hypothesized that the conflict of strong ethnic identity, coupled with the awareness and activation of negative stereotypes about their ethnic group, may result in a de-coupling of their academic and ethnic identities (Armenta, 2010; Guyll et al., 2010). We found a positive correlation between academic self-concept and ethnic identity centrality for the White students and no correlation between them for Hispanic students.

One contributor to this disconnect between academic and ethnic identity for Latino college students may be nonconscious associations that link ethnicity with achievement. Using an Implicit Associations Test (IAT), we found that White college students responded more quickly when success words (e.g., "Achievement," "Graduate") were associated with the word "White" than with the word "Hispanic." Similarly, they responded more slowly when failure words (e.g., "Dropout," "Hopeless") were associated with the word "White" than when it was paired with the word "Hispanic." Importantly, this same stereotypical pattern of associating success with being White and failure with being Hispanic was found with the Latino sample. The results of the IAT suggest that the Hispanic college students in this study, despite being academically successful and proud of their ethnic group, held unconscious associations favoring the academic achievement of White students. We suspect that these unconscious associations may influence the association between academic self-concept and ethnic identity, particularly for Latino students attending colleges in which they are in the minority, and therefore frequently exposed to stereotype threat activation.

In our second study, we conducted an experiment to see if we could reduce or eliminate this stereotypical IAT pattern (Urdan, Herr, Coushon, & Stenchever, 2014). Approximately 100 college students were assigned to one of three conditions: Letter-writing, Possible Selves, or Control. All participants first completed a survey to assess ethnic identity and academic self-concept, among other variables. They also completed the same IAT that was used in Study 1. After completing the survey and the IAT, participants in the Letter-writing condition read a brief article that described the academic successes and accomplishments of Hispanic students. After reading the article, participants were asked to write a letter to a fictitious Latino high school student who was considering applying to college. The purpose of the letter was allegedly to encourage the fictitious student to apply to college, but for our purposes we hoped writing such a letter would solidify what participants had learned about the academic success of Hispanic students. We modeled this intervention on the work of Walton and Cohen (2011) with African American students at a predominantly White, selective private university. In the Possible Selves condition, participants read a brief article discussing the importance of being able to envision oneself as academically successful in the future (i.e., a positive academic future self). Participants were then asked to quickly (within 15 minutes) develop a program that could be used to help high school students develop positive academic future selves. This intervention was based on the work of Oyserman, Terry, and Bybee (2002). In the control condition, participants read a brief article about plants and were asked to write a summary of what they learned from the article.

Immediately after the interventions, participants again completed the survey and the IAT. Although we expected that the Letter-writing and Possible Selves interventions would reduce or eliminate the stereotypical IAT pattern, the elimination of stereotypical implicit associations only occurred in the Possible Selves group. We saw no change in the IAT pattern for participants in the Letter-writing group. We suspect that the Letter-writing condition may not have required enough of a cognitive commitment to really produce changes in explicit (i.e., survey) or implicit attitudes. We are currently examining the actual letters and plans students in the experimental conditions produced to see if there is evidence of differences in depth of thought and engagement in the task.

Our research on this topic, to date, indicates that for Latino students attending a selective 4-year university with a majority-White student body, there may be a disconnect between ethnic identity and academic self-concept. Rather than viewing one's connection to his/her ethnic identity as a fundamental source of academic achievement, for the students in our study, ethnic identity was unrelated to the academic self. This disassociation may have been fueled in part by implicit associations, even among high-achieving Latino students, that link academic

What Schools Can Do

Many Hispanic college students are first-generation college students with financial stressors and inadequate academic preparation. Lower-income students are more likely to remain in college if they are receiving financial assistance and access to opportunities to earn money through work (Elmers & Pike, 1997; Lascher, 2008). Similarly, students who enter college with inadequate academic preparation are more likely to persist in school if they receive academic remediation (Lascher, 2008). First-generation college students also benefit from bridge programs that help familiarize students with college life, both before and immediately after the beginning of their first year of college. Students are also more likely to persist in college if they feel safe and welcome on campus, so programs designed to increase such feelings (e.g., orientation programs, residential learning communities, one-on-one faculty–student advising) tend to increase retention (Tinto, 1975). These programs may be particularly important for Hispanic college students who may feel less safe and welcome on campus because of cultural differences or racial biases (Villapando, 2004).

Research has found that students, particularly minority students attending majority-White colleges, benefit from conscientious efforts to promote diversity on campus. This includes creating diverse groups of students (e.g., through learning communities), presenting diverse perspectives in course content, and promoting intergroup dialogues (Umbach & Kuh, 2003). Increasing the diversity of the student body and the faculty may also promote feelings of inclusion and belonging among minority students on campus.

Our own research suggests that for some Latino students, even those who are performing well academically, the strain of stereotype threat and of the challenge of integrating academic and ethnic identities can be difficult. Research conducted with other stereotyped or underrepresented groups in college suggests that confronting these issues directly may improve students' achievement and feelings of belonging. For example, research conducted with girls and women in math reveals that talking openly about and debunking the negative stereotypes about females in math can greatly reduce the effects of stereotype threat (Johns, Schmader, & Martens, 2005). Similarly, Walton and Cohen (2011) found that manipulating African American college students' attributions for their feelings of isolation during their first year of college away from race and toward a normative freshman experience improved their feelings of belonging in school, achievement, and health outcomes. Our own research with Latino college students indicates that asking students to think about ways of promoting the development of healthy academic identities among Latino youth can reduce implicit stereotypes. Taken together, this research suggests that one way to increase Latino college student retention, in addition to the economic and academic supports schools can provide, is to explicitly address the beliefs and perceptions of students in an effort to promote feelings of belonging and value on campus.

Conclusion

Although Hispanic students are quickly becoming a larger segment of the population in higher education, we still know very little about how to foster the enrollment and retention of Latino students through graduation from a 4-year college. Part of this knowledge gap stems from the fact that the Latino population is quite diverse—in country of origin, generational status, academic background, and perceptions of school. Many Latino students enter college with economic and academic challenges, and programs designed to help students with such challenges (e.g., financial aid, academic remediation) are effective for Hispanic students. Institutional efforts to increase feelings of connection and belonging in the school, such as residential learning communities and advising programs, are also effective. There is some evidence that Latino students face specific challenges that include perceptions of racism at school, negative stereotypes, and coordinating multiple aspects of ethnic and academic identities. More research is needed about the specific challenges that Hispanic college students face and the best ways to overcome these challenges and promote college retention and completion.

Note

1 Throughout this chapter we use the terms "Hispanic" and "Latino" interchangeably.

References

Altschul, I., Oyserman, D., & Bybee, D. (2008). Racial-ethnic self-schemas and segmented assimilation: Identity and the academic achievement of Hispanic youth. *Social Psychology Quarterly, 71*, 302–320.

Armenta, B. E. (2010). Stereotype boost and stereotype threat effects: The moderating role of ethnic identification. *Cultural Diversity and Ethnic Minority Psychology, 16*, 94–98.

Bassili, J. N. (1995). Response latency and the accessibility of voting intentions: What contributes to accessibility and how it affects vote choice. *Personality & Social Psychology Bulletin, 21*, 686–695.

Berry, J. W. (2005). Acculturation: Living successfully in two cultures. *International Journal of Intercultural Relations, 29*, 697–712.

Berry, J. W., Phinney, J. S., Sam, D. L., & Vedder, P. (2006). Immigrant youth: Acculturation, identity, and adaptation. *Applied Psychology: An International Review, 55*, 303–332.

Cervantes, R. C., & Castro, F. G. (1985). Stress, coping, and Mexican American mental health: A systemic review. *Hispanic Journal of Behavioral Sciences, 7*, 1–73.

Chavous, T., Bernat, D., Schmeelk-Cone, K., Caldwell, C., Kohn-Wood, L., & Zimmerman, M. (2003). Racial identity and academic attainment among African American adolescents. *Child Development, 74*, 1076–1090.

Coll, C. G., Flannery, P., Yang, H., Suarez-Aviles, G., Batchelor, A., & Marks, A. (2009, March). *The immigrant paradox: A review of the literature.* Paper presented at the conference Is Becoming American a Developmental Risk: Children and Adolescents From Immigrant Families. Brown University, Providence, RI.

Cross, W., & Vandiver, B. (2001). Nigrescence theory and measurement: Introducing the Cross Racial Identity Scale (CRIS). In J. G. Ponterotto, J. M. Casas, L. M. Suzuki, & C. M. Alexander (Eds.), *Handbook of multicultural counseling* (2nd ed., pp. 371–393). Thousand Oaks, CA: Sage.

Elmers, M. T., & Pike, G. R. (1997). Minority and non-minority adjustment to college: Differences or similarities? *Research in Higher Education, 38*, 77–97.

Fazio, R. H., & Dunton, B. C. (1997). Categorization by race: The impact of automatic and controlled components of racial prejudice. *Journal of Experimental Social Psychology, 33*(5), 451–470.

Fry, R. (2004). *Latino youth finishing college: The role of selective pathways.* Washington, DC: Pew Hispanic Center.

Fry, R., & Taylor, P. (2013). *Hispanic high school graduates pass Whites in rate of college enrollment.* Washington, DC: Pew Research Center.

Fuligni, A. J., & Tseng, V. (1999). Family obligation and the academic motivation of adolescents from immigrant and American-born families. In T. Urdan (Ed.), *Advances in motivation and achievement, Vol. 11* (pp. 159–183). Stanford, CT: JAI Press.

Fuligni, A., Witgow, M., & Garcia, C. (2005). Ethnic identity and the academic adjustment of adolescents from Mexican, Chinese, and European backgrounds. *Developmental Psychology, 41*, 799–811.

Gibson, M. A. (1988). *Accommodation without assimilation: Sikh immigrants in an American high school.* Ithaca, NY: Cornell University Press.

Gitlin, A., Buendia, E., Crosland, K., & Doumbia, F. (2003). The production of margin and center: Welcoming-unwelcoming of immigrant students. *American Educational Research Journal, 40*, 91–122.

Guyll, M., Madon, S., Prieto, L., & Scherr, K. C. (2010). The potential roles of self-fulfilling prophecies, stigma consciousness, and stereotype threat in linking Latino/a ethnicity and educational outcomes. *Journal of Social Issues, 66*, 113–130.

Hudley, C., & Irving, M. (2012). Ethnic and racial identity in childhood and adolescence. In T. Urdan (Ed.), *APA educational psychology handbook, v. 2* (pp. 262–292). Washington, DC: American Psychological Association.

Ishitani, T. T. (2003). A longitudinal approach to assessing attrition behavior among first-generation students: Time-varying effects of pre-college characteristics. *Research in Higher Education, 44*, 433–449.

Johns, M., Schmader, T., & Martens, A. (2005). Knowing is half the battle: Teaching stereotype threat as a means of improving women's math performance. *Psychological Science, 16*, 175–179.

Krogstad, J. M., & Fry, R. (2014, 24 April). *More Hispanics, blacks enrolling in college, but lag in bachelor's degrees.* Pew Research Center. Retrieved from http://www.pewresearch.org/fact-tank/2014/04/24/more-hispanics-blacks-enrolling-in-college-but-lag-in-bachelors-degrees/

Lascher, E. L. (2008). Retrieved from http://www.csus.edu/ihelp/PDFs/R_ResearchBrief_0809.pdf

Lee, Y., & Ottati, V. (1995). Perceived in-group homogeneity as a function of group membership salience and stereotype threat. *Personality & Social Psychology Bulletin, 21*, 610–619.

Ogbu, J. U. (1992). Understanding cultural diversity and learning. *Educational Researcher, 21*, 5–14.

Oyserman, D., Terry, K., & Bybee, D. (2002). A possible selves intervention to enhance school involvement. *Journal of Adolescence, 25*, 313–326.

Padilla, A. M. (2006). Bicultural social development. *Hispanic Journal of Behavioral Sciences, 28*, 467–497.

Perez, P. A. (2010). College choice process of Latino undocumented students: Implications for recruitment and retention. *Journal of College Admission, Winter*, 21–25.

Pew Hispanic Center (2009). *Between two worlds: How young Latinos come of age in America*. Washington, DC: Pew Research Center.

Phinney, J., Cantu, C., & Kurtz, D. (1997). Ethnic and American identity as predictors of self-esteem among African American, Latino, and White adolescents. *Journal of Youth and Adolescence, 26*, 165–185.

Phinney, J., & Devich-Navarro, M. (1997). Variations in bicultural identification among African American and Mexican American adolescents. *Journal of Research on Adolescence, 7*, 3–32.

Plunkett, S. W., & Bámaca-Gómez, M., Y. (2003). The relationship between parenting, acculturation, and adolescent academics in Mexican-origin immigrant families in Los Angeles. *Hispanic Journal of Behavioral Sciences, 25*, 222–239.

Portes, A., & Fernández-Kelly, P. (2008). No margin for error: Educational and occupational achievement among disadvantaged children of immigrants. *The Annals of the American Academy of Political and Social Science, 620*, 12–36.

Schleicher, A. (2006). Where immigrant students succeed: a comparative review of performance and engagement in PISA 2003. *Intercultural Education, 17*, 507–516.

Schneider, M. E., & Ward, D. J. (2003). The role of ethnic identification and perceived social support in Latinos' adjustment to college. *Hispanic Journal of Behavioral Sciences, 25*, 539–554.

Steele, C. M. (1997). A threat in the air: How stereotypes shape intellectual identity and performance. *American Psychologist, 52*, 613–629.

Steele, C. M., & Aronson, J. (1995). Stereotype threat and the intellectual test performance of African-Americans. *Journal of Personality and Social Psychology, 69*, 797–811.

Suarez-Orozco, C., & Suarez-Orozco, M. M. (1995). *Transformations: Immigration, family life, and achievement motivation among Latino adolescents*. Stanford, CA: Stanford University Press.

Tinto, V. (1975). Dropouts from higher education: A theoretical synthesis of the recent literature. *A Review of Educational Research, 45*, 89–125.

Umbach, P. D., & Kuh, G. D. (2003, May). *Student experiences with diversity at liberal arts colleges: Another claim for distinctiveness*. Paper presented at the meeting of the Association for Institutional Research, Tampa, FL.

Urdan, T. (2013, April). *The weight of stereotypes and minority status for successful Latino college students*. Paper presented at the annual meetings of the American Educational Research Association, San Francisco, CA.

Urdan, T., Herr, V., Coushon, C., & Stenchever, N. (2014, June). *Ethnic identity, academic motivation, and stereotype threat: Breaking the cycle*. Paper presented at the biannual meeting of the International Conference on Motivation. Helsinki, Finland.

U.S. Department of Commerce. (2013). *Changing nation: Percent Hispanic of the U.S. population, 1980–2050.* Retrieved from https://www.census.gov/content/dam/Census/newsroom/facts-for-features/2014/cb14-ff22_graphic.pdf

Villapando, O. (2004). Practical considerations of critical race theory and Latino critical theory for Latino college students. *New Directions for Student Services, 105,* 41–50.

Waldinger, R., & Feliciano, C. (2004). Will the new second generation experience 'downward assimilation'? Segmented assimilation re-assessed. *Ethnic and Racial Studies, 27,* 376–402.

Walton, G. M., & Cohen, G. L. (2011). A brief social-belonging intervention improves academic and health outcomes for minority students. *Science, 331,* 1447–1451.

12

DESEGREGATING GIFTED EDUCATION FOR CULTURALLY DIFFERENT STUDENTS

Recommendations for Equitable Recruitment and Retention

Donna Y. Ford

> *No person in the United States shall, on the basis of sex, be excluded from participation in, be denied the benefits of, or be subjected to discrimination under any education program or activity receiving federal financial assistance.*
> *Civil Rights Act of 1964, Pub. L. No. 88–352, 78 Stat. 241, 255 (July 2, 1964)*

In addition to general education, students with special needs are served in special education and gifted education. General education and special education specifically are increasingly segregated along racial lines. In general education, this takes the form of zoning policies that result in districts that are majority White or Black (Frankenberg, 2012). In this work, Frankenberg (2012) argues and shares data that point to undeniable racial segregation that mirrors the 1960s—a clear sign of regression and lack of progress along racial lines. Gifted education also has its share of racially segregated programs and classrooms. Black students are significantly underrepresented nationally and in most states (Ford & King, 2014). Hispanic students are also underrepresented but to a lesser degree than Black students (Ford, 2013). In the pages that follow, I discuss segregation in gifted education, along with goals for schools to target to achieve equity.

There is no place in educational settings for segregation, and the idea and ideals of integration have been elusive in U.S. schools and gifted programs in particular. *Brown v. Board of Education* (1954), in which segregated schools, classrooms, and programs based on race were declared illegal and unconstitutional, has yet to be realized. The Supreme Court mandated an end to separate and unequal education in America; and desegregation was to occur with all deliberate speed. Some six decades later, *Brown* and associated legal mandates have yet to be

184 Donna Y. Ford

fulfilled, particularly in gifted education, Advanced Placement (AP) classes, and other courses for advanced learners (e.g., honors and International Baccalaureate classes).

It is unprofessional and unethical to allow, be it intentional or unintentional, the inequitable distribution of resources and opportunities to students based on race (Title VI, 1964). Title VI was enacted as part of the landmark Civil Rights Act of 1964. It prohibits discrimination on the basis of race, color, and national origin in programs and activities receiving federal financial assistance. Most funding agencies have regulations implementing Title VI that prohibit practices that have the effect of discrimination on the basis of race, color, or national origin. Noteworthy is that Title VI prohibits intentional discrimination. As former President Kennedy expressed in 1963:

> Simple justice requires that public funds, to which all taxpayers of all races [colors, and national origins] contribute, not be spent in any fashion which encourages, entrenches, subsidizes or results in racial [color or national origin] discrimination.
>
> *(see http://www.justice.gov/crt/about/cor/coord/titlevi.php)*

An important clause overall and certainly relevant to gifted education is that of intent. As noted, Title VI prohibits *intentional* discrimination. It is often difficult and sometimes (many times) impossible to discern intentional from unintentional discrimination. This said, meaning intent notwithstanding, the impact is the same—access and rights denied when discrimination exists. An auto accident analogy sheds light on intent and outcome. Imagine being in an accident in which someone hits your vehicle. The person apologizes, stating that he/she is sorry and did not mean to hit you. Regardless of intent, your car is damaged, along with other expenses and inconveniences. Intent does not erase the damage, expenses, and inconveniences.

Inequitable opportunities contribute to and promote educational disparities and create a vicious cycle in which Black and Hispanic students are denied access to school programs that are important to closing achievement gaps and reaching one's potential. Gifted education promotes and reinforces these racial inequities. For decades, educators, policy makers, and legal personnel have failed to recruit and retain an equitable percentage of Black and Hispanic students in gifted education and courses for advanced learners. This lack of accountability and discriminations contributes to de facto and de jure segregation.

A recent court case in gifted education demonstrating de facto and de jure segregation is *McFadden v. Board of Education for Illinois School District U-46*, settled in 2013 (Ford & Russo, 2015). In Grades 4 through 6, the district operated two physically separate gifted programs based on and thus segregated by race and ethnicity. Gifted Hispanic and White students never interacted in race-based classes. Specifically, this district created a separate gifted program for Hispanic students

Desegregating Gifted Education **185**

who had *exited* English language learner (ELL) programs. Thus, the students were English proficient; they did not require their primary instruction in Spanish, but language need was used as an excuse to separate Hispanic from White students. The court affirmed that, in creating a separate gifted education program for Hispanic students only, this school district violated the United States and Illinois constitutions' equal protection clauses. The court noted that establishing a separate gifted education program based on race perpetuates the problems that our nation's civil rights laws were created and authorized to prevent.

Considering discrimination and segregation, I present patterns in the representation of Black and Hispanic students in gifted education using the Office for Civil Rights's Civil Rights Data Collection[1] (CRDC) from 2009 to 2011. Next, these data are placed within the context of *Brown v. Board of Education* (1954). Gifted education must become desegregated and integrated. Segregation pertains to numbers and placement; integration refers to quality of life once placed (Ford, 2013). De facto *and* de jure segregation in gifted education must end, with all deliberate speed, before another 60 years passes (Ford & King, 2014; Ford & Russo, 2015).

Gifted Education Definitions: Overview With Cultural Implications

There is no consensus on the definition of "gifted" (also known as gifted and talented). The U.S. Department of Education has adopted six definitions of giftedness between 1970 and 2001. Per Table 12.1, the only explicit mention of culture appears in 1993; others are colorblind, including the later 2001 definition, which is regressive. The emphasis on potential and talent development is equitable. Talent development—the focus on early identification and potential and ongoing supports—holds much promise for recruiting and retaining underrepresented gifted students. The unprecedented 1993 definition addressed two historically ignored or trivialized notions specific to culturally different students: (1) gifted students must be compared with others of their age, experience, or environment and (2) outstanding talents are present in students from all cultural groups, across all economic strata, and in all areas of human endeavor. (Also see Sternberg, 2007a, 2007b.) This definition calls for much-needed attention to local norms and, more importantly, school building norms. In every school building and zip code, there are gifted students. In every racial and ethnic group, there are gifted students.

Definitions of giftedness are normed and conceptualized on middle-class Whites (Sternberg, 2007a, 2007b). They have been operationalized by intelligence tests and achievement tests, respectively. In the majority of schools, students are required to obtain an IQ score of 130 or higher to be identified as intellectually gifted and/or they must score at or above 96th percentile on an achievement test. These criteria are based on the belief that giftedness is synonymous with intelligence and achievement and that both can be measured validly and reliably by standardized tests. Both assumptions and associated criteria discount

TABLE 12.1 Federal definitions of gifted and talented (1970–2001)

YEAR	DEFINITION
1970	The term "gifted and talented children" means in accordance with objective criteria prescribed by the Commissioner, children who have outstanding intellectual ability or creative talent, the development of which required special activities or services not ordinarily provided by local education agencies.
1972	Gifted and talented children are those identified by professionally qualified persons who by virtue of outstanding abilities are capable of high performance. These are children who require differentiated educational programs and/or services beyond those normally provided by the regular school programs in order to realize their contributions to self and society. Children capable of high performance include those with demonstrated and/or potential ability in any one of the following areas, singly or in combination: (1) general intellectual ability; (2) specific academic aptitude (grades in a particular subject area(s)); (3) creative or productive thinking; (4) leadership ability; (5) ability in the visual or performing arts; and (6) psychomotor ability.
1978	The term "gifted and talented children" means children and, whenever applicable youth, identified by professionally qualified persons and who, by virtue of outstanding abilities, are capable of high performance. These abilities, either potential or demonstrated, include (1) general intellectual ability, (2) general and specific academic ability, (3) creative or productive thinking, (4) leadership ability, and (5) ability in the performing arts.
1988	The term "gifted and talented" students means children and youth who give evidence of high performance capability in areas such as intellectual, creative, artistic, or leadership capacity, or in specific academic fields, and who require services or activities not provided by the school in order to fully develop such capabilities.
1993	Children and youth with outstanding talent perform or show the potential for performing at remarkably high levels of accomplishment when compared with others of their age, experience, or environment. These children and youth exhibit high performance capacity in intellectual, creative, and/or artistic areas, and unusual leadership capacity, or excel in specific academic fields. They require services or activities not ordinarily provided by the schools. Outstanding talents are present in children and youth from all cultural groups, across all economic strata, and in all areas of human endeavor.
2001	The term "gifted and talented," when used with respect to students, children, or youth, means students, children, or youth who give evidence of high achievement capability in areas such as intellectual, creative, artistic, or leadership capacity, or in specific academic fields, and who need services or activities not ordinarily provided by the school in order to fully develop those capabilities.

Source: Ford (2013)

and otherwise negate the importance of culture, language, and experience in test performance.

Because gifted education is not federally mandated, states have a great deal of discretion regarding identification and services, including the troubling option to neither identify, serve, nor fund such programs, and the bizarre or perplexing option of identifying but not serving and/or not funding. Therefore, it is essential to consider state definitions in desegregating gifted education. All states must revise definitions to include cultural dimensions, talent development, and under-achievement. Another crucial step is to analyze data and set measurable equity goals, which is described in the next section.

Having presented an overview of U.S. Department of Education definitions and sample criteria for intelligence and achievement, I now focus on data and setting equity goals to reduce underrepresentation in racially segregated gifted programs.

Gifted Underrepresentation Formula and Equity Allowance Formula

Underrepresentation is the primary focus when targeting inequities in gifted edu-cation. The significant underrepresentation of Black and Hispanic students is a major source of tension and discomfort in this field, with data and longstanding patterns revealing segregation (de facto and de jure) in gifted education (see Ford, 2011, 2013).

Several statistics can be adopted to analyze disproportionality or representa-tion discrepancies. The Relative Difference in Composition Index (RDCI) is used in this chapter. The RDCI for a racial group is the difference between its gifted education composition and general education composition, expressed as a discrepancy percentage. The focal question is: "What is the difference between the composition (percentage) of Black or Hispanic students in general education compared to the composition of Black or Hispanic students in gifted education?" This formula allows for the comparison of disproportionality. A discrepancy is sig-nificant when underrepresentation exceeds a threshold determined legally and/ or by decision makers, as discussed next with an equity allowance formula (Ford, 2013; McFadden, 2013).

Thresholds are not racial quotas, which are illegal but still being debated at the time of this writing. With quotas, group representation in school enrollment and gifted education enrollment is proportional; hence, if Black or Hispanic students comprise 65% of a school district (state or even school building), they must com-prise 65% of gifted education enrollment. After sharing examples using the RDCI, I present an equity allowance formula to help determine whether underrepresen-tation is beyond statistical chance—that is, whether such imbalance is primarily influenced by human-made barriers (subjectivity, deficit thinking, prejudice; Ford, 2014; Ford & Grantham, 2003; Valencia, 2010) and, thus, possibly discriminatory.

188 Donna Y. Ford

The RDCI for underrepresentation is computed as [100%—((Composition (%) of Black students in gifted education)/(Composition (%) of Black students in general education)]. Using decimals will yield the same results.

Each year, more than 250,000 Black students are not identified as gifted and lack access to classes, programs, and services. If not identified as gifted, they are not likely to be served in gifted education classes and programs. Black students are the *most underrepresented* group of gifted students per data from the Office for Civil Rights's CRDC (2006, 2009, 2011); and this group is more often the focus of complaints and litigation in gifted education (Ford, 2010, 2013; Ford & Russo, 2015).

Tables 12.2 and 12.3 present the national Civil Rights Data Collection (CRDC) for 2006, 2009, and 2011. For Black students, underrepresentation ranged from 43% to 47%; for Hispanic students, the range was from 31% to 37% (see Table 12.3). Underrepresentation exists in the majority of states and school districts for Black students, as reported by Ford and King (2014), who listed data for each state. They did not conduct state-by-state analyses in that article for Hispanic students. And like Black students, some 250,000 Hispanic students have not been identified as gifted, as noted in Ford (2013).

Debates and discussions are plentiful regarding ways to determine when underrepresentation (in referrals, screening, identification, and placement) is unreasonable and when discrimination is in operation. "When is underrepresentation significant?" "How severe must underrepresentation be in order to require changes?" "How severe must underrepresentation be to be considered

TABLE 12.2 Black student underrepresentation in gifted education nationally (2006, 2009, 2011)

	National Enrollment	Gifted Enrollment	Underrepresentation
2006	17.13%	9.15%	47%
2009	16.17%	9.9%	43%
2011	19%	10%	47%

Sources: U.S. Department of Education, Office for Civil Rights, Civil Rights Data Collection (2006, 2009, 2011); Ford (2013); Ford and King (2014)

TABLE 12.3 Hispanic student underrepresentation in gifted education nationally (2006, 2009, 2011)

	National Enrollment	Gifted Enrollment	Underrepresentation
2006	17.13%	9.15%	47%
2009	16.17%	9.9%	43%
2011	19%	10%	47%

Source: U.S. Department of Education, Office for Civil Rights, Civil Rights Data Collection (2006, 2009, 2011)

Desegregating Gifted Education **189**

discriminatory?" In the McFadden court case, I relied on the U.S. Department of Education Office for Civil Rights's (2006) 20% Equity Allowance Formula (also see *Griggs v. Duke Power*, 1971, also described in Ford, 2013) to guide decision makers in determining a targeted goal for the *minimally* accepted degree of under-representation for each racial group (and disaggregated by race, gender, income, etc.). When the percentage of underrepresentation *exceeds* the designated threshold in the Equity Allowance Formula, it is beyond statistical chance; therefore, human error is operating—attitudes, instruments, and policies and procedures may be discriminatory and biased (see Table 12.4).

When examining underrepresentation, intent matters, depending on the law being applied. In District U-46 (Elgin), the court found that school personnel *intentionally* discriminated against Hispanic students by running two racially identifiable programs. Disparate impact was found. The doctrine of disparate impact holds that practices may be considered discriminatory and illegal if they have a disproportionately "adverse impact" on students regarding a protected trait. The protected traits vary by statute, but most federal civil rights laws (e.g., Title VI) include race, color, religion, national origin, and gender as protected traits (Ford & Russo, 2014).

Under the disparate impact doctrine, a violation of Title VI of the 1964 Civil Rights Act may be proven by demonstrating that an instrument, practice, and/or policy has a disproportionately adverse effect on Black and Hispanic students. Therefore, the disparate impact doctrine prohibits school personnel from using a facially neutral practice that has an unjustified adverse impact on members of a protected class. Note that a facially neutral employment practice is one that does not appear to be discriminatory on its face/on the surface; instead, it is one that is discriminatory in its application and/or its effect. More information on disparate impact appears at http://en.wikipedia.org/wiki/Disparate_impact.

TABLE 12.4 Black students' underrepresentation and equity allowance index nationally (2006, 2009, 2011)

Black Students	National Public School Enrollment	National Gifted Enrollment	Underrepresentation	Equity Allowance Goal
2006	17.13%	9.15%	47%	13.7% (increase from 9.15% to 13.7%)
2009	16.17%	9.9%	43%	12.9% (increase from 9.9% to 12.9%)
2011	19%	10%	47%	15.2% (increase from 10% to 15.2%)

Source: Ford (2013); Ford and King (2014)

190 Donna Y. Ford

Note that the authors refer to the 20% rule also as the 80% rule. Terminology notwithstanding, the targeted goal is the *same* for minimal representation goals that are equitable.

Used in isolation and devoid of context, the RDCI is not adequate for determining unacceptable or possibly discriminatory underrepresentation. This is where the Equity Index (EI) is useful. Calculating the Equity Index (EI) is a two-step process. Step 1: [(Composition (%) of Black students in general education) × Threshold of 20% = B. This is abbreviated as C × T = B. Step 2: (Composition (%) of Black students in general education) − B = EI. This is abbreviated as C − B = EI. For example, if Black students were 19% of school enrollment in 2011 (see Table 12.2), the Equity Index using a 20% allowance would be: B is 19% × 20% = 3.8% and EI is 19% − 3.8% = 15.2%. Thus, as indicated in Table 12.4, Black students should represent at *minimum* 15.2% of students in gifted education. Nationally, the percentage for 2011 is 10%. The underrepresentation for Black students is not only significant but also beyond statistical chance. To achieve the minimal equity target, educators must increase Black students' representation nationally from 10% to at least 15.2%. These data illustrate the troubling reality that our states' and nation's gifted programs are segregated for Black students. The same formula applies to Hispanic students, who are also underrepresented but not to the same degree. We, as a national and educational system, are far from fulfilling the mandates of *Brown* in gifted education.

Why Access to Gifted Education Matters: Equality Versus Equity

Access to an equitable education is related to racial stratification. Regardless of the reason(s) for underrepresentation—inequitable access to gifted education—this jeopardizes the development of ability and achievement and social and economic success for Black and Hispanic students. Denied opportunities, regardless of motive and intent, have resulted in segregated gifted education. Underachievement is almost inevitable for many of these underrepresented and underserved gifted students (Ford, 2010). This cycle of educational inequity is predictable.

When not challenged, regardless of gifts and talents, students become unmotivated, underachieve, and act out in academically and socially. As noted in Ford (2010), gifted students represent some 20% of students who drop out of school. How this breaks down by race is unclear due to not being studied; but it cannot be denied that some or many students who drop out of school are not only Black and Hispanic but also gifted Black and Hispanic students.

How are these gifted students expected to be and remain motivated and engaged when poorly challenged in schools? How are Black and Hispanic gifted students expected to be and remain motivated and engaged when they lack access to rigorous educational courses and programs? How are they expected to achieve and excel, to retain motivation, goals, and dreams, when denied access to curriculum, instruction, and supports needed to reach their potential?

Undeniably, gifted education classes and services are disproportionately represented by and serving higher-income White and Asian students; and gifted education gives them a boost up the social and fiscal hierarchy that is fueled by racial and social privileges (e.g., McIntosh, 1988) and the larger inequity of the myth of meritocracy. Social inequities and race-based underrepresentation are inseparable—social, racial, and educational inequities feed underrepresentation; underrepresentation feeds injustices and poor motivation, disengagement, and low achievement or underachievement.

Unquestionably and unfortunately, social pressures, racism, and elitism influence efforts to recruit and retain non-White students in gifted education (Ford, 2013, 2014). Teachers, administrators, decision makers, and policy makers acquiesce to the status quo (Kohn, 1998; Sapon-Shevin, 1994, 1996). One result is two types of schools and gifted programs—those that are inequitable and those that are equitable.

Equality is the cornerstone of *Brown v. Board of Education* (1954). Equality refers to sameness. Thus, all students are entitled to high-quality teachers. All students are entitled to have access to the same technology and to the same supports and resources. Problematic is that equality fails to consider students' context and, accordingly, different needs. Thus, doing the same when there are different needs is in and of itself an injustice. While race is not directly addressed, the ecological work of Bronfenbrenner (1979) is informative here. Given the aforementioned problems, I summarize key points by juxtaposing these very different types of schools.

Equality District

This district promotes sameness and fails to consider different opportunities, issues, and needs. Not surprisingly, Black and Hispanic students are sorely underrepresented in gifted education. While Hispanic students are 30% of their schools, they are 20% of gifted classes—almost a 40% discrepancy. Even more underrepresented are Black students. Despite being 45% of the school district, they are only 22% of gifted education. The discrepancy is around 50%. The discrepancies are large and may point to discrimination in recruitment and retention policies, procedures, and instruments (Ford, 2013).

Equality District relies on teacher referrals for screening of students in the third grade. Gifted programming begins the next year, even though reports and consultants have urged that screening, identification, and programming begin earlier. *If* students are referred by their teachers, then testing begins.

The administration recognizes that teachers underrefer Black and Hispanic students. They also know that certain schools and teachers rarely if ever refer these two groups. But they continue this practice of allowing teachers to be gatekeepers. They also accept referrals from parents/primary caregivers and have found that higher-income and more educated parents overrefer their children, while those with less social (cultural and economic) capital underrefer their children. These families complain that the procedures and forms are confusing and very time consuming. Equality District has failed to reach out to inform and support this group of parents and families.

There is no screening phase in Equality District. Rather, once referred by teachers or parents, identification begins. A traditional test of intelligence containing three subscales—verbal, math, and nonverbal—is used. Equality District also includes achievement test scores in its criteria and has set the cutoff percentile at 96. Local and building norms are not adopted, and income is not considered.

Equity District

This district considers differences in students and their contexts. Gifted Black and Hispanic students are underrepresentated but not to the extent that they are in Equality District. Hispanic students are 30% of their school enrollment and 25% of gifted classes. Black students are 45% of the school district and 34% of gifted education enrollment. The discrepancies are less but equitable, as described shortly. As much as this district wants gifted education enrollment to mirror district enrollment, it recognizes that racial quotas are illegal.

This district supports teacher input but not as referral agents. Equity District has read reports on referrals (Ford, Moore, Whiting, & Grantham, 2008) and hired a consultant to study teacher and parental referrals by students' race and income in their district. They understand that parents are their children's first and forever teachers; caregivers have 6 years to raise their children before formal education. Educators have studied the achievement gap in a developmental way; children spend those first 6 years with different access to language, literacy, preschool, and educational experiences. They knew that underreferral by teachers is a problem in their district and that low-income, and Black and Hispanic parents also underrefer compared to higher-income and more educated White parents.

As a result, rather than relying on referrals by teachers and parents, Equity District adopted universal screening in the first grade using both a traditional and nontraditional test (i.e., nonverbal). For screening, they have adopted the same traditional test used by Equality District, but for screening, they screen students who score an IQ of 110 or more on *one* of the three subscales. Schools can also replace this traditional instrument with a nonverbal measure, especially when students are limited English proficient and/or low income. Rather than using racial quotas, Equity District has set goals that target *minimal* representation enrollments for underrepresented students (see Table 12.5).

Desegregating Gifted Education **193**

TABLE 12.5 Gifted education in equality district versus equity district

Criteria	Equality District	Equity District
Screening	N/A	Universal
Teacher Referral	Yes; grade 3	No
Family/Caregiver Referral	Yes; grade 3	No
Intelligence Tests	Traditional (IQ of 130+ on verbal *and* math subscales)	Traditional (for screening, an IQ of 110 on *one* of the three subscales; for identification, IQ of 120+)
		Nontraditional (Nonverbal; IQ of 110 for screening or 120+ for identification)
Achievement Test	96th percentile	Based on Building Norms
Norms	National	Local and School Building
Income Considerations	No	Yes
Gifted Programming	Grade 4	Grade 1
Equity Goals	No	Yes

Source: Ford (2015)

Recommendations

Too many Black and Hispanic students fail to achieve to their potential because they are denied access to gifted classes and opportunities. Prejudices, stereotypes, and deficit-oriented paradigms contribute to segregated gifted programs (which violate the principles and mandates of *Brown*) that are sorely inadequate at recruitment and retention (Ford, 2013, 2014; Ford & Grantham, 2003; Valencia, 2010). Recent court cases, specifically *McFadden v. Board of Education for Illinois School District U-46* (2013), remind and compel us to continue advocating for underrepresented groups, that discrimination is not only unintentional but also intentional, and that discrimination exists in both de facto and de jure segregation. The will and accountability to *eliminate* human-made barriers, to take on the status quo, and to advocate for underrepresented gifted Black and Hispanic students is crucial.

Analyze and Disaggregate Underrepresentation Data

Attitudes (prejudice, deficit thinking, and racism) and inequitable policies and practices must be acknowledged, examined, analyzed, challenged, and addressed to recruit and retain underrepresented students in gifted education. Are Black and Hispanic students being screened and referred by teachers in proportion to their representation in the district and state? How pervasive and severe is underrepresentation? Which factors contribute to underrepresentation (e.g., subjectivity in beliefs, attitudes, and values; subjective instruments such as checklists and nomination forms; biased and unfair tests; and discriminatory policies and procedures)? Which policies and procedures contribute to and exacerbate underrepresentation (e.g., reliance on teacher referral or checklist versus schoolwide grade-level screening: parent/caregiver referral or checklists: designated cutoff scores; grade at which gifted programs begins; ongoing screening; convenience and location of testing sites; modes of communicating in neighborhoods)? Which educators underrefer Black and Hispanic students, and how are they being assessed for accountability? How effective are family referrals for such students, and what is being done to increase such referrals?

Determine Equity Allowance Goals

After studying the magnitude of and causes for underrepresentation, equity goals must be set to desegregate gifted education using the 20% equity allowance (Ford, 2013). The equity allowance is a recognition that giftedness exists in *every* racial group. Students' lived experiences, resources, and supports are not always equally and equitably distributed. This equity allowance, which is measurable, takes such differences and injustices into account, thereby opening doors for many non-White students who might otherwise not be identified and served in gifted education.

Collect Data on the Experiences of Gifted Black and Hispanic Students

What are the experiences of former and current Black students in gifted education? Disaggregate data by gender and income—What are the experiences of Black males compared to females and low-income students compared to high-income Black students? Surveys, interviews, focus groups, and case studies from such students and families regarding their experiences can be useful for both recruitment and retention. It is essential to study what encourages or motivates students to persist in gifted classes. Study relationships with classmates and with peers in the community. Do students feel welcome in gifted classrooms? Do these gifted students feel valued and appreciated by their teachers? How do gifted Black and Hispanic students find ways to fit in and be welcomed in gifted education? How supportive are their families?

Evaluate and Promote Educators' Preparation in Gifted Education

Educators are seldom formally prepared in gifted education, despite their responsibility for referrals, nominations, and teaching gifted students. Gifted education preparation is essential and can take place via courses, degree programs, and professional development. Training must be continuous and substantive, which means targeting equitable identification and assessment instruments, policies and procedures, and development—affective, psychological, academic, social, and cultural (Ford, 2010, 2011).

Culturally responsive educators are adept at motivating their gifted students and know that Black and Hispanic students may face more challenges than their White classmates and peers, as already noted. They recognize that several goals must be addressed: motivate students cognitively, motivate students academically, motivate students socially-emotionally, and motivate students culturally.

Evaluate and Promote Cultural Competence Among Educators

Culturally incompetent educators risk undermining the educational experiences of Black students and thus contribute to segregated gifted education programs. Formal, substantive, and comprehensive multicultural preparation helps ensure educational equity (Banks, 2010, 2015). Professional development on culture and cultural differences must be ongoing and deep, including defining and understanding culture and cultural differences without a deficit orientation and recognizing how culture impacts teaching and learning, testing and assessment, and classroom environment (e.g., relationships with teachers and classmates, classroom management). Sample opportunities consist of field experiences, attending community events, and visiting families. Again, it is vital that educators connect with students culturally and that their work is culturally responsive and affirming.

Increase the Demographics of Black and Hispanic Educators in Gifted Education

White teachers comprise a significant proportion of the education profession nationally (Kena et al., 2014). Specifically, at the national level, Whites comprise 85% of teachers, while Blacks represent 7% of teachers, as do Hispanics. Asians are 1% of teachers. Ford (2011) reported that Black teachers are virtually invisible in gifted education. Thus, students from every racial and cultural background continue to graduate without ever having a Black or Hispanic teacher, counselor, educational psychologist, and/or administrator; and this is rarer in gifted education. Culturally different educators can and do serve as cultural brokers, role models, mentors, and strong advocates for Black and Hispanic students (Delpit, 2012; Ford, 2011; Gay, 2010; Ladson-Billings, 2009).

Summary and Conclusion

In *Brown v. Board of Education* (1954), the Supreme Court ruled that segregating children on the basis of race was unconstitutional. It signaled the end of legalized racial segregation in the U.S. schools, overruling the "separate but equal" principle set forth in the 1896 *Plessy v. Ferguson* case. Yet segregation persists in school settings and gifted education.

Discrimination in gifted education was found in the *McFadden* (2013) court case. While other districts may not have been found guilty of *intentional* discrimination, it is clear that de facto and de jure segregation is operating—unintentionally and intentionally—in many school districts.

In principle and in practice, gifted education professionals must abide by the spirit and law of *Brown* (1954) regarding desegregating classrooms, programs, and services. Progress in gifted education underrepresentation has been insignificant and inequitable. Educators must be proactive, deliberate, and diligent about eliminating intentional *and* unintentional barriers to recruiting and retaining Black and Hispanic students in gifted education—to desegregating and integrating gifted education.

Note

1 These Civil Rights Data Collection files are state and national estimations. The 2009–10 estimations are based on a rolling stratified sample of approximately 7,000 districts and 72,000 schools and on reported data from those districts that responded to the survey.

References

Banks, J. A. (2010). Approaches to multicultural curriculum reform. In J. A. Banks & C.A.M. Banks (Eds.), *Multicultural education: Issues and perspectives* (7th ed., pp. 233–258). Hoboken, NJ: John Wiley & Sons.

Banks, J. A. (2015). *Cultural diversity and education: Foundations, curriculum and teaching* (6th ed.). Boston: Pearson, Allyn & Bacon.

Bronfenbrenner, U. (1979). *The ecology of human development: Experiments by nature and design.* Cambridge, MA: Harvard University Press.

Brown v. Board of Education, 347 U.S. 483 (1954).

Delpit, L. D. (2012). *Multiplication is for White people: Raising expectations for other people's children.* New York: The New Press.

Ford, D.Y. (2010). *Reversing underachievement among gifted Black students* (2nd ed.). Waco, TX: Prufrock Press.

Ford, D.Y. (2011). *Multicultural gifted education* (2nd ed.). Waco, TX: Prufrock Press.

Ford, D.Y. (2013). *Recruiting and retaining culturally different students in gifted education.* Waco, TX: Prufrock Press.

Ford, D. Y. (2014). Segregation and the underrepresentation of Blacks and Hispanics in gifted education: Social inequality and deficit paradigms. *Roeper Review, 36,* 143–154.

Ford, D.Y. (2015). Recruiting and retaining Black and Hispanic students in gifted education: Equality vs. equity schools. *Gifted Child Today, 38*(3), 187–191.

Ford, D.Y., & Grantham, T. C. (2003). Providing access for gifted culturally diverse students: From deficit thinking to dynamic thinking. *Theory into Practice, 42*(3), 217–225.

Ford, D.Y., & King, R. A. (2014). No Blacks allowed: Segregated gifted education in the context of *Brown vs. Board of Education. Journal of Negro Education, 83*(3), 300–310.

Ford, D. Y., Moore III, J. J. Whiting, G. W., & Grantham, T. C. (2008). Conducting cross-cultural research: Cautions, concerns, and considerations. *Roeper Review, 30*(2), 82–92.

Ford, D. Y. & Russo, C. (2014, March). Point/counterpoint. Needed: The law and spirit of the law in overcoming persistent racial divides in gifted and disabled programming. *UCEA Review*, 33–35.

Ford, D. Y., & Russo, C. J. (2015). No child left behind . . . unless a student is gifted and of color: Reflections on the need to meet the educational needs of the gifted. *Journal of Law in Society, 15*, 213–239.

Frankenberg, E. (2012). Understanding suburban school district transformation: A typology of suburban districts. In E. Frankenberg & G. Orfield (Eds.), *The resegregation of suburban schools: A hidden crisis in education* (pp. 27–44). Cambridge, MA: Harvard Education Press.

Gay, J. (2010). *Culturally responsive teaching: Theory, research, and practice* (2nd ed.). New York: Teachers College Press.

Griggs v. Duke Power Co., 401 U.S. 424 (1971).

Kena, G., Aud, S., Johnson, F., Wang, X., Zhang, J., Rathbun, A., Wilkinson-Flicker, S., and Kristapovich, P. (2014). *The Condition of Education 2014* (NCES 2014–083). Washington, DC: U.S. Department of Education, National Center for Education Statistics.

Kohn, A. (1998). Only for my kid: How privileged parents undermine school reform. *Phi Delta Kappan, 79*(8), 568–577.

Ladson-Billings, G. (2009). *The dreamkeepers: Successful teachers of African American children* (2nd ed.). New York: Jossey-Bass.

McFadden v. Board of Education for Illinois School District U-4. (2013). Retrieved from http://www.maldef.org/news/releases/maldef_u46_discrimination_case/

McIntosh, P. (1988). *White privilege: Unpacking the invisible knapsack*. Working Paper #189. Wellesley, MA: Wellesley College Center for Research on Women.

Office for Civil Rights. (2006). *Elementary and secondary school civil rights survey*. Retrieved from http://ocrdata.ed.gov/flex/Reports.aspx?type=school

Office for Civil Rights. (2009). *Elementary and secondary school civil rights survey*. Retrieved from http://ocrdata.ed.gov/StateNationalEstimations/Projections_2009_10

Office for Civil Rights. (2011). *Civil rights data collection*. Retrieved from http://ocrdata.ed.gov/flex/Reports.aspx?type=school

Plessy v. Ferguson, 163 U.S. 537 (1896).

Sapon-Shevin, M. (1994). *Playing favorites: Gifted education and the disruption of community*. Albany: SUNY Press.

Sapon-Shevin, M. (1996). Beyond gifted education: Building a shared agenda for school reform. *Journal for the Education of the Gifted, 19*(2), 194–214.

Sternberg, R. J. (2007a). Who are the bright children? The cultural context of being and acting intelligent. *Educational Researcher, 36*(3), 148–155.

Sternberg, R. J. (2007b). Cultural concepts of giftedness. *Roeper Review, 29*(3), 160–166.

Title VI, 42 U.S.C. § 2000d et seq., (1964).

Valencia, R. R. (2010). *Dismantling contemporary deficit thinking: Educational thought and practice*. London: Routledge.

PART IV

Future Directions in Examining Race and Ethnicity in the Study of Motivation

13

A FUTURE AGENDA FOR RESEARCHING RACE AND ETHNICITY IN THE STUDY OF MOTIVATION IN EDUCATIONAL CONTEXTS

Jessica T. DeCuir-Gunby, Paul A. Schutz, and Sonya D. Harris

In motivation research, we often shy away from examining race/ethnicity as a central construct (Graham & Hudley, 2005). When race/ethnicity is used, it is often subsumed under the broad category of culture or just seen as a demographic variable (Helms, Jernigan, & Mascher, 2005). Doing so inadvertently devalues the importance of race and ethnicity and the critical roles they play in the study of motivation in education. As such, the impetus for this volume was to illustrate why the study of race and ethnicity is important in teaching and learning, as well as to demonstrate how such studies are being currently conducted in motivation research. Although we provided a variety of examples of research on race and ethnicity throughout this volume, more work is needed in this area. The goal of this chapter is to continue the dialogue on helping to advance this research agenda and expand the use of race-reimaged and race-focused approaches in the study of motivation in education (DeCuir-Gunby & Schutz, 2014). We initiate the dialogue with a brief discussion of the major themes that were presented in the chapters. We then provide future research directions for inquiry on race and ethnicity in the study of motivation in education. Next we discuss the need for expanding our methodological considerations in the study of race and ethnicity. Last, we provide implications for teaching, learning, and educational policy as they pertain to motivation.

Examining Race and Ethnicity in Motivation: Race-Reimaged and Race-Focused Approaches

The chapters presented in this book were organized into two major sections: race-reimaged and race-focused approaches. Within these sections, the authors explored a variety of relevant issues related to teaching, learning, and motivation

202 Jessica T. DeCuir-Gunby et al.

within K–16 education contexts. In discussing these issues, the authors explored a variety of constructs that are essential to the understanding of the experiences of students of color.

Race-Reimaged Approaches to Examining Race and Ethnicity

Using race-reimaged approaches involves reconceptualizing traditional constructs to include sociocultural perspectives (DeCuir-Gunby & Schutz, 2014). A variety of the chapters in this volume utilized this approach (see Section II of this volume). These race-reimaged approaches were used to focus on some of the more "traditional" motivation constructs such as persistence, retention, self-regulation, belonging, achievement motivation, academic expectations, and school engagement. These researchers foregrounded race and ethnicity while engaging in research to investigate the lived experiences of students of color. As such, these chapters help us further our understanding of the experiences of students of color as well as the constructs themselves. By coupling "traditional" motivation theories and constructs with racialized experiences of students of color, these chapters also illustrated the necessity of framing motivation research within sociocultural and sociohistorical perspectives.

Race-Focused Approaches to Examining Race and Ethnicity

On the other hand, race-focused approaches place race (or ethnicity) at the center of analysis, with the goal of viewing race itself as a construct (DeCuir-Gunby & Schutz, 2014). Several chapters in this volume utilized this approach (see Section III of this volume). In doing so, such chapters focused on a variety of race-based constructs including Black racial identity, ethnic identity, intersectionality, acculturation, assimilation, asset-based pedagogy, and culturally relevant assessment, among others. The authors of these chapters demonstrated how students of color are influenced by cultural issues and the impact of the sociohistorical nature of race, as well the roles that schooling can play in these experiences. In addition, the chapters illustrated a variety of ways in which race-focused approaches or perspectives can be used in motivation research, demonstrating the relevance of race-centered constructs in the study of motivation in educational contexts, thus providing windows into the potential future of motivational research from sociohistorical perspectives.

Future Directions for Inquiry on Race and Ethnicity

The chapters in this volume highlight some of the research by both leading and emerging researchers in the field of motivation in K–16 education that engage in both race-reimaged and race-focused work. Their research showcases the myriad of ways in which race/ethnicity can be explored in the study of motivation.

However, there are still many constructs and areas that need further exploration regarding race and ethnicity in the study of motivation in education. Specifically, we need to expand both the use of race-reimaged and race-focused approaches. In order to do so, we should focus on inter- and intraracial/ethnic group dynamics. We also should explore the impact of race/ethnicity on school structures/functioning. Last, more work is needed on external influences on race/ethnicity and motivation.

Intergroup Interactions

Expanding the use of race-reimaged and race-focused constructs within motivation research will involve exploring the experiences of racial/ethnic groups within the school context. School contexts are filled with opportunities for interactions between racial/ethnic groups (Pettigrew & Tropp, 2013). One the various ways in which motivation researchers can better comprehend the impact of race/ethnicity on schooling is to further explore the ways in which racial/ethnic groups interact with each other. Within the school context, there are many potential intergroup interactions in which race/ethnicity plays a significant role including peer relationships, student–teacher relationships, parent–teacher relationships, and administration–teacher relationships, among others. By focusing on these interpersonal interactions, researchers can gain insight on how issues surrounding race/ethnicity can support or hinder the development and maintenance of such relationships.

There are a number of unanswered questions about intergroup relationships in schools and their influence on motivation. For instance, research indicates that racial identity moderates the relationship between experiences with discrimination and motivation in school (Chavous et al., 2003). However, researchers have limited understanding as to the many ways in which racial identity impacts motivation in schools. How is racial identity shaped by relationships with peers and adults from diverse racial and ethnic backgrounds in the school context? How do relationships with people in different racial/ethnic groups affect racial/ethnic and academic identities? Are intergroup interactions less or more impactful than intragroup interactions? By focusing on these interpersonal interactions, researchers can gain insight on how issues surrounding race/ethnicity can support or hinder student motivation.

Intragroup Dynamics

In addition to better understanding interactions or relationships among racial/ethnic groups within the school context, we also need more research about the racial/ethnic groups themselves, or intragroup dynamics. Education researchers often describe racial/ethnic groups as though they are monolithic, in essence essentializing what it means to be a part of the group (Chao, Hong, & Chiu, 2013).

For instance, it is common to hear phrases like "THE Black experience," as if there is only one way to experience Blackness. Instead, we should focus on understanding the multidimensionality of race/ethnicity within the school context. Researchers need to focus more on understanding the experiences of members of individual racial/ethnic groups and their specific histories.

Issues such as racial identity development, racial socialization, colorism, intersectionality, and generational status, for example, are all important issues that can have an impact on what occurs within the school context. Each has a role in shaping both the individual and the school. More research is needed to better understand how such issues impact students within the school context. Specifically, how do students develop their identities within the school context? Which identities are most salient within the school context? What is the relationship between identity development and motivation? In order to better understand the nuances and complexities of identity development, it is necessary for us to have comprehensive models and measures of identity. Sellers, Smith, Shelton, Rowley, and Chavous's (1998) model for Black racial identity, for instance, is multidimensional and captures how African Americans feel about their race, their affinity for their race, and their perception of how others feel about their race. However, there is a need for other models to improve our ability to investigate the impact of these relationships as well as similar relationships within the school context.

School Structures and Functioning

Although it is important to understand the experiences of individuals, it is also essential for researchers to better comprehend the roles that race/ethnicity have in school structures and functioning. The structure, such as its rules, policies, and priorities, establishes what is valued and deemed important within a school context (Gillborn, 2005). For instance, understanding policies for school admissions, program placement (e.g., gifted and special education programs; see Ford, Chapter 12, this volume) and disciplinary procedures, all of which have the capability to disproportionately impact students of color in a negative manner, are necessary to comprehend how schools function and are maintained. In addition, structures such as how school curricula are chosen as well as what is included in the curricula are essential to creating a school's culture. The manner in which school structures are impacted by issues of race/ethnicity can also impact the experiences of underrepresented racial/ethnic groups.

School culture helps influence students' experiences. School belonging, a measure of students' sense of connectedness with their classmates and teachers, is critical for retention and moderates the risk of dropout and other negative behaviors (Finn, 1989; Wehlage, Rutter, Smith, Lesko, & Fernandez, 1989). Research suggests that belonging is facilitated when students perceive fewer differences between themselves and the student body, and these perceptions are shaped by feelings of comfort and tolerance (Booker, 2007). Further, teachers report that they have difficulty in sustaining academic engagement and commitment in environments in which students do not feel valued and welcomed (Batcher, 1981; Tinto, 1987; Zeichner, 1980). As such, more research is needed to better understand school culture, climate, and belonging. Specifically, how does school policy impact school climate? How does curriculum influence student motivation and engagement? How does school climate impact student racial identity development?

External Impacts

The last major area of inquiry that needs more exploration is the role of external influences on school contexts. Race-related issues outside of the school context can have a significant impact on what occurs within schools because schools are susceptible to external influences (Johnson, 2008). Thus it is important to better understand the roles that external influences can have on what occurs within schools. For instance, social movements (e.g., Black Lives Matter), popular culture (e.g., music, television, etc.), social media (e.g., Facebook, Instagram, Twitter, Black Twitter, etc.), and political priorities (e.g., No Child Left Behind) can all have racial/ethnic implications within schools. As such, it is important for motivation researchers to examine the role that external influences can have on schools.

The overall racial climate in society and race-related policies impacts what occurs in school (Thapa, Cohen, Guffey, & Higgins-D'Alessandro, 2013). As the United States has been experiencing a shift in overall racial/ethnic demographics as well as elected its first Black president, racial discussions and race-related issues have permeated the political and social climate. As such, we need to understand how this has impacted schools and learning. How does the media coverage of controversial cases with racial undertones (e.g., Trayvon Martin, Eric Garner, the Black Lives Matter movement, etc.) impact student motivation and student interactions in school? Similarly, how does school choice impact school climate? Is this relationship moderated by racial identity, racial socialization, or other aspects of social development? How does the growth of "no excuse" charter schools and alternatives to traditional public education in a community impact student development? As described, race and school outcomes are entangled with a web of external factors; motivation researchers should explore these relationships.

Methodological Considerations in the Study of Race and Ethnicity

In order to better explore race and ethnicity within school contexts, it is also necessary to consider the importance of methodology. As demonstrated throughout the various chapters in this book, race and ethnicity has been examined using multiple methodological approaches including quantitative, qualitative, and mixed methods. Although this is the case, more work still needs to be done to better explore race and ethnicity in the study of teaching, learning, and motivation.

206 Jessica T. DeCuir-Gunby et al.

Specifically, we need to move beyond traditional methodological approaches and incorporate more culturally responsive theoretical, methodological, and assessment approaches.

Moving Beyond Traditional Methodologies

Motivation researchers tend to rely heavily on traditional methodological approaches (e.g., single study, mostly quantitative, mostly survey). In order to better understand race/ethnicity within the school context, we will need to expand our approaches. We should utilize quantitative, qualitative, and mixed-methods approaches. We should also consider conducting more cross-sectional studies involving various developmental ages within a study as well as longitudinal studies. In addition, we should also contemplate moving beyond self-reports. For instance, some racial identity research has begun to explore the impact of racism on the stress and coping of African American college students, using psychophysiological indicators such as heart and respiratory rates (Neblett & Roberts, 2013). We need to continue to add to our uses of self-report measures to include other methodologies such as ethnographies, observations, historical analyses, psychophysiological methods, and neuroimaging (for example, see Gray, Hill, Bryant, Wornoff, Johnson, & Jackson, Chapter 4, this volume). These approaches will allow us to have a richer understanding of race/ethnicity within the school context.

Embracing Culturally Responsive Approaches

In addition to utilizing nontraditional methodologies, it is necessary that researchers begin to embrace more culturally responsive approaches to examining motivation within schools. The importance of culture should be imperative to all aspects of the research process, particularly the design and implementation of instruments or assessments (Tran, 2009). Too frequently motivation researchers utilize instruments that are not culturally sensitive and attempt to use them on racially/ethnically diverse populations (Knight, Roosa, & Umana-Taylor, 2009). Doing so may result in claims that are not accurate. Thus, motivation researchers should implement more culturally responsive assessment practices. For example, research should take into consideration cultural or multicultural validity when conducting research (Kirkhart, 1995). Multicultural validity is "the accuracy or trustworthiness of understandings and judgments, actions, and consequences, across multiple, intersecting dimensions of cultural diversity" (Kirkhart, 2010, p. 401). Addressing the multidimensionality of culture (e.g., participants, context, history, researchers, etc.) should be a common component of the validation process.

Similarly, motivation researchers should embrace culturally relevant theoretical approaches. When examining issues involving race/ethnicity, it is necessary that motivation research is grounded in culturally relevant theories or theories that are centered on sociocultural issues (e.g., race, gender, SES, sexuality, etc.). For instance, when researching issues involving race/ethnicity within the teaching and learning process, motivation researchers should consider theories such as culturally relevant pedagogy (Ladson-Billings, 1995, 2014), culturally responsive teaching (Gay, 2010), culturally sustaining pedagogy (Paris, 2012), or asset-based pedagogy (López, Chapter 9, this volume). In addition, when examining systemic issues involving racism and power, theories such as Black feminist thought (Collins, 2002), critical race theory (DeCuir & Dixson, 2004; Ladson-Billings & Tate, 1995), or postcolonial theory (Gandhi, 1998) would be helpful. Framing motivation research using such theories or similar theories coupled with motivation theories would allow for a more comprehensive theoretical approach.

Implications for the Examination of Race and Ethnicity in the Study of Motivation in Education

Although additional research is indeed needed, as previously discussed, research is not the only way to further our understanding regarding race and ethnicity in the study of motivation. Assistance is needed from practitioners that are operating within a variety of educational contexts. Specifically, more work is needed in terms of practice in the areas of teacher/professor training, student development, and policy.

Teacher Training

With the growing racial/ethnic diversity of schools, it is imperative that teachers/professors embrace the diversity of their classrooms (PK–16). One of the ways in which to accomplish this is for teacher education programs to incorporate multicultural curricula (Milner, 2006, 2010). Preservice teachers should be trained using approaches that question traditional theories that privilege the White, middle-class perspective. Similarly, there should be more diversity courses available in higher education in order to expose students to diverse perspectives. Another way to better understand issues of race and ethnicity in the study of motivation in education is to increase the recruitment and retention efforts of teachers/professors of color. According to the U.S. Department of Education, in the 2011–12 school year, 81.9% of K–12 teachers were White, while only 7.8% were Hispanic, 6.8% were African American, and 1.8% were Asian (Goldring, Gray, & Bitterman, 2013). In higher education, the statistics are similar: 84% of full-time professors were White while only 3% were Hispanic, 4% were African American, and 9% were Asian/Pacific Islander (U.S. Department of Education, National Center for Education Statistics, 2015). Concerted efforts should be made to increase the diversity of teachers and professors in order to better mirror the racial demographics of the U.S. populace. Last, although the presence of people

208 Jessica T. DeCuir-Gunby et al.

of color in education is imperative, it is also necessary for White educators to be both receptive and supportive of diversity efforts. As such, it is necessary to develop White allies (Reason, 2005; Tatum, 1994). White allies understand issues surrounding diversity, particularly systemic racism and White privilege. They serve as sources of support for people of color as well as agents of change within social systems.

Student Development

A focus of education is to help ensure positive student development (Chickering & Reisser, 1993). As such, it is essential that schools (K–16) place emphasis on helping students develop positive identities, particularly racial and ethnic identities. Schools have to create atmospheres in which multiple identities are valued. Students need to feel valued and that their racial and ethnic backgrounds are considered assets rather than deficits. In other words, students need to feel as though they belong to the school community (Osterman, 2000). There are several ways to increase students' sense of belonging. One approach is to provide opportunities for student involvement (Moore, Lovell, McGann, & Wyrick, 1998). Schools should have access to a variety of multicultural or cultural activities and organizations. This will enable students to interact with other students with similar interests and backgrounds. Another way is to provide opportunities to engage students' voices. It is important for students to voice their opinions as well as for faculty to listen to the voices of students. Students need to feel as though their voices matter (Mitra, 2004). Ultimately, the more students feel they belong, the more likely they will be engaged in school and academically successful (Wang & Eccles, 2012).

Policy

Oftentimes motivation researchers focus on issues pertaining to intra- and interpersonal interactions. Rarely do we focus our attention to structural issues and how they may impact the school context. As such, it is necessary that motivation researchers attend to bigger issues such as school policy and how it affects students and teachers. For instance, many school systems are making new busing and school assignment plans that are resulting in school resegregation (Donnor & Dixson, 2013; Reardon, Grewal, Kalogrides, & Greenberg, 2012). Such policy choices are disproportionately negatively impacting students of color. In addition, examining policy implications can help us address larger issues like the overrepresentation of students of color in special education programs and the underrepresentation of students of color in gifted education (Ford, 2014, this volume; Harry & Klingner, 2014). Also, using a motivation lens to refocus the achievement gap discussion to one of an opportunity gap would help provide more opportunities to support achievement within the school context.

Conclusion

The 21st century is an exciting time for education researchers. With the growing racial and ethnic diversity of our schools comes the opportunity to explore new and exciting questions while utilizing novel approaches. This volume provides a foundation to better understand issues of race and ethnicity in motivation. With such a foundation, motivation researchers are poised to lead the way to better understanding the role of race and ethnicity in education.

References

Batcher, E. (1981). *Emotion in the classroom: A study of children's experience*. New York: Praeger Publishers.

Booker, K. C. (2007). Likeness, comfort, and tolerance: Examining African American adolescents' sense of school belonging. *The Urban Review, 39*(3), 301–317.

Chao, M. M., Hong, Y.Y., & Chiu, C.Y. (2013). Essentializing race: Its implications on racial categorization. *Journal of Personality and Social Psychology, 104*(4), 619–634.

Chavous, T. M., Bernat, D. H., Schmeelk-Cone, K., Caldwell, C. H., Kohn-Wood, L., & Zimmerman, M. A. (2003). Racial identity and academic attainment among African American adolescents. *Child Development, 74*(4), 1076–1090.

Chickering, A. W., & Reisser, L. (1993). *Education and identity: The Jossey-Bass higher and adult education series*. San Francisco, CA: Jossey-Bass Inc.

Collins, P. H. (2002). *Black feminist thought: Knowledge, consciousness, and the politics of empowerment*. New York: Routledge.

DeCuir, J. T., & Dixson, A. D. (2004). "So when it comes out, they aren't that surprised that it is there": Using critical race theory as a tool of analysis of race and racism in education. *Educational Researcher, 33*(5), 26–31.

DeCuir-Gunby, J. T., & Schutz, P. A. (2014). Researching race within educational psychology contexts. *Educational Psychologist, 49*(4), 244–260.

Donnor, J. K., & Dixson, A. (2013). *The resegregation of schools: Education and race in the twenty-first century* (Vol. 95). New York: Routledge.

Finn, J. D. (1989). Withdrawing from school. *Review of Educational Research, 59*(2), 117–142.

Ford, D. Y. (2014). Segregation and the underrepresentation of Blacks and Hispanics in gifted education: Social inequality and deficit paradigms. *Roeper Review, 36*(3), 143–154.

Gandhi, L. (1998). *Postcolonial theory: A critical introduction*. New York: Columbia University Press.

Gay, G. (2010). *Culturally responsive teaching: Theory, research, and practice*. New York: Teachers College Press.

Gillborn, D. (2005). Education policy as an act of white supremacy: Whiteness, critical race theory and education reform. *Journal of Education Policy, 20*(4), 485–505.

Goldring, R., Gray, L., & Bitterman, A. (2013). *Characteristics of public and private elementary and secondary school teachers in the United States: Results from the 2011–12 schools and staffing survey* (NCES 2013–314). Washington, DC: U.S. Department of Education.

Graham, S., & Hudley, C. (2005). Race and ethnicity in the study of motivation and competence. In A. Elliot & C. Dweck (Eds.), *Handbook of competence and motivation* (pp. 392–414). New York: Guilford.

Harry, B., & Klingner, J. (2014). *Why are so many minority students in special education?* New York: Teachers College Press.

Helms, J., Jernigan, M., & Mascher, J. (2005). The meaning of race in psychology and how to change it: A methodological perspective. *American Psychologist, 60*(1), 27–36.

Johnson, E. S. (2008). Ecological systems and complexity theory: Toward an alternative model of accountability in education. *Complicity: An International Journal of Complexity and Education, 5*(1), 1–10.

Kirkhart, K. E. (1995). Seeking multicultural validity: A postcard from the road. *Evaluation Practice, 16*, 1–12.

Kirkhart, K. E. (2010). Eyes on the prize: Multicultural validity and evaluation theory. *American Journal of Evaluation, 31*(3), 400–413.

Knight, G. P., Roosa, M. W., & Umana-Taylor, A. J. (2009). *Studying ethnic minority and economically disadvantaged populations: Methodological challenges and best practices.* Washington, DC: American Psychological Association.

Ladson-Billings, G. (1995). Toward a theory of culturally relevant pedagogy. *American Educational Research Journal, 32*(3), 465–491.

Ladson-Billings, G. (2014). Culturally relevant pedagogy 2.0: Aka the remix. *Harvard Educational Review, 84*(1), 74–84.

Ladson-Billings, G., & Tate IV, W. (1995). Toward a critical race theory of education. *The Teachers College Record, 97*(1), 47–68.

Milner, H. R. (2006). Preservice teachers' learning about cultural and racial diversity Implications for urban education. *Urban Education, 41*(4), 343–375.

Milner, H. R. (2010). What does teacher education have to do with teaching? Implications for diversity studies. *Journal of Teacher Education, 61*(1–2), 118–131.

Mitra, D. (2004). The significance of students: Can increasing "student voice" in schools lead to gains in youth development? *The Teachers College Record, 106*(4), 651–688.

Moore, J., Lovell, C. D., McGann, T., & Wyrick, J. (1998). Why involvement matters: A review of research on student involvement in the collegiate setting. *College Student Affairs Journal, 17*(2), 4–17.

Neblett, Jr., E. W., & Roberts, S. O. (2013). Racial identity and autonomic responses to racial discrimination. *Psychophysiology, 50*(10), 943–953.

Osterman, K. F. (2000). Students' need for belonging in the school community. *Review of Educational Research, 70*(3), 323–367.

Paris, D. (2012). Culturally sustaining pedagogy a needed change in stance, terminology, and practice. *Educational Researcher, 41*(3), 93–97.

Pettigrew, T. F., & Tropp, L. R. (2013). *When groups meet: The dynamics of intergroup contact.* New York: Psychology Press.

Reardon, S. F., Grewal, E. T., Kalogrides, D., & Greenberg, E. (2012). Brown fades: The end of court-ordered school desegregation and the resegregation of American public schools. *Journal of Policy Analysis and Management, 31*(4), 876–904.

Reason, R. D. (Ed.). (2005). *Developing social justice allies: New directions for student services, number 110* (Vol. 84). San Francisco: Jossey-Bass.

Sellers, R. M., Smith, M. A., Shelton, J. N., Rowley, S. A. J., & Chavous, T. M. (1998). Multidimensional model of racial identity: A reconceptualization of African American racial identity. *Personality and Social Psychology Review, 2*(1), 18–39.

Tatum, B. (1994). Teaching White students about racism: The search for White allies and the restoration of hope. *The Teachers College Record, 95*(4), 462–476.

Thapa, A., Cohen, J., Guffey, S., & Higgins-D'Alessandro, A. (2013). A review of school climate research. *Review of Educational Research, 83*(3), 357–385.

Tinto, V. (1987). *Leaving college: Rethinking the causes and cures of student attrition*. Chicago, IL: University of Chicago Press.

Tran, T. V. (2009). *Developing cross-cultural measurement*. New York: Oxford University Press USA.

U.S. Department of Education, National Center for Education Statistics. (2015). *The condition of education 2015* (NCES 2015–144). Characteristics of Postsecondary Faculty.

Wang, M. T., & Eccles, J. S. (2012). Social support matters: Longitudinal effects of social support on three dimensions of school engagement from middle to high school. *Child Development, 83*(3), 877–895.

Wehlage, G. G., Rutter, R. A., Smith, G. A., Lesko, N., & Fernandez, R. R. (1989). *Reducing the risk: Schools as communities of support*. London: Falmer.

Zeichner, K. M. (1980). Myths and realities: field-based experiences in preservice teacher education. *Journal of Teacher Education, 31*(6), 45–55.

ABOUT THE CONTRIBUTORS

Rhonda S. Bondie is an assistant professor of special education at Fordham University. Her research focuses on differentiated instruction and teacher preparation through digital teaching platforms. Her innovative learning strategies have been published in books such as *Making Thinking Visible and Igniting Creativity in Gifted Learners, K–6: Strategies for Every Teacher* and on websites such as the National History Education Clearinghouse. She maintains two websites for teacher learning, Project REACH Online.org and ALL-ED.org.

Lauren H. Bryant is the Director of Innovation and Evaluation with the SMART Collaborative and a Research Scholar at the Friday Institute for Educational Innovation at NC State. Her research interests include achievement motivation, individual differences, and research methodologies, including innovative evaluation methods such as scale and developmental evaluation. Currently, she leads a collaborative project with local educators to collect data on student motivation and uses those data to make changes in classroom practice. She is also leading the development of a framework that helps motivation researchers demonstrate the relevance of their work in the everyday lives of educators and students.

Tabbye M. Chavous is a Professor of Education and Psychology at the University of Michigan. She is codirector of the Center for the Study of Black Youth in Context and Associate Dean for Academic Programs and Initiatives in the Rackham Graduate School. Her research focuses on social identity development among Black adolescents and young adults; achievement motivation processes, including relations among racial, gender, and academic identities; and diversity and multicultural climates in secondary and higher education.

About the Contributors **213**

Su-je Cho is an associate professor of Special Education and the Director of the Childhood Special Education programs in the Division of Curriculum and Teaching at Fordham University. Dr. Cho has also directed the federally funded Project REACH to better prepare prospective teachers for students with disabilities by redesigning the teacher education program. Her research areas include school adjustment of Asian students and assessment and interventions for children with challenging behavior.

Danya M. Corkin is the director of research and evaluation for the Rice University School Mathematics Project. She is also an adjunct assistant professor of psychology in the School of Social Sciences at Rice University. She earned her Ph.D. in educational psychology and individual differences from the University of Houston. Her research interests include investigating the role of student motivation in academic achievement, specifically in math and science.

Lyn Corno is formerly a Professor of Education and Psychology at Teachers College, Columbia University and currently a member of the Teachers College EdLab as well as co-editor of *Teachers College Record*. She has served as president of Division 15 of the American Psychological Association, chair of the Visiting Panel for Research at ETS, and chair of the board for the National Society for the Study of Education. She has also served as the editor of the *American Educational Research Journal* and *Educational Psychologist*.

Jessica T. DeCuir-Gunby is an Associate Professor of Educational Psychology and University Faculty Scholar in the Department of Teacher Education & Learning Sciences at NC State University. Her research interests include race and racial identity development, critical race theory, mixed-methods research, and emotions in education. She is currently an associate editor for the *American Educational Research Journal*.

Samantha Drotar is a research team lead at the Center for the Study of Black Youth in Context at the University of Michigan. She is also the project manager for the center's College Academic and Social Identities Study. Sam received her B.A. with high honors in psychology and sociology and a minor in moral and political philosophy from the University of Michigan in 2009. Her research interests span a variety of topics related to social and personal identities, with an emphasis on the significant role of context.

Gloryvee Fonseca-Bolorin is a doctoral candidate at the Center for the Study of Higher and Postsecondary Education at the University of Michigan. Her dissertation project uses data from the Center for the Study of Black Youth in Context to explore the role of racial/ethnic identity in understanding student experiences and resilience in higher education.

214 About the Contributors

Donna Y. Ford is Professor of Education and Human Development at Vanderbilt University. Her research focuses on (1) the achievement gap; (2) recruiting and retaining culturally different students in gifted education; (3) multicultural curriculum and instruction; (4) culturally competent teacher training and development; (5) African American identity; and (6) African American family involvement. She has also received numerous awards, including the Early Career Award and the Career Award from the American Educational Research Association.

Sandra Graham is a Professor in the Human Development and Psychology division in the Department of Education at UCLA and the University of California Presidential Chair in Education and Diversity. Her major research interests include the study of academic motivation and social development in children of color, particularly in school contexts that vary in racial/ethnic diversity. Professor Graham has published widely in developmental, social, and educational psychology journals and received many awards. Most recently, in 2015 she was elected to the National Academy of Education.

DeLeon L. Gray is an Assistant Professor of Educational Psychology at NC State University. He also directs The SMART Collaborative (www.thesmartlab.org). Dr. Gray has previously held appointments at the Association for Psychological Science (APS), the American Institutes for Research, and the National Institutes of Health. He focuses on how students' achievement motivation and in-school behavior may be traced back to interpretations of their own social encounters. His recent honors and awards include the Research on Socially and Economically Underrepresented Populations Award (RiSE-UP) from APS and dissertation fellowships from the National Academy of Education/Spencer Foundation and American Education Research Association (AERA).

Sonya D. Harris is a Graduate Student in the Educational Psychology program in the Department of Teacher Education & Learning Sciences at NC State University. Her research interests include racial socialization, racial identity, peer relationships, adolescent development, and achievement.

Veronica Herr graduated from Santa Clara University in 2014 with a bachelor's degree in psychology. Currently, she is enrolled in the forensic psychology master's program at The George Washington University. After earning her master's degree, she hopes to travel to Antarctica, completing her goal of traveling to every continent, before pursuing her Ph.D.

LaBarron K. Hill is an Assistant Professor at Duke University's Medical Center in the Department of Psychiatry and Behavioral Sciences. His research interests include parasympathetic influences on physical and mental health (e.g., hypertension) and physiological responses to environmental stimuli that induce worry and discrimination. His recent work examines the independent and interactive influence of psychosocial factors and underlying hemodynamic mechanisms on cognitive health and aging in African Americans.

Cynthia Hudley is a Professor Emerita at the University of California, Santa Barbara, in the Department of Education; she specializes in child and adolescent development and educational psychology. Dr. Hudley has edited two volumes on achievement motivation (*Academic Motivation and the Culture of Schools*, Oxford University Press; *Adolescent Identity and Schooling*, Routledge). She is former president of Division E of AERA, former associate editor of the *American Educational Research Journal*, former member of the Board of Educational Affairs for APA, and former chair of the Committee on Socioeconomic Status for APA. She is currently member at large and chair of the Fellows Committee for APA Division 15.

Lisa Jackson is a doctoral student in the School of Education at Virginia Commonwealth University in Richmond, Virginia (focus: educational psychology). Her research interests include education policy and racial achievement gaps in education and the influence of motivation constructs on minority achievement in both K–12 education and higher education populations. Lisa's research also focuses on the belongingness and collective efficacy of minority populations in schools, as well as the role of policy in the success of marginalized student groups.

Oriana Johnson is a doctoral student in North Carolina State University's Department of Teacher Education and Learning Sciences (focus: educational psychology). She has taught second and fifth grades in Title I public schools in New York City and North Carolina. Her research interests include critical race feminism, motivation, racial identity development, and hip-hop culture's impact on Black girls' education.

Stuart A. Karabenick is a Research Professor in the Combined Program in Education and Psychology (CPEP) and the Department of Psychology. His research interests focus on student and teacher motivation and self-regulated learning, especially students' use of and access to helping resources and social networks, as well as the study of cultural influences on learning and motivation. Research projects in progress include how teachers' beliefs about their professional responsibilities influence their approaches to teaching and professional commitment, teachers' motivation for professional development, and student help seeking.

Revathy Kumar is a Professor of Educational Psychology at the University of Toledo and Adjunct Assistant Research Scientist at the Institute for Social Research's Survey Research Center, University of Michigan. Her research focuses on social and cultural processes involved in constructing a sense of self and identity among adolescents in culturally diverse societies. Of particular interest are the

216 About the Contributors

role of teachers, teacher-education programs, schools, communities, and families in facilitating minority and immigrant adolescents' development, learning, and motivation.

Seanna Leath is a doctoral candidate in the Combined Program for Education and Psychology at the University of Michigan and fellow in the University's Center for the Study of Black Youth in Context. Her research interests include racial and gender identity development processes among African American girls and women; racial discrimination impacts on academic and psychological well-being; and family, school, and community influences on girls' racial and gender identity.

Francesca López is an Associate Professor in the Educational Psychology department at the University of Arizona. Her research, which is focused on the ways educational settings inform Latino student identity and achievement, has been funded by the American Educational Research Association Grants Program, the Division 15 of the American Psychological Association Early Career Award, and the National Academy of Education/Spencer Postdoctoral Fellowship. She is currently a coeditor for the *American Educational Research Journal.*

Donald Lyons is an upper-division undergraduate studying psychology and intergroup relations at the University of Michigan and research assistant in the university's Center for the Study of Black Youth in Context (CSBYC). He is currently working on a psychology honors thesis, using qualitative data from the CSBYC regarding the college experiences of Black women attending predominately White institutions.

Julie P. Martin is an Assistant Professor of Engineering and Science Education at Clemson University. She earned her Ph.D. in materials science and engineering from Virginia Polytechnic Institute and State University. Her research interests focus on social factors affecting the recruitment, retention, and career development of underrepresented students in engineering. She is a 2009 National Science Foundation CAREER awardee for her research titled "Influence of Social Capital on Under-Represented Engineering Students' Academic and Career Decisions."

Faheemah Mustafaa is a doctoral candidate in the Combined Program in Education and Psychology at the University of Michigan. Her research examines practices and contexts that support Black youth's holistic development. As an extension of her focus on youth well-being, Faheemah's current work focuses on the underpinnings of culturally grounded pedagogy among K–12 Black educators.

Kelly A. Rodgers is an Assistant Professor of Psychology at Borough of Manhattan Community College in the City University of New York. She received a B.A. in mathematics and Spanish from Westminster College and a Ph.D. in educational psychology from the University of Missouri. Dr. Rodgers's research centers around the motivational and socioemotional aspects affecting the retention of students of color in college in general and in STEM in particular.

Paul A. Schutz is currently a Professor in the Department of Educational Psychology at the University of Texas at San Antonio. His research interests include the nature of emotion, emotional regulation, and teachers' understandings of emotion in the classroom. He is a past president for Division 15: Educational Psychology of the American Psychological Association and a former coeditor of the *Educational Researcher: Research News and Comment*, a lead journal for the American Educational Research Association.

Tim Urdan is a Professor of Psychology and Liberal Studies at Santa Clara University. He studies the intersection of ethnic identity and academic motivation, adolescent development, and contextual influences on student motivation and achievement. He is the coeditor of the Advances in Motivation and Achievement book series and an Associate Editor for the *Merrill-Palmer Quarterly*. He is also a huge San Francisco Giants fan.

Jeffery H. Warnke is a Ph.D. candidate in the philosophy of education. His previous research focused on identity and schools as sites of intercultural contact, social development, and educational opportunity. Current research is focused on developing a normative theoretical framework for sustainability located within a conception of justice amenable to the demands of citizenship developed through civic education. His interests span identity, civic education, democracy, sustainability, and justice.

Jason R. Wornoff is a doctoral student in North Carolina State University's Department of Teacher Education and Learning Sciences (focus: educational psychology). His research aims to understand the influence of students' social encounters on academic motivation and physiological biomarkers of wellness. He has held several appointments outside of academia, including his work as a research analyst for the United States Department of Defense Education Activity (DoDEA) and the United States Army—North Carolina National Guard.

Shirley L. Yu is an associate professor of educational psychology in the Department of Educational Studies at the Ohio State University. She earned her Ph.D. in education and psychology from the University of Michigan. Her research is focused on motivation and self-regulated learning in science, technology, engineering, and mathematics, especially among women and ethnic minority students.

Akane Zusho is an Associate Professor of Educational Psychology at Fordham University. Her research focuses on examining the intersection of culture,

218 About the Contributors

achievement motivation, and self-regulation. The overarching goal of her research is to develop informed, less prescriptive, culturally sensitive theories of motivation and self-regulated learning that take into consideration the academic and motivational processes of urban youth from culturally diverse backgrounds. With Dr. Rhonda Bondie, she is currently working on developing a motivationally supportive professional development program called All Learners Learning Everyday (all-ed.org).

INDEX

Note: Italicized page numbers indicate a figure or table on the corresponding page.

academic activities, outcome expectations 70
academic adjustment 122
academic contexts, racial stereotypes (salience) 125
academic dis-identification 120
academic expectations 202; ethnicity differences 104–5; ethnic variation 108; examination, ANOVA (usage) 106; U.S. high school students 99
academic functioning, HRV (link) 59
academic identification 120; operationalization 121
academic identity: associations, conceptual model *118*; concept 120
academic integration 38
academic motivation: ethnic identity, association 173–4; increase 22; problems, impact 21
academic self-concept (Latino students) 174
academic self-esteem, low level 19
academic success, expense 60
acculturation 73–5, 202; costs (Latino youth) 171; description 73–4; Hispanic college students 171–8; process 171–2; term, usage 171
Acculturation Rating Scale for Mexican Americans (ARSMA-II), usage 74–5
achievement: direct influences 122–3; domain, model 14; ethnicity,

nonconscious associations 176–7; goal theory 8, 154–5; identity 140; motivation 83, 202
active participation, increase 83–4
adaptive learning outcomes, increase 155
adaptive motivation, facilitation 84–8
adjustment relationships, ethnic contexts *29*
adolescent identity negotiations: culture, role 152; proximal minority/majority status, role 152; schooling, relationship 158–64
adolescents of Arab descent (ArD) 152; Arab/national identity, adoption 159; cultural minority, shaping 164; haven (United States) 162; identities, fluidity 157; learning environment 164; multifaceted identities 160; school cultural responsiveness 162; school numerical majority/minority status 162–4; societal dominant/subordinate status 162–4; students, needs (meeting) 162; teachers, beliefs/attitudes 164
adolescents, self-regulating learning/ behavioral participation 51
adult-like negative intent 31
African Americans: boys, aggressive label (attributions) 20–4; collectivistic communities 43; males/females, school social environment response 52; undergraduates, focus group interviews

220 Index

77; youth, social misbehavior/behavior (judgments) 25–6

African Americans (adolescents): negative racial stereotypes, consequences 24; offenders, stereotypes/attributions 24–6

African Americans (adolescents), fitting in/heart rate variability (associations) 50; Body Mass Index (BMI) 56; cardiovascular recording 55; discussion 59–62; fitting in, opportunity structures (consideration) 59–60; fitting in (function), significance/confidence bands (Johnson-Neyman regions) 58; means/standard deviations/correlations 56; method 54–6; Need to Belong Scale 55; Patient-Centered Assessment and Counseling for Exercise Plus Nutrition (PACE+) Adolescent Physical Activity Measure 55–6; physical activity measure 55–6; procedure 54–5; progress/theory development, methodological considerations 61–2; research 53; results 56–9; Standing Out and Fitting In (SOFI) measures 55; survey administration 54

African Americans (students): gender gap, persistence 125; sample, impact 28; science persistence, intrinsic motivation (relationship) 41–2

aggressive behavior, impact 20

algebra unit, mastery calculations usage (performance summary) 87

alienation, potential 41

All Learners Learning Every Day (ALL-ED) 6; active participation, increase 83–4; adaptive motivation, facilitation 84–8; assumptions 87; belonging, promotion 86–7; competence, promotion 84–5; defining 83–8; *Domino Share* GRLP, usage 92–3; ELLs, relationship 88–9; experienced math teacher, case study 94–5; GPLRs, features 83–4; impact 82; instructional routines, descriptive routines 92; novice math teacher, case study 93–4; principles 84–8; rubrics 87; science department teacher team, case study 92–3; value, promotion 85–6

All Learners Learning Every Day professional development (ALL-ED PD): attendance 89; description 90; goals 84–5; math teacher participation, example 93–4

American schools, Arab American/ Chaldean students (presence) 155–6

amotivation 39

anger: attributional cues 18; psychological distress factor 50

Anglo orientation 74–5

ANOVA, usage 105–6

anxiety, psychological distress factor 50

Arab American adolescents: adolescents of Arab descent (ArD) 152; cultural considerations, complexity 158–60; focus group interviews 157–8; identity negotiation/school experiences 157–8; national/religious/gender/ American identity 158–60; sample selection/interview process 157–8; sliding identity 158–60; study, research methodologies 157

Arab American students: American school presence 155–6; learning environments 164; teachers, beliefs/attitudes 164

Arabness 161

Arabs, group heterogeneity 155–6

Asian American students, model minority assumption 101–2

Asian American subgroups, health disparities/lifestyles 104

Asian identification, model minority stereotype (usage) 109–10

Asian-Pacific Islander (API): ethnic diversity 100; high school students, aggregated sample 102–3

Asian students, intragroup analyses 109

asset-based pedagogy (ABP) 7, 133, 202; constructs, denotation 134; empirical evidence, paucity 140–1; framework 134; literature, limitations 137; programmatic inquiry framework 134–5; student outcomes 144; teacher-reported ABP beliefs/ behaviors 144

assimilation 202

assumptive help 19

attribution: dispositional attributions 164; importance 28; relationships, ethnic contexts 29; relations, structural model 26; theory, summary 14–17

attributional ambiguity 29

attributional analyses, usage 27

attributional beliefs, written survey (usage) 103

attributional content, variation 14

autonomic nervous system (ANS) 53

Index 221

autonomous adolescent social system 51
autonomy 44–5

background contextual affordances 75–7
Barker, George 18
behavioral engagement: behaviors,
combination 105; data *107*
beliefs: behaviors, correspondence 143–4;
knowledge, distinguishing 135–6
belonging 202; promotion 86–7; sense,
increase 208
belongingness, factor 40
Best Foot Forward 30; design 22–4
bias: hostile attributional bias 20; impact
133–4; positive feedback bias 19;
societal racial bias, racial identification/
awareness (increase) 122–3
Black achievement, racial identity
(relationship) 122–3
Black college students, identity/
motivation/resilience (example) 117
Black, construct (examination) 25
Black educators, demographics
(increase) 195
Black Lives Matter 205
Black men, STEM involvement 124–5
Black racial identity 202
Black students, educational experiences
(undermining) 195
Black students, underrepresentation *189*;
data, analysis/disaggregation 193–4;
gifted Black students, experiences
(data collection) 194; gifted education,
relationship *188*; recommendations
193–5
Black women, STEM involvement
123–4
Body Mass Index (BMI) 54, 56
Bondie, Rhonda 5, 6, 82, 212
brain, executive center (deactivation) 53
Brainpower (curriculum) 21, 30;
elaboration 22
Brown, Michael (shooting) 14
Brown v. Board of Education of Topeka 3, 183,
185; mandates, fulfilling 190, 193
Bryant, Lauren H. 5, 50, 212
bullying 26; victims, feeling 27

cardiovascular activity, physiological arousal
index 52–3
career-related activities, outcome
expectations 70
causal dimensions 16

Chaldean adolescents: cultural
considerations, complexity 158–60;
cultural minority, shaping 164; focus
group interviews 157–8; identity
negotiation/school experiences 157–8;
multifaceted identities 160; national/
religious/gender/American identity
158–60; sample selection/interview
process 157–8; sliding identity 158–60;
study, research methodologies 157
Chaldean Christians, emigration 156
Chaldean students: American school
presence 155–6; learning environment
164; school numerical majority/
minority status 162–4; societal
dominant/subordinate status 162–4;
teachers, beliefs/attitudes 164
characterological self-blame attributions,
endorsement 27
Chavous, Tabbye 7, 117, 212
Cho, Su-Je 5, 6, 99, 213
Civil Rights Act (1964) 184, 189
Civil Rights Data Collection (CRDC),
usage 185, 188
classmates, admiration 39
classroom: active participation, increase
83–4; adaptive motivation, facilitation
84–8; belonging, promotion 86–7;
competence, promotion 84–5; dynamics
research, constructs (representation)
134; motivational/self-regulated
learning theories, application 82;
observations, conducting 142; perceived
climate 102–3; self-regulated learning
(SRL), promotion 87–8; value,
promotion 85–6
classroom climate: importance 102–3;
perception 102, 106, 108–9
cognitive evaluation theory (CET) 39;
usage 42
Coie, John 20
collectivistic communities 43
college: enrollment, Latino decisions 170;
enrollment/retention process (Hispanic
students) 170–1; Latino student
retention, impact 170; racial climate 119
colorblind perspectives 123
colorism, issues 204
Common Core State Standards (CCSS) 88
competence 42–3; feelings, impact 44;
promotion 84–5
confirm and contribute routine, usage
88–9

222 Index

connectedness 43–4; importance 44; sense 204–5
context-level factors, associations (conceptual model) *118*
contextual risk factors 118
controllability (causal dimension) 16
Corkin, Danya M. 5, 6, 67, 213
Corno, Lyn 213
creativity 139
critical awareness 7, 133–4, 136–7
critical bicultural pedagogy 135
critical culturally sustaining revitalizing pedagogy 135
cultural connectedness 135
cultural content integration 139
cultural diversity, dimensions (intersection) 206
cultural identities, ethnic identities (combination process) 172
cultural knowledge 139; beliefs, relationship (discrepancy) 143–4
culturally appropriate/congruent/compatible approaches 135
culturally different students: gifted education, desegregation 183; recruitment/retention, recommendations 183
culturally relevant assessment 202
culturally relevant pedagogy 135
culturally responsive approaches, usage 206–7
culturally responsive education 135
culturally responsive teaching 135
culturally sustaining pedagogies 135
cultural minority, shaping 164
culture: contextually situated interpretations 152–3; role 152
culture of poverty 135

daily instruction, motivational/self-regulated learning theories (application) 82
Darwin, Charles 53
DeCuir-Gunby, Jessica T. 3, 9, 201, 213
deficit orientations 135
depression: feeling 28; psychological distress factor 50
difference orientations 135
differential student treatment, biases (impact) 133–4
direct-instruction mini-lesson, usage 95
disciplinary procedures, impact 204
discrimination, risk (enhancement) 123
disparate impact doctrine 189–90

dispositional attributions 164
Dodge, Kenneth 20
double jeopardy 123
Drotar, Samantha 7, 117, 213

East Asian Confucian cultural values, attribution 103
East Asian immigration histories, research 104
education: motivation (study), race/ethnicity examination (implications) 207–8; multicultural education 135
educational attainment 108
educational contexts (motivation study), race/ethnicity (research) 3; agenda 201
educational disparities 184
educators, cultural competence (evaluation/promotion) 195
effectiveness studies 7
elitism, impact 191
engagement 100–1; construct, usage 101
English classes, self-report data (collection) 105
English language learners (ELLs): belonging, promotion 86–7; daily instruction, motivational/self-regulated learning theories (application) 82; number, increase 82; relationships *96*; self-regulation struggle 89
English language learners (ELLs), ALL-ED (relationship) 88–9; data sources 90–1; discussion 95–6; method 89–91; participants/schools, description 89–90; qualitative methods/analyses 91; qualitative results 92–5; quantitative measures/analyses 90–1; quantitative results 91–2; results 91–5
Equality District: screening phase, absence 192
equality district 191–2; gifted education, relationship *193*
Equality District, reliance 191
equality, equity (contrast) 190–2
equity: equality, contrast 190–2; pedagogy 135; promotion 145
equity allowance: costs, determination 194; formula 187–90; index *189*
Equity District: universal screening, adoption 192
equity district 192; gifted education, relationship *193*
ethnic diversity contexts 28
ethnic enclaves: schooling 160–1; schools, status hierarchy 161–2

ethnic identity 71–3, 140–1; academic identity, association 174; academic motivation, association 173–4; cultural identities, combination process 172; formation patterns 172–3; Hispanic college students 171–8; strength (second-generation youth) 173; term, usage 172

ethnicity: achievement, nonconscious associations 176–7; data *106*, *107*; ethnicity-related context variables, examination 28; importance 31; inquiry, future directions 202–5; study 3; study, methodological considerations 205–7; variations 99

ethnicity, examination 201–2; implications 207–8; race-focused approach 202; race-reimaged approach 202

ethnic minority: adolescents, school belonging 51–2; groups, adolescent members (identity problems) 172

ethnic minority students: motivation/ performance, undermining 19; self-report data, usage 175

ethnic minority youth: achievement-related experiences 14; motivation, attributional perspective 13; motivation-relevant experiences 31; motivation, study 32

ethnic variability 100

evidence-based arguments, engagement 88

expectancy, relations (structural model) 26

expectancy-value theory 37

expectations: enhancement, self-confidence (impact) 109; high level 125; school satisfaction/peer cohesiveness, relationship 103

experienced math teacher, ALL-ED case study 94–5

face validity 146

failure: attribution 17; failure-prone students, self-esteem (protection) 19; preintervention/postintervention attributions, treatment condition function *23*

family members, approval 39

fight or flight reaction 53

fit: ethnic minority adolescent perception 51–2; stage-environment fit theory 60

fitting in: function prediction 54; gender/ mean-adjusted heart rate variability (conditional relation), significance/ confidence bands (Johnson-Neyman

regions) *58*; heart rate variability, associations 50; opportunity structures, consideration 59–60

Fonseca-Bolorin, Gloryvee 7, 117, 213

Ford, Donna Y. 8, 183, 214

formative assessments 6

future academic expectations (U.S. high school students) 99; ethnicity/grade level, data *106*; perceived climate/ ethnicity, impact *107*

gender: consideration 123–5; processes, study 123

gender/mean-adjusted heart rate variability (conditional relation), significance/confidence bands (Johnson-Neyman regions) *58*

generational status, issues 204

gifted Black/Hispanic students, experiences (data collection) 194

gifted, definition 185

gifted education: access, importance 190–2; Black/Hispanic educators, demographics (increase) 195; Black student underrepresentation *188*; cultural implications 185–93; definitions 185–93; desegregation 183; educator preparation, evaluation/promotion 194–5; educators, cultural competence (evaluation/promotion) 195; equality district, equity district (contrast) *193*; Hispanic student underrepresentation *188*; preparation, importance 194–5

gifted, federal definitions *186*

giftedness, definitions 185–7

gifted students, motivation/engagement (expectations) 190–1

gifted underrepresentation formula 187–90

grade level, data *106*

Graham, Sandra 5, 13, 214

Gray, DeLeon L. 5, 50, 214

Griggs v. Duke Power 189

group learning routines (GPLRs) 83; assessment 91; creation 93–4; observations 95; roles *83*

group routines 6

group threat theory 153–4

harassment, impact 26–7

Harris, Sonya D. 9, 201, 214

HBCUs 42–6

heart rate variability (HRV): academic functioning, link 59; cardiovascular

224 Index

recording 55; conceptualization 61; confidence interval 58–9; fitting in, associations 50–1; fitting in, conditional effects (gender distinctions) 57; gender differences 59; high-frequency power spectrum analysis, unstandardized regression coefficients 57; mean-adjusted heart rate variability/gender (conditional relation), significance/confidence bands (Johnson-Neyman regions) 58; measure 53; role 52–3

Heider, Fritz 14

Herr, Veronica 8, 168, 214

high-frequency power spectrum analysis, unstandardized regression coefficients 57

Hill, LaBarron K. 5, 50, 214–15

Hispanic college students: acculturation 171–8; demographics 169–71; Latino students, college (relationship) 169–70; motivation/achievement 168; population 169; recommendations 193–5; retention, factors 170–1; schools, impact 178–9; subconscious processes 174–8

Hispanic college students, ethnic identity 171–3; academic motivation, association 173–4; academic motivation, association (research summary) 175–8; formation, patterns 172

Hispanic educators, demographics (increase) 195

Hispanic population, history (complexity) 168–9

Hispanic-serving institutions (HSIs) 46

Hispanic students, college enrollment/ retention processes 170–1

Hispanic students, underrepresentation: data, analysis/disaggregation 193–4; gifted education, relationship *188*; gifted Hispanic students, experiences (data collection) 194; recommendations 193–5

home/school dissonance, feelings (exacerbation) 153

hostile attributional bias 20

Hudley, Cynthia 5, 6, 21, 99, 215

I Am My Language (González) 139

identity 117; adolescents, concerns (increase) 60; problems 172

Implicit Association Test (IAT) 157; stereotypical pattern 177; usage 176–7

individual self-concept, derivation 153

inferiority, suspicion 19

in-group members, out-group members (comparison) 153

in-group variability, masking 110

injustices, teacher creation (condemnation) 136

institution-level factors 118–19

instructional routines, descriptive statistics *91*

intentional discrimination, prohibition 184

interbeat interval (IBI) series 55

interest (values) 70–1

intergroup contact hypothesis 8, 154

intergroup interactions 125, 203

interpersonal experiences 119

interpersonal interactions, focus 203

intersectionality 202; issues 204

intragroup dynamics 203–4

intrinsic motivation 42–5; African American student science persistence, relationship 41–2; positive effect 44

Jackson, Lisa 5, 50, 215

Johnson-Neyman regions *58*

Johnson, Oriana 5, 50, 215

juvenile delinquency, childhood aggression (risk factor) 24

juvenile justice system, racial disparities (mirroring) 25–6

Karabenick, Stuart A. 8, 152, 215

Kelly, George 32

Kennedy, John F. 184

knowledge, belief (distinguishing) 135–6

Kubios HRV analysis software, Version 2.0 (usage) 55

Kumar, Revathy 8, 152, 215–16

language, cultural knowledge/content integration (relationship) 139–40

Latinos: academic self-concept 176; discriminatory/segregative practices 142; negative academic stereotypes, impact 174; youth, acculturation costs 171

Latino students: academic abilities, negative abilities 173–4; academic/ ethnic identities, integration (challenge) 178–9; academic self-concept 174; achievement/identity, asset-based pedagogies 133, 138–40; college, relationship 169–70; context 142; ethnic identity 140–1; ethnic identity, academic self-concept (disconnect)

177–8; framework, application 141–6; high expectations, operationalization 145–6; identity 140–1, 144–5; programmatic inquiry framework 134–5; sample, hypothesis 28; stereotype threat, strain/difficulty 178–9; study 142–5; teacher behaviors 137–40; teacher beliefs 135–7
learning: constructivist views 139; environment 155, 164
Leath, Seanna 7, 117, 216
locus (causal dimension) 16
López, Francesca 7, 133, 216
low-level skills, focus 138
Lyons, Donald 7, 117, 216

maladjustment: strength 28–9; weakness 29
male role socialization, historical cultural norms 125
Martin, Julie P. 5, 6, 67, 216
math problem solving, GPLR (role) *83*
math self-efficacy, level (increase) 72–3
McDonald, LaQuan (shooting) 14
McFadden v. Board of Education for Illinois School District U-46 184–5, 193
mean-adjusted heart rate variability/ gender (conditional relation), significance/confidence bands (Johnson-Neyman regions) *58*
Mendez v. Westminster School District 3
minority group, threat 163
minority-serving institutions (MSIs) 46
minority student success, contextual factors 125–6
model minority stereotype, usage 109–10
monolithic model minority identity 100
monolithic racial categories, unpacking 110
moodiness, psychological distress factor 50
motivation 117; attributional perspective 13; attributional theory *15*; classic theories, posit 101; constructs 202; methodological approaches 206; race/ethnicity, examination 201–2; race-reimaged/race-focused approaches 201–2; social cognitive theory 8; study 3; study, race/ethnicity examination (implications) 207–8; theory 37–39
motivational interventions 32–3
motivational learning theories, application 82
motivational methods 31–2
multicultural education 135
Mustafaa, Faheemah 7, 117, 216

need-satisfying opportunity structures 60
Need to Belong Scale 55
negative stereotypes, fulfilling (threat) 176
neighborhood characteristics, school context (relationship) 156
New York City Department of Education (NYC DoE) teachers, ALL-ED PD instruction 89–90
Next Generation Science Standards (NGSS) 88
No Child Left Behind 205
no excuses approach, proliferation 138–9
nonethnic enclaves, schooling 160–1
novice math teacher, ALL-ED case study 93–4
numerical minority status, impact 163–4

one-on-one faculty-student advising, impact 178
operationalized academic identification 121
orientation programs, impact 178
originality 139
other ethnic identity, high levels 145
outcome expectations 69–70

parasympathetic nervous system (PNS) 53; activity, increase 59
parent-teacher relationships 203
Patient-Centered Assessment and Counseling for Exercise Plus Nutrition (PACE+) Adolescent Physical Activity Measure 55–6
Patterns of Adaptive Learning Scales (PALS) 90
peer cohesiveness, expectations (relationship) 103
peer harassment 26
peer nomination procedures, studies 52
peer victimization, attributions 26–9; examination 27–8
peer victimization, ethnicity (relationship) 28
perceived climate 102–3; data *107*
persistence 37–9; retention, contrast 38–9; treatment 39–41
personal-level factors, associations (conceptual model) *118*
person inputs 71–5
phenomenological variant of the ecological systems theory (PVEST) 154
Plessy v. Ferguson 3
Polar™ RS800CX Heart Rate (HR) Monitor, usage 55

226 Index

political priorities, impact 205
positive feedback bias 19
predominantly White institutions (PWIs) 38, 41, 46; Black college students, survey 72
prefrontal cortex (PFC), deactivation 53
priming effects, documentation 25
priming methodology, usage 25
problem finding 139
problem solving 139
professional development (PD) 6, 83; cases 91; description 90; impact, assessment 92; relationships *96*
programmatic inquiry, ABP framework 134–5
proximal contextual influences 75–7
proximal minority/majority status, role 152
psychological distress: biomarker 51; increase 27; indicators 50; prediction, self-perceptions (impact) 110; proxy 52–3; race-related stress, association 61–2
Psychology of Interpersonal Relations, The (Heider) 14
punishment, relations (structural model) *26*
Pygmalion Effects in the Classroom (Rosenthal) 136

qualitative interview methods 76
quantitative survey methods 76

race: consideration 123–5; inquiry, future directions 202–5; race-focused approaches 201–2; race-focused constructs, usage 4; race-reimaged approaches 201–2; race-reimaged constructs, usage 4; race-related factors 24; race-related issues 205; race-related stress, psychological distress (association) 61–2; research 3; study 123; study, methodological considerations 205–7
race, examination 201–2; implications 207–8; race-focused approaches 202; race-imaged approaches 202
racial achievement gap, problem 32
racial climate, impact 205
racial disparities, mirroring 25–6
racial identity 71–3; Black achievement, relationship 122–3; development, issues 204; resilience factor (STEM achievement) 121–3
racial prime, relations (structural model) *26*
racial quotas, thresholds (contrast) 187
racial slurs, usage 26

racial socialization, issues 204
racial stigma, experience/vulnerability 124–5
racism: ethnic identities 141; impact 191
reading competence, high levels 144–5
reciprocal determinism 103
Regulation of Learning Questionnaire (RLQ), development 90–1
Relative Difference in Composition Index (RDCI) 187–8; inadequacy 190
Relevance, measurement 90–1
residential learning communities, impact 178
resilience 117; contextual factors 125–6; factor (STEM achievement) 121–3; factors 118–19
rest and digest system 53
retention 37–9, 41–2; persistence, contrast 38–39; term, meaning 38
Rice, Tamir (shooting) 14
rigor: ALL-ED definition 85; equation *85*; provision 146
Rodgers, Kelly A. 5, 36, 216–17
rounds, usage 84, 86–7

scholastic achievement, basis 60
school engagement 202; classroom climate, importance 102–3; U.S. high school students, relationship 99
schooling: adolescent identity negotiations, relationship 158–64; ethnic enclaves, nonethnic enclaves (contrast) 160–1
schools: adolescents, self-regulating learning/behavioral participation 51; American schools, Arab American/ Chaldean students (presence) 155–6; belonging 51–2; climate, perceptions 108–9; context, external impacts 205; context, neighborhood characteristics 156; cultural diversity, study (theoretical perspectives) 153–5; cultural focus 145; cultural responsiveness 162; culture, impact 204–5; ethnic enclave schools, status hierarchy 161–2; fitting, function prediction 54; functioning 204–5; impact (Hispanic college students) 178–9; numerical majority/minority status 162–4; racial context, attributions 26–9; racial/ethnic diversity 207–8; satisfaction, expectations (relationship) 103; social environment, African American males/females (response) 52; structures 204–5; study, theoretical perspectives 153–5

Schutz, Paul A. 3, 9, 201, 217
science department teacher team, ALL-ED case study 92–3
science identity, development 40–1
science self-efficacy, level (increase) 72–3
science, technology, engineering and mathematics (STEM): academic adjustment/persistence, associations (conceptual model) *118*; academic identification, stigma (experience/impact) 119–21; awards 36–7; belongingness, factor 40; Black men, involvement 124–5; Black students, degrees 46; Black women, involvement 123–4; contexts 126; curriculum difficulty, factor 40; degrees/careers, pursuit 121; disciplines, URM population (increase) 67; out-of-class interactions, support 76–7; settings, stigma (experience) 121; student academic identification 120; student motivation, impact 76–7; student persistence 40; student pursuit, discouragement 77; URM persistence/achievement, influences (understanding) 68
science, technology, engineering and mathematics (STEM), Black college students (identity/motivation/resilience): associations, conceptual model *118*; conceptual framework 118–19; example 117; race/gender, consideration 123–5; resilience, contextual factors 125–6; STEM academic identification, stigma (experience/impact) 119–21; STEM achievement, racial identity (resilience factor) 121–3; summary 126
science, technology, engineering and mathematics (STEM) careers: family pursuits, incompatibility (perception) 124; interest/pursuit 42; selection 74
science, technology, engineering and mathematics (STEM) fields 36; Black student achievement 117; Black student stigma experiences, analysis 119–20; degrees, student of color pursuit 42; students of color, motivation (understanding) 37; White male domination 43–4
science, technology, engineering and mathematics (STEM) motivation: ethnic identity, impact 72–3; importance 75; influences 76; persistence 67

science, technology, engineering and mathematics (STEM) persistence 72; promotion/hindrance, racial/ethnic identity (impact) 73
science, technology, engineering and mathematics (STEM) programs 5; culture, comfort 38; culture, description 43
Scott v. Sanford 3
second-generation youth, ethnic identity (strength) 173
self-blame 28; negative outcomes 27
self-blame relationships, ethnic contexts *29*
self-blaming tendencies 29
self-concept 122; formation, assertion 141; renegotiation 120
self-confidence, impact 109
self-determination, quest 44
self-determination theory (SDT) 5, 37, 39–45
self-efficacy 69; math/science self-efficacy, level (increase) 72–3; outcome expectations, relationship 69–70
self-esteem: low level 27; protection 19
self-evaluation 120
self-fulfilling prophecy, vulnerability 136
self-perceptions, impact 110
self-regulated learning (SRL) 6, 83; promotion 87–8
self-regulated learning theories, application 82
self-regulatory processes, disruption 50–1
self-reported affective engagement, increase 106
self-responsibility, assumption 22
self, student conceptualizations 45
self-worth, low level (psychological distress factor) 50
situational demands, meeting 109
sleep, expense 60
sliding identity, Arab American/Chaldean students 158–60
social anxiety, feeling 28
social behavior problems, impact 21
social cognitive career theory (SCCT) 68–71; acculturation 73–5; background contextual affordances 75–7; barriers 77; ethnic identity 71–3; extended framework, usage 77; interest (values) 70–1; model, test 74; outcome expectations 69–70; personal/cultural/contextual influences 71–7; person inputs 71–5; proximal contextual influences 75–7; racial identity 71–3;

228 Index

self-efficacy 69; studies, variation 74–5; supports 75–7
social cognitive theory, SCCT (consistency) 69
social identity: contextually situated interpretations 152–3; function 161
social identity theory 8, 153–4
social integration 38; fostering, difficulty 41
social media, impact 205
social movements, impact 205
social order, status quo (challenge) 141
social pressures, impact 191
social support, decrease 50
societal dominant/subordinate status 162–4
societal racial bias, racial identification/ awareness (increase) 122–3
socioeconomic status (SES) 161; adjustment, absence 61
somatic complaints 50–1
Southeast Asian immigration histories, research 104
stability (causal dimension) 16
stage-environment fit theory 60
Standing Out and Fitting In (SOFI) measures 55
stereotype threat research 120–1
stigma: associations, conceptual model *118*; experience/impact 119–21
structural equation modeling, usage 25
students: academic identification 120; achievement identity 140; adverse impact 189; backgrounds, teacher beliefs (interrelationships) 134–5; belonging, sense (increase) 208; culturally different students 183; development 208; disaggregated data, examination 103–4; engagement 99–101; identity 140–1, 144–5; individuality, focus 143; needs, variables 99; positive identities, development 208; reading achievement 144; self, conceptualization 45; social support, decrease 50; somatic complaints 50–1; STEM motivation, influences 76; student-level factors 118–19; supportive needs 41; teachers, relationships 203; U.S. high school students, school engagement/future academic expectations 99–102
students, future academic expectations 99, 101–2; behavioral engagement/ ethnicity *107*; ethnicity/grade level,

data *106*; findings 105–6; measures 105; perceived climate/ethnicity *107*; sample 105; study 104–7
students of color, motivation theory (application) 37–8
students, outcomes: asset-based pedagogy, relationship 144; teacher behaviors, relationship 137
subconscious processes, Hispanic college students 174–8
sympathetic nervous system (SNS) 53
sympathy condition, participants 18

talented, federal definitions *186*
task performance, affective reactions 22
teacher behaviors 137–40; perception 102; student outcomes, relationship 137
teacher beliefs 135–7, 164; behaviors, correspondence 143–4; student backgrounds, interrelationships 134–5
teachers: affective displays 18; asset-based pedagogy 138–40; attitudes 164; condemnation 136; critical awareness 133–4; differential expectations 137–8; effectiveness 137–40; expectancy 7, 135–6; feedback, attributional antecedent 17–19; high expectations 138–9; operationalization 145–6; parents, relationship 203; preparation 137; relationship, directionality 140; sympathy, attributional cues *18*; teacher-reported ABP beliefs/behaviors 144; training 207–8
Teacher Sense of Efficacy Scale, usage 91
theory-guided interventions, usage 32
threat, perception (induction) 109
thresholds, racial quotas (contrast) 187
Tinto, Vincent 38
Title VI (Civil Rights Act of 1964) 184, 189
traction planner, steps *86*
treatment condition, function *23*

unconscious stereotypes, impact 24–5
underrepresented minority (URM) 6, 67; career development, issues/ challenges 71; participation/viewpoints, waste (cessation) 67–8; persistence/ achievement, influences (understanding) 68; STEM motivation/persistence 67; STEM population, increase 67
United States population, U.S. Census Bureau figures 169

universal screening, adoption 192
Urdan, Tim 8, 168, 217
U.S. high school students: disaggregated
data, examination 103–4; discussion
108–10; perceived climate 102–3;
school engagement 99, 100–1
U.S. high school students, future academic
expectations 99, 101–2; behavioral
engagement/ethnicity, data *107*;
ethnicity/grade level, data *106*; findings
105–6; measures 105; perceived
climate/ethnicity, data *107*; sample 105;
study 104–7

value, promotion 85–6
varied identities, development 161

victimization-maladjustment relations,
attributional analyses (usage) 27

Warnke, Jeffery H. 8, 152, 217
Weiner, Bernard 14
well-being, low level (psychological distress
factor) 50
Whites: ethnic identity, numerical
minority status (impact) 163–4;
identity, foregrounding 163; language
stratification 157–8
Wornoff, Jason R. 5, 50, 217

Yu, Shirley L. 5, 6, 67, 217

Zusho, Akane 5, 6, 82, 217–18